THE RELIGIOUS LIFE OF RICHARD III

Daniel Wright

For Venetia and Timothy

THE RELIGIOUS LIFE OF RICHARD III

PIETY AND PRAYER IN THE NORTH OF ENGLAND

JONATHAN HUGHES

FOREWORD BY
JEREMY CATTO

SUTTON PUBLISHING

First published in 1997 by
Sutton Publishing Limited · Phoenix Mill
Thrupp · Stroud · Gloucestershire · GL5 2BU

Paperback edition first published in 2000

British Library Cataloguing in Publication Data
A catalogue record for this book is available from the British Library

ISBN 0 7509 2446 2

Cover illustration: a king, his queen, courtiers and staff of a chapel attend mass being celebrated by a bishop (By permission of The British Library, Add. MS. 28962 fo. 281v)

Typeset in 10/15pt Baskerville.
Typesetting and origination by
Sutton Publishing Limited.
Printed in Great Britain by
MPG, Bodmin, Cornwall.

CONTENTS

LIST OF ILLUSTRATIONS

BLACK AND WHITE ILLUSTRATIONS

COLOUR PLATES

FOREWORD

'Blessed is the man to whom the Lord hath not imputed sin; and in whose spirit there is no guile.'
These words from the second of the penitential psalms may have been well known
to Richard III – certainly, they were written in his book of hours, a verse out of a
common devotion which was used to induce a spirit of penitence. The penitential
psalms had been a monastic observance; by the fifteenth century they, with their
companion prayers, had been all but universally adopted by the sophisticated and
educated cadre of European society on whom the conduct of affairs, with its
inevitable pressure on consciences, almost entirely rested.

Among the political leaders of the generation before Machiavelli, none has
raised more passionate and more starkly contrary judgements than Richard III.
Universally condemned for a series of political murders after his death, and
even in his lifetime, Richard enjoyed an equivocal rehabilitation in the
seventeenth and eighteenth centuries, and a more confident if not unchallenged
reappraisal by Sir Clements Markham, enthusiastically followed by the Richard
III Society, in the twentieth century. The more recent partisans of Richard have
had the pleasure of debunking the 'Tudor myth' or propaganda on which the
case against him allegedly rested. However, the historical if not the legal verdict
of the majority of scholars is still the same – Richard was beyond reasonable
doubt at least complicit in the murders of Henry VI and George, Duke of
Clarence, and the prime mover in those of Edward V and his brother, Richard.
These deaths, together with that of Lord Hastings in 1483 in which no regard
whatever was paid to due process, were by no means typical of late fifteenth-
century England; only the possible murder of Humphrey, Duke of Gloucester in
custody in 1447 forms a precedent, one which shocked contemporaries as much
as did the bloodstained reputation of Richard III. It would be perverse to
imagine that deeds which revolted public opinion could sit easily upon the
consciences of their perpetrators. Henry IV's moral authority and peace of
mind seem to have dissolved with his youthful charm and *franchise*, after his
usurpation and the violence which followed. At a lower level of tension

ministers like Henry, Cardinal Beaufort, only one of the politicians who resorted to stern confessors at Sheen Charterhouse, had to face a painful examination of conscience. It is not surprising that evidence for the religious life of Richard III should recently be adduced in aid of the debate on his life and reign, especially his book of hours and the 'prayer of King Richard' inserted in the text. These have now been examined in detail by Anne Sutton and Livia Visser-Fuchs and as a result of their analysis, fortified by their earlier studies of his other books, it is no longer possible to treat Richard as the cardboard Machiavellian, the mechanically ruthless operator working his will in an indifferent world who has appeared in numerous popular histories. Whatever the difficulties it may raise, the conscience of the king must be taken into account, and his 'contrariety of character', perceived by William Hutton in 1788, allowed its proper scope.

Jonathan Hughes takes on the challenge of relating Richard III's career to the political and social ethic of his age. He places Richard's devotions in the perspective of two layers of his moral and cultural formation. First of all, the court chivalry of the Yorkists, subtly modified by the cult of ancient virtue and the propensity to stoic resignation which his brother-in-law, Anthony Woodville, celebrated in his translation of Christine de Pisan's *Livre de corps de policie*; sophisticated, cultivated, worldly, the courtiers of Edward IV had been formed by the civility of the Burgundian and French *beaux mondes* and by the literary taste of the Valois kings Charles V and Charles VI. The France of the Lancastrian conquest and the circle of John, Duke of Bedford had been one of the principal conduits of French literary taste and manners; Jacquetta of Luxemburg, dowager Duchess of Bedford had married Richard, Lord Rivers and was the mother of Queen Elizabeth and of Anthony Woodville. It is probable that part of the library of Charles V, which had come into the possession of the Duke of Bedford, passed through her to the Woodvilles. Another part, or texts copied from books in the collection, was in the possession of the retired master of Bedford's household, Sir John Fastolf; his copies of Cicero, Seneca and the *Epistle of Othea* in French translation were the basis of English renderings by William Worcester and Stephen Scrope. A library of these popular texts in English seems to have been assembled for wider distribution in printed form by William Caxton in the 1470s. All the texts illustrated the bias of Edward IV's nobility and courtiers towards a chivalry of manners and a cult of ancient heroes and antique virtue as defined in the France of a century before. If there was a place in this world for civil responsibility and the duties of the citizen, duties well understood by contemporary Italians, the martial virtues and the cult of the hero or the *vir illustris* were better attuned to English ears. The rather unsettled youth of Richard of Gloucester, spent under the care at various times of Cardinal Bourchier and Richard, Earl of Warwick, with one short spell at the Burgundian court, throws little light on his affinity with these cultural norms. But his books, which included Giles of Rome's *De regimine principum*, the *Historia destructionis Troiae* of Guido delle Colonne, and Geoffrey of Monmouth's *Historia regum Britanniae*, together with the standard military author Vegetius, is so entirely typical of them that it must be assumed that Richard could have found, had he wished, a comfortable role model among the heroes of the ancient world as they were presented in contemporary Franco-Burgundian guise.

The second, more pervasive and abiding cultural or moral layer of English public life had been laid down somewhat earlier, in the time of Henry IV's minister Thomas Arundel, Archbishop of Canterbury, and of Henry V. This was founded on the concept of the 'mixed life', the way of life of men immersed in public affairs, 'temporal men with much possession of worldly goods' who could nevertheless 'in party savour of ghostly occupation'. The words are those of Walter Hilton, the great contemplative author who was, however, concerned to infuse into public life the saving grace which came from meditation and sober reflection. He and his contemporaries, the northern contemplative writers from Richard Rolle to Nicholas Love, were the subject of Jonathan Hughes's earlier ground-breaking work *Pastors and Visionaries* (Woodbridge, 1988). Their enormous influence, both through the power and attraction of their teaching to the lay nobility and gentry and to a wider circle of readers, and through the seal of official approval set upon their writings by Archbishop Arundel and by the government of Henry V, is made clear by the proliferation of their works and the use of their words in popular prayers and devotions. Hilton's *Scale of Perfection* and Nicholas Love's translation of the pseudo-Bonaventuran *Meditationes vitae Christi* were copied and circulated by the Carthusians at Sheen, Mountgrace and the London Charterhouse and by the Brigittine community at Syon, together with Netherlandish and German works of spirituality of which the *Imitation of Christ* is the best known. These houses had had the firm support of Henry V's government, which had continued during Henry VI's minority. After about 1440, however, the model of the public servant whose conscience was guided by intense personal spirituality seems to have been slowly superseded, at the highest social levels, by the French ideal of the chivalrous but wordly wise courtier. It remained a potent paradigm of the just governor outside the court – among Londoners, especially perhaps the preachers at the great London churches, who most faithfully supported the royal houses of Sheen and Syon in the later fifteenth century; and as the further proliferation of spiritual texts indicates, probably among the provincial gentry, such as Robert Thornton, the owner of the Thornton manuscripts of devotional works and romances. Richard III also possessed works of this kind, including the *Booke of Gostlye Grace*, an English translation of a work of Mechtild of Hackeborn. Indeed his long residence in the north may have brought him into more intimate contact with northern spiritual authors than the majority of his peers. It cannot have been a great step, as Jonathan Hughes shows, for him to contrast their honest and plain concept of sober duty with the worldly equivocations and vanities of the Edwardian court. The relationship between his apparently sincere sense of duty and awareness of conscience and his path to the throne is a problem which has only grown more acute as the relevant circumstances are more clearly established.

In the following pages Jonathan Hughes works out the theme in fascinating detail and against a wide canvas of fifteenth-century moral and religious conceptions. Much of the most interesting work on this once neglected era has begun to focus on the development of ideas, political, ethical and in the stricter sense religious. Their application to the government of England and to the ambitions of the main protagonists in the struggle to control it is necessarily complex and fraught with pitfalls, and we can be sure that these will not be the last pages devoted to the topic. But they represent the first serious attempt to place the career of Richard III and the court culture of the Yorkist kings in the larger context of the spirituality of the fourteenth and fifteenth centuries, and what they have to say will be fundamental in any future assessment of that complex and mysterious figure.

Jeremy Catto
Oriel College, Oxford

ACKNOWLEDGEMENTS

My interest in Richard III was first roused when Professor Tony Pollard of the University of Teeside asked me to deliver a paper to the fifth triennial conference of the Richard III Society in April 1993 at University College, Durham on Richard III's piety. He first suggested that I expanded this paper into a book, and his advice and encouragement has been crucial in its formulation. I would also like to express my gratitude to Dr Jeremy Catto of Oriel College, Oxford who has read the proofs with care and who has shared his enthusiasm and ideas with me over many cups of coffee. Professor James Campbell of Worcester College, Oxford and Dr Maurice Keen of Balliol College, Oxford have always been willing to discuss the fifteenth century with me and to share their insights; and Dr Keith Dockray and Professor Barrie Dobson, of Christ's College, Cambridge, have read earlier drafts of the book and offered helpful advice. I would also like to thank members of the Yorkshire branch of the Richard III Society for the interest they have shown in the project and in particular, Anne-Denise Worsnop, who showed me some of the places associated with Richard. Finally I would like to acknowledge the help of the staff of the following libraries: the Bodleian Library, Oxford; the British Library; and Lambeth Palace library.

This book has been written under difficult circumstances in the past two years and aware as I am of Richard III's belief in the importance of loyalty and his sense of betrayal I am grateful that I have been able to count on the support and loyalty of a number of friends including: Katherine Duncan-Jones of Somerville College, Oxford, John Gidney of St Edward's School, Oxford, and Timothy Baines. Above all I would like to express my gratitude for the faith shown in me by a special friend, Bethe, to whom this book is also dedicated.

PICTURE CREDITS

Photographs were supplied by, or are reproduced by courtesy of and the kind permission of the following: Bibliothéque Nationale (p. 83); Bodleian Library (colour plate 5, p. 148); British Library (colour plates 1, 2, pp. 30, 110, 143); Her Majesty the Queen (colour plate 3); Royal Society of Antiquaries (colour plate 4); Geoffrey Wheeler (pp. 111, 112, 113, 114); A.D. Worsnop (pp. 45, 46, 109); Lambeth Palace (colour plate 6, p. 120).

1

THE RELIGION AND PERSONALITY OF RICHARD III

Controversy surrounding this king's reign continues after 500 years and to some extent the opinions voiced have had a regional bias. The well-attested popularity Richard III enjoyed in the north of England, while he was duke of Gloucester and largely resident in the north and which continued during and immediately after his reign, is still evident in York today. Among such circles as the Yorkshire branch of the Richard III Society he is regarded as England's only 'northern king', deposed and subsequently discredited by envious southerners. To some extent Richard's complex and often contradictory personality can be understood in terms of the conflicting influences on the north and south, though this should not be overstated. As a younger brother of the king he occupied an important role in the court, largely resident in the Thames valley, and he was, therefore, subjected to the intellectual, moral influences (primarily writings on public duty and chivalry) of this court from such people as William Caxton and Anthony Woodville, Earl Rivers. However, he was also, through his mother, Cicely Neville, and by adoption, considering the amount of time he spent in Yorkshire, a northerner. As we shall see he was, therefore, subjected to the intellectual and spiritual influences of his mother and northern servants and friends who represented the devotional traditions of this region. These influences shaped Richard's character and religious personality which has been largely ignored until now.

Before studying Richard's religion and all the moral standards and attitudes this embraces it is necessary to show briefly where I stand in relation to the much disputed crimes attributed to this king; in any assessment of Richard's practices and beliefs they are of central importance. To me it is clear that Richard was guilty of, or implicated in, most if not all of the crimes of which he has been accused – the killing of Henry VI and his son, Edward the Prince of Wales, in 1461 (he was certainly present); the elimination of George the Duke of Clarence in the Tower in 1478 (he did nothing to prevent it and initiated the act of attainder against George's children); the killing of members of Elizabeth Woodville's family and affinity, including Anthony Woodville the Earl Rivers, Sir Richard Grey and Sir Thomas Vaughan; the elimination of his own friend, William, Lord Hastings; the murder of Edward IV's two sons, Edward V and Richard, Duke of York; the death of his wife, Anne Neville, formerly widow of Edward, Prince of Wales (he was accused of poisoning her and had to make a public denial); the usurpation of the crown which rightfully belonged to Edward IV's son, Edward; and his intention to commit incest by marrying his niece, Elizabeth of York, sister of the murdered princes (which he also had publicly to deny). What is beyond dispute is that his subjects (especially in the south) and other European rulers and their observers thought he was guilty of most if not all of these things and this must have played an important part in his religious convictions and his self-image. The so-called 'Tudor propaganda campaign' against the last Plantagenet has been over emphasized. The black legend created by Shakespeare was merely a reflection of widespread public opinion that existed before Bosworth and which was endorsed by the earliest chroniclers, reporters and historians using firsthand observation and eyewitness testimony.

Dominic Mancini, the Roman poet and diplomat in the service of Angelo Cato, Archbishop of Vienne at the court of Edward IV, wrote an account of the usurpation of Richard III for his patron after leaving England on 6 July 1483. He had completed this by 1 December 1483 and in it he admitted he had not been able find out how the princes had died. However, earlier in the same work he described Richard as the Duke of Gloucester 'who destroyed Edward's children and, then claimed for himself the throne'.[1] Mancini's general picture is of a man who 'violated the ties of kin and friendship' in his lust for power, for which the people 'cursed him with a fate worthy of his crimes'.[2] Another Italian observer, Carmeliano, in a poem written in 1486 celebrating the birth of Prince Arthur, charged Richard with the murder of Henry VI and his nephews.

Another observer in court circles was the author of the continuation of the *Crowland Chronicle*, a Londoner in the diplomatic service and a chancery clerk. This was probably John Sharpe, the protonotary in charge of state papers who accompanied Bishop Russell on a visit to Crowland Abbey after twenty-five years' service.[3] While there he completed an account of Edward IV's and

Richard III's reigns by April 1486. He hinted that Richard was personally involved in the murder of Henry VI, and while he was sympathetic towards Edward IV, this is what he had to say about events after Tewkesbury: 'I shall say nothing, at this time, about the discovery of King Henry's lifeless body in the Tower of London; may God have mercy upon and give time for repentance to him, whoever it might be, who dared to lay sacrilegious hands on the Lord's Anointed! And so, let the doer merit the title of tyrant and the victim that of glorious martyr'.[4] When discussing the killing in 1478 of George, Duke of Clarence, Edward IV's brother, he pointed out that the sentence was carried out by Richard's friend and confidant, Henry, Duke of Buckingham. This firsthand observer of events close to the crown also judged that the rebellion in the south east in August 1483 occurred because of the widespread rumour that Richard had done away with the princes and that Buckingham had joined it because he repented of the deed.[5] As a guest at the Christmas festivities in 1484 the Crowland Chronicler noted that Queen Anne and Elizabeth of York, who were alike in complexion and figure, exchanged clothes and that it was rumoured that Richard was 'applying his mind in every way' to contract a marriage with Elizabeth, either after the death of the Queen or by means of a divorce. Shortly afterwards, he added that Anne fell ill and the king spurned her bed, to which the author cryptically added 'What more is there to be said'.[6] When the newly widowed king's plans to marry Elizabeth were revealed he was told by his squires of the body, Sir Richard Ratcliffe and William Catesby, that if he proceeded with the marriage he would be faced with a rebellion (like the one in August 1483) this time charging him with causing the death of the queen to complete his incestuous association with a kinsman, to the offence of God. Other chronicles of the period are also hostile. *Warkworth's Chronicle*, and *The Great Chronicle of London* state that the Duke of Gloucester was involved in the murder of Henry VI and *Fabyan's Chronicle* that he killed Edward, Prince of Wales.[7]

Another official who was a firsthand observer of events of this period was Philippe de Commynes, an ambassador to England while in the service of Charles the Bold, the Duke of Burgundy from 1467 to 1472. Commynes entered the service of Louis XI, King of France from 1472 to 1483 when he became counsellor of the regent Anne of Beaujeu. In 1524 he completed his

Memoirs, which included the events of June to August 1483: 'The government of the two sons was committed to the Duke of Gloucester, King Edward's brother, who barbarously murdered them, slew those of the nobility whom he thought would oppose his designs, and usurped the crown.'[8] When he became king, Richard, according to Commynes, who was a firsthand witness, desired to continue the alliance with Louis XI as his brother had done and to receive his pension: 'but our king looked upon him as an inhuman and cruel person, and would neither answer his letters nor give audience to his ambassador; for King Richard, after his brother's death, had sworn allegiance to his nephew as his king and sovereign, and yet committed that inhuman action not long after; and in full parliament caused two of his brother's daughters, who were remaining to be degraded and declared illegitimate upon a pretence.'[9] Commynes added that it was not long 'after the murder of his nephews, as you have heard; but he lost his wife, some say he made away with her too'.[10]

A more humble observer of these events was John Rous, a chantry chaplain of Guy's Cliff near Warwick Castle, an antiquary and author of the *Rous Roll*, a history of the earls of Warwick. He also wrote a *History of the Kings of England*, and when he came to the reign of Richard III he would, as an employee of the Nevilles, have been able to rely on some firsthand information. Also he would not have been unfavourably disposed to Richard, who was himself a Neville. However, having praised the Warwick heiress, Anne Neville, and her husband, Richard, in 1483, some time between the Battle of Bosworth and his own death in 1492, he launched into a description of Richard as a deformed tyrant who 'caused others to kill the holy man Henry VI, or as many think, did so by his own hands, ascended the throne of the slaughtered children whose protector he was himself; beheaded Lord Hastings the chamberlain of King Edward IV without trial and Lady Anne, his queen, daughter of the Earl of Warwick, he poisoned.'[11]

The most forthright condemnation of Richard III was in Sir Thomas More's *History of King Richard III*, completed by 1513. More, five years old at the time of Richard III's usurpation, was brought up in the household of John Morton, Bishop of Ely, who was a royal counsellor present at such key events as the arrest of William Hastings. More, in his *History of King Richard III*, drew on oral traditions and eyewitness accounts such as the testimony of a group of ladies including: Elizabeth Mowbray, dowager Duchess of Norfolk and mother-in-law of the younger of the princes, Richard, Duke of York, Jane Talbot, Elizabeth Brackenbury, daughter of Richard III's keeper of the Tower, Mary Tyrell, niece of John Tyrell, and Joyce Lee to whom More dedicated his first book. These ladies were inmates of the Minories just outside the Tower of London.[12] More applied a critical legal mind to his history and was not as has been maintained providing propaganda for the Tudor dynasty. He was quite capable of expressing criticism of Henry VII and at the very least his account reflects what people thought shortly after Richard III's death. According to More, Richard slew with his own hand, and without the knowledge of Edward IV, Henry VI. He claimed 'some wise men I also ween that his drift covertly conveyed, lacked not in helping forth his brother of Clarence to his death'. More further maintained that Richard anticipated Edward IV's death through overeating while his children were young and 'for this intent he was glad of his brother's death'.[13] While admitting that there was no certainty on these points, More claimed that Richard, observing that Edward was likely to die young because of his diet, coveted the throne. On the night of Edward's death, William Mistlebrook, the king's servant and auditor, reported to one of Richard's servants, Richard Potter, who was to be his attorney in chancery in 1483, that it was likely that the duke would be king. More did not believe that Buckingham was the prime mover at the time of Edward's death and said those who knew 'the subtle wit of the protector' denied he revealed his enterprise to the Duke of Buckingham until he had control of the queen's sons and and persuaded him to crown him.[14] More then added that Richard began his reign of cruel death and slaughter with 'the most piteous, wicked, I mean the lamentable murder of his innocent nephews'. His description of the murder of the princes in the Tower is very precise and he names John Tyrell, who was still alive, as the one who carried out Richard's orders.[15]

One other writer who could call on oral tradition and eyewitnesses was the Italian, Polydore Vergil, the historian and chamberlain to Pope Alexander VI who came to England in 1502. With Henry VII's encouragement he wrote in Latin, *A History of England*, the first draft of which was completed in 1513. Like More, Virgil was an independently minded scholar (he rejected the Arthurian myths of Geoffrey of Monmouth) and no Tudor hack. Vergil claimed that Edward, Prince of Wales, was slain in the presence of Edward IV, George, Duke of Clarence, Richard, Duke of Gloucester and William, Lord Hastings. His verdict on the fate of Henry VI was that 'The contynuall report is that Richard Duke of Gloucester killyd him with a sword'.[16] According to Vergil, after Edward IV's death Richard 'from thenceforth determyned to assay his purposyd spytefull practyse by subtyltie and sleight, which yf by that meane should not foule owt so fortunately as he hopyd, than lastelye, with malice apert, to attempt the same'.[17] This account continues by claiming that Richard's mind was inflamed with the desire of usurping the kingdom but the crown brought little peace. After the coronation he went to York via Gloucester, but 'he lyvyd in contynuall feare, for thexfelly whereof by any kind of meane he determyned by death to dispatche his nephewys, because so long as they lyvyd he could never be out of hazard'. Brackenbury, the Constable of the Tower, refused to carry out the task which fell to John Tyrell and the deed was done, 'King Richard, delyveryd by this fact from his care and feare, kept the slaughter not long secret, who with a few days after, permyttyd the rumor of ther deth to go abroad'.[18] Vergil also hinted that Richard practised the death of his queen. The king had it broadcast abroad that she was ill, complained of her barreness and 'whether she wer dispatchyd with sorowfulnes or poyson, dyed within a few days after'.[19] Vergil's final assessment of Richard was 'he had a sharp witt provydent and subtyle, apt both to counterfayt and dissemble' and he had a 'sharp and sowre cowntenance, which semyd to savor of mischief, and utter evydently craft and deceyt'.[20]

None of the above is new but what is interesting, and something that has not been fully investigated, is that this ruthless, inscrutable man was also religious, an austere practitioner of a chivalric code of ethics, a public benefactor and protector of the church, a founder of chantries. In his public pronouncements he upheld a strict, puritanical code of sexual morality in marked contrast to many of his fellow courtiers. In his private life he can be considered a man of piety, a practitioner of the mixed life to rank with his mother, Cicely Neville and his sister Margaret, Duchess of York and Burgundy. Richard III owned a Middle English verse translation of the Old Testament and a Wycliffite translation of the New Testament, a copy of the *Revelations of St Mechtild* and a beautiful but unostentatious book of hours acquired for his personal daily use. It contains a number of devotions written for the king including a Collect of St

Ninean, a Litany asking for deliverance from suffering and a long prayer which was added at the king's request in which Richard's name and title was added in two places, probably by himself, in which 'your servant Ricardus Rex' asks God to deliver him from tribulation and his enemies as he has delivered a number of Old Testament leaders.[21]

Few have attempted to investigate Richard III's religion closely and to consider the way it related to his usurpation of the throne and his crimes. The earliest accounts of his reign make little reference to his religion. Contemporaries clearly found Richard an inscrutable, private man, which is why he took everyone by surprise by his ruthless, decisive actions between June and August 1483. Vergil said he was inscrutable; Mancini described him as a 'good dissembler';[22] and More said he was 'closed and secret, a deep dissimuler'.[23]

These early accounts of Richard's reign have little specific to say about his personality because the authors and their informants probably just did not know what he was like; but they all attempted to make sense of his apparent religiosity and moral austerity. Mancini saw him as a hypocrite – after Clarence's death Richard set out to acquire the loyalty of the people through favours and justice; the good reputation of his private life and public activities; his chivalric prowess which powerfully attracted the esteem of strangers; and 'By these *arts* Richard acquired the favour of the public'.[24] According to Mancini, Richard used the church and his own high moral stance to push the princes aside and obtain power: 'he so corrupted preachers of the divine word, that in the sermons to the people they did not blush to say in the face of decency and all religion, that the progeny of the king should be instantly eradicated for neither had he been a legitimate king nor would his issue be so'.[25] He then got these priests to stress that he, the Duke of Gloucester, was the only survivor of the royal stock and 'his previous career and blameless morals would be a sure guarantee of his good government'. Although Mancini dismissed Richard's puritan morality as political expediency, he did go a little deeper in his analysis to suggest that Richard drove himself mad through ambition and beyond the pale of decent values: 'But whom will insane lust for power spare if it dares violate the ties of kinship and friendship'.[26] The author of the continuation of the *Crowland Chronicle* was the first to suggest, in 1486, that there was a degree of delusion in Richard, that he believed it was his mission to rule, when in Latin hexameters concluding his account of Richard's reign, he referred to those who enter the place of power by a back door and 'confounding at the same time themselves and their own – not to mention mixing up the public with the private'.[27] This author also saw the last Plantagenet as a representative of the devil, describing how the night before Bosworth he was surrounded by a host of demons. The notion of the demonic king was popularized during his lifetime. Daffyd ap Llewelyn ap Griffid of Mathafarn composed a prophetic ode on the outcome of the Battle of Bosworth in 1485/6 describing Richard as the 'sad lipped saracen, . . . the little caterpillar of London, . . . a servile boar' who 'wrought penance upon Edward's sons' who 'slew Christ's angels' showing 'the bravery of cruel Herod' and who ended his life as 'a dog slain in a ditch'.[28] John Rous, writing at about the same time as the Crowland Chronicler, described Richard's birth as a deliverance of the beast that had been retained within his mother's womb for two years emerging with teeth and hair to his shoulders. His reign was described in apocalyptic terms as presaging that of Antichrist: 'King Richard, who was excessively cruel in his days, reigned for three years and a little more, in the way that Antichrist is to reign. And like Antichrist to come he was confounded at his moment of greatest pride'.[29] It could be said that Rous' account of Richard lacks subtlety and owes much to credulous and superstitious rumour, but the same could not apply to the two most intellectually distinguished contemporary (or near contemporary) writers on Richard III, Polydore Vergil and Sir Thomas More.

Vergil also saw Richard as an instrument of the forces of darkness. He saw the elimination of George, Duke of Clarence, because of the prophecy that a certain G would reign, as a trick of the devil's allowing Richard to come to power: 'And because the devels ar wont in that sort to envegle the mynds of them who conceave pleasures in suche illusions, with ther crafty conceytes and subtylties men sayd afterwardes that the same prophecy took effect, when after Edward the duke of Gloucester usurpyd the kyndom'.[30] Vergil's Richard anticipates Shakespeare's Macbeth as he sees him driven by ambition and his own deceptions and cruelty to madness: 'Surely so yt happeneth to graceless people, that who seketh to overthrow an other, his own frawd, wicked and mischevouus intent, his owne desperate boldness, maketh him frantyke and mad.'[31] Like Macbeth, Vergil's Richard is driven to distraction by a disturbed conscience 'Richard, whose mynd partly ws enflamyd with desire of usurping the kingdom, partly was trubblyd by guyltyness of intent to commyt so haynous wickednes, for a guiltie conscience causeth thoffender to have dew punishment alway in imagination before his eyes'.[32] Guilt and repentance was, however, soon followed by a realization that he could not undo his crimes, and by a hypocritical desire to change his reputation: 'he fell from so great felycytie into a feare and heavynes of hart, and, because he could not reforme the thing that was past, he determyned to abolishe by all dewtyfulnes the note of infamy wherwith his honor was staynyd'.[33] Religion subsequently became a tool to persuade people of his innocence. Vergil suggests Richard may have come to believe in his own performance and through such gestures as the foundation of a chantry of one hundred priests at York to merit salvation: 'But hard yt ys to alter the naturell disposition of ones mynde, and suddaynly to exterp the thing therin settyld by dayly conversation. And so, whether yt wer for that cause or (as the brute commonly goeth) because he now repented of his evell dedes, he began afterward to take an hand a certayne new forme of lyfe, and to geave the shew and cowntenance of a good man, wherby he might be accowynted more righteous, more mylde and so first might meryte pardon for his offences at God's hand.'[34] But, Vergil maintains, the hollowness of his reformation and divine disapproval was made all too clear as the king's misfortunes, such as the death of his son, multiplied and served to increase his torments and fears: 'But anon afteryt appearyd evydent that feare, which seldomm causeth continewance of dewtyfull dealing, made King Richard so suddainly good . . . but counterfayt waxed cold agane quickly; by reason wherof all his proposyd practyses began straightaway to com to naught', and he began 'more dowtynge than trusting in his owne cause', and 'was vexyd, wrestyd and tormentyd in mynd with feare almost perpetuyally wherefor he had a myserable lyfe'.[35] Vergil's Richard, because of this sense of despair of grace, was seen as a scheming, ruthless and brave monster: 'to ryd hymself of this inward gryfe, determynd fynally to pull up by the rootes all matter of feare and tumult and by guyle of fere to bring the same about'.[36] There are, as we shall see, many other dimensions to Richard and his religion, but Vergil's portrait is nevertheless a compelling and coherent account. He presents a man driven by ambition who had a reputation in his own lifetime for having a possibly insane belief in his own destiny and who, well aware of his isolation and his demonic reputation, maintained the forms of religious piety to gain acceptance and a following and from an intermittent sense of remorse. It is a portrait which could be ratified by contemporary descriptions of the king's reputation and behaviour.

The most perceptive view of Richard's religion is Sir Thomas More's account. This subtle and devout lawyer saw Richard as one who was 'indifferent to friend and foe when ambition was at stake', a self-righteously proud man 'arrogant of heart'.[37] More hints that what motivated Richard was a degree of religious self-delusion: 'God never gave this world a more notable example neither in what unsurety standeth this worldly weal, or what mischief worketh the proud enterprise of a high heart'.[38] In his treatise on *The Four Last Things*, the spiritual sin of pride (Richard's sin according to More) is the most deadly, almost incurable without God's special mercy.[39] More presents a Richard whose self-righteousness isolated him from ordinary, decent values. This is shown in his analysis of Richard's apparent puritanism, his austere code of sexual ethics (which emerged in the protector's condemnation of the immorality of his brother's court; his treatment of the Mistress Elizabeth (Jane) Shaw, the king's mistress; and his posthumous attack on the sexual morality of her lover, William, Lord Hastings). This analysis shows that Richard III's self-righteousness isolated him from the warmth of his fellow men. No one, More implies, took Richard's condemnation of Mistress Shaw's immorality seriously: 'the thing that herself could not deny, that all the world wist was true, and that nevertheless every man laughed at to hear it then so suddenly so highly taken-that she was naught (immoral) of her body'.[40] In fact More celebrated her femininity, describing her appearance when performing her penance: 'so womanly . . . so fair and lovely . . . a homely red colour in her cheeks.' that many good folk pitied 'more her penance than rejoiced therein'.[41] Though More personifies her as lechery, he sees her sexual licence as one aspect of a warm, impulsive, compassionate and generous person, who used her influence as the king's mistress to help people and who 'never abused to any man's hurt, but to many man's comfort and relief'.[42] Consequently, unlike Richard, she had many friends. The image of Mary Magdalene is not far below the surface of this portrait and More is suggesting what he explicitly states in the *The Four Last Things*. He proposes that compulsive sins like lechery and gluttony (also the vices of Edward IV) contain the sins of their own repentance and do not isolate the sinner from the rest of the human family in the way that Richard's pride, which impels him towards cruelty and isolation, does: 'And for this cause (as a goodly and continent prince, clean and faultless of himself, sent out of heaven into this vicious world for the amendment of men's manners) he caused the Bishop of London to put her to open penance'.[43] In *The Four Last Things*, More argues there are those who would do well to exchange the spiritual vices of pride, wrath and envy for the beastly carnal sins of gluttony, sloth and lechery.[44] He implies that Edward IV, who embodied these three carnal sins, and his immoral courtiers were, in contrast to the Duke of Gloucester, easygoing, sane and motivated in general by tolerance and compassion.

This is explicitly stated in More's account of Richard's treatment of William, Lord Hastings. Hastings, like Shaw, was 'somewhat desolate [dissolute]', yet he was 'a good knight and a gentle, . . . plain and open to his enemy and secret to his friend, eth [easy] to beguile, as he that of good heart and courage [disposition] forestudied [anticipated] no perils; a loving man and passing well beloved; very faithful and trusty enough, trusting too much'.[45] This, of course, is in marked contrast to the portrait of Richard III given by More and his contemporaries, which emphasizes the king's proud, suspicious, close, friendless nature, the sort of suspicious watchfulness celebrated in many of the psalms and devotions in Richard's prayer book which we will examine later. More is in many ways the key to the approach of this book. His humanist tolerance of human nature emerges in his portrait of Hastings, and he has little sympathy for Richard's intolerant and aloof brand of piety; but he does appreciate that the king was an isolated and, therefore, somewhat deluded zealot. It is my intention to look closely at ways in which Richard would have received encouragement to maintain this stance from his private devotions and prayers.

More was the last writer to draw on eyewitness accounts of the behaviour of Richard III and the further we get away from the beginning of the sixteenth century the more remote a figure Richard becomes, especially in the area of religious belief and practice. It is Shakespeare's vision that still dominates popular perception of Richard III and indeed of the fifteenth century. He created in his history plays (*Richard II*, *Henry IV Parts I* and *II*, *Henry V*, *Henry VI Parts I*, *II* and *III*, and *Richard III*) an epic story of an original sin, regicide, the killing of Richard II; a false dawn in the reign of Henry V that presaged

England's eventual greatness; and the punishment and expiation for the original regicide in the civil wars culminating in the reign of the Antichrist Richard III. Out of this apocalypse, in which most members of the York and Lancaster families died, there emerged a strong nation. This picture has similarities with Polydore Vergil's and there is no doubt that Shakespeare drew on the historical figure of Richard as described by More and Vergil and mediated to the Tudor chroniclers, especially Hall. Richard III can be seen in the character of Macbeth, the good man undone by ambition. This tradition was started by the Crowland Chronicler, who noted with regret the destructive rivalry between the three Yorkist brothers and their outstanding talent. This was continued by Robert Fabyan, who sadly noted that if Richard had allowed the children to have prospered he would have triumphed over all. Richard is also present in the incestuous and ambitious Claudius; in the scheming and talented Iago; and above all in the disinherited younger son, Edmund, Duke of Gloucester. Shakespeare's portrait of the personality of Richard III is compelling – a gifted man whose relationship with his family, especially his mother, and his monstrous egotism and intellectual strengths gave him a contempt for humanity and set him apart from the human family and the values of his day. This assessment remains truest to the individualistic spirit of the real Richard III, but, for all his perceptive insights into political and family strife, Shakespeare ignored the crucial dimension to Richard's personality, his religion, which he dismissed as cynical propaganda. What Shakespeare distorts is the image of Richard at prayer, which he and subsequent historians have seen as a cloak of hypocrisy to give moral credibility to a ruthless usurpation of power. Shakespeare dramatized Buckingham orchestrating a scene where representatives of the city of London attempt to interrupt the king at his private devotions to persuade him to take the crown. The king, feigning reluctance to renounce the pleasures of the contemplative life for the burdens of kingship, exclaims: 'Will you enforce me to a world of cares?' This crucial area of Shakespeare's ignorance explains why he was able to create the impression that there was a seismic rift between the fourteenth and sixteenth centuries by ignoring the religious continuity that existed between them. He was very much a product of lay literacy and the popularization of the literature of antiquity; a clever grammar school boy brought up on authors such as Seneca, Cicero and Livy. He, therefore, had a profound understanding of ancient Rome, which he dramatized in a number of his plays, but very little understanding of his immediate religious history. His only reference to the late medieval church occurs in Sonnet no. 73, when he looks at the 'bare ruined choirs' of a monastery with the same level of respect and incomprehension as the modern English poet Philip Larkin, when explaining in *Church Going* the appearance of a medieval parish church. It is perhaps a measure of the successful dissemination of classical education in England by the sixteenth century that it was not only chantries and religious houses that disappeared, but, in the minds of many intelligent laymen, much understanding of late medieval religion and, therefore, a complete understanding of the personality of Richard III.

This failure to appreciate the role of religion in Richard's actions increased with the years and it became an element in the increasingly polarized arguments about the relative merits of this last Plantagenet king. The first writer to give a favourable account of the king and to use his religious conduct to strengthen his case was Sir George Buck, a great grandson of John Buck who was taken prisoner at Bosworth for fighting for Richard III. Buck, in his *History of King Richard III*, which he completed in 1619, was sympathetic to Richard's puritanism and gives credit to his resolve to 'love and honour the clergy and to revere the holy church' and his attempt to win over his enemies by his good life. Buck ingeniously explains Richard's defeat at Bosworth as God's taking away a good and godly just prince because of the iniquities and transgressions of the people 'whom God deems in his divine judgment to be utterly unworthy of a good and virtuous king'.[46] John Milton, however, as a puritan, had little sympathy with Richard's chantry foundations and public good works and in *Eikonoklastes* he discerned in Richard 'a deep dissembler, not of his affections only but of his religion'. Horace Walpole, in his *Historic Doubts on the Life and Reign of King Richard III* in 1768, attempted to undo what he saw as the Tudor myth, but in doing so he paid little attention to religious motivations as befitted a writer of the Enlightenment. Instead he submitted Richard's crimes, such as his alleged attempt to dishonour his mother, to the dictates of common sense and found no evidence of motive on the king's part.[47] The first writer to suggest that Richard was a mixture of contradictions was the antiquary, William Hutton, who said in his *Battle of Bosworth Field* in 1788 that Richard bore 'the greatest contrariety of character which like every man's had two sides though most writers display but one'.[48] Such subtlety of analysis was displayed in the hostile biography of James Gairdner, *The Life and Reign of Richard III* in 1898. Gairdner, writing on Richard's religious benefactions, endorsed the now orthodox line of hypocrisy, but recognized that 'hypocrite as he was in many things, we may believe, nevertheless, that he acted in these matters from mixed motives in which some real sense of religion had its share. For there is surely a religious element even in the hope, so eagerly cherished by wrongdoers, that they may possibly buy back the favour of God as they do of men, and mitigate his displeasure in some degree by costly contributions.'[49] Gairdner also saw in Richard's attempt to win over his subjects by his good life a degree of religious motive: 'His public religion and his reign was conceived in the spirit of a penitent man who in the speech attributed to him by chroniclers before Bosworth calling on his subjects to forget his crimes and remember only the relations that ought to subsist between a sovereign and his people'.[50]

In the twentieth century the debate over Richard III has intensified and a society, the Fellowship of the White Boar (now the Richard III Society) was established to redeem the king's reputation. The first major revisionist work was Sir Clements Markham's *Richard III: his Life and Character*, published in 1906. Markham was a patriot writing before the discovery of Mancini's *Usurpation of Richard III* in 1934. He saw the vilification of Richard's reputation as a plot on the part of the Welsh Tudors who employed an Italian, Vergil, to create an Italian tyrannical figure far removed from the real king, who was an English-born patriot. Markham exonerated Richard of all the crimes he had been accused of, but, curiously, in his rehabilitation, he paid scant attention to Richard's piety, only remarking: 'He was devout and religious, striving to provoke greater activity among the clergy in improving the morals of the people'. In the next sentence he adds: 'Richard was a keen sportsman devoted to the chase'.[51] Perhaps this Edwardian portrait of a quintessentially hearty Englishman could not embody too fervid or popish a brand of Catholic religiosity. Another revisionist, who paid more attention to Richard's religion, was P.M. Kendall in his *Richard III*, 1955. Kendall detected a preoccupation with witchcraft in the second half of the fifteenth century and saw it colouring a number of political judgements such as the arrests of Clarence and Hastings.

He also saw religious motivations in many of Richard's pronouncements against his political opponents. Kendall considered that Richard was a rudimentary puritan because of his ownership of a Wycliffite New Testament; his attacks on the immorality of his brother's court and of the dead Hastings; his treatment of Mistress Shaw; his descriptions of the Marquis of Dorset and Henry Tudor as the leaders of a rabble of adulterers; and his communication to his bishops in March 1484 instructing them to reform public morals.[52]

It is surprising that until this time no attention had been paid to Richard III's book of hours and in particular the prayer containing his name which was added at his request. The first attempt to use this prayer as a window into Richard's mind was made in an imaginative work of fiction, *We Speak No Treason*, by Rosemary Hawley, 1971. The hero of this novel is a good man innocent of the crimes imputed to him. After the death of his son, Richard agonizes over the necessary execution of his friend, Hastings, for treason, something that he regrets, and relates the circumstances that force him to take the throne: 'A bastard cannot rule. Ah holy God! Did I do right to wear the crown. He turns to his prayer book and his personal prayer and asks his companion and knight at arms to read to him from his book of hours and his personal prayer, identifying himself with the innocent and wrongly accused Susannah: 'He knew this prayer by heart; I could hear him echoing my voice in a breath ". . . Even as . . . even as . . .". A cry was choking in my throat. My power of sight was gone. There was only silence; mine and his. "Even as thou didst save Susannah from false accusation" he said, in his beautiful voice.'[53]

The first scholarly descriptions of Richard III's book of hours and Richard's prayer occurs in Pamela Tudor-Craig's *Catalogue of the 1973 Richard III Exhibition*. She saw the prayer as playing a key role in reconciling Richard to his misfortunes and to expressing his feeling that he was misunderstood by his subjects. She suggests plausibly that he asked for it to be inserted into his prayer book after the death of his wife and son. She too places emphasis on the reference to the false accusations against Susannah and suggests he either believed he was innocent of the charges against him or that he was 'a very advanced schizophrenic'.[54] In 1980 J.R. Lander was less equivocal. He too saw the prayer as written for the king after the deaths of his wife and son and claimed that the prayer reveals an attitude of mind more than a form of persecution. Citing the highly charged reference to Susannah as prominently standing out, Lander claimed that 'considering the accusations against him, the knowledge he slandered his brother's memory, the probablility that he impugned his mother's chastity, that he authorized judicial murder, that he prepared to contemplate incest, that he cheated his nephews out of their inheritance if not far worse the prayer must indicate that either Richard thought he was innocent of the charges or that towards the end of his life he had become in the highest degree schizophrenic, a criminal self righteously invoking the protection of the almighty.'[55] Lander's suggestive use of modern, psychological terminology has the virtue of recognizing that Richard was both religious and unusual. He conceded that Richard's piety was more than skin deep or merely conventional with his neurotic awareness of hostility, his obsession with sexual morality and his morbid sense of persecution.

In the following year Charles Ross in his standard biography, *Richard III*, was more cautious in his estimation of Richard's prayer, commenting that it revealed a distracted emotional condition following the death of his son and the threat of invasion from the Earl of Richmond.[56] Ross, like Lander, was prepared to consider Richard's religion on its own terms and said there was no reason to doubt that he was a genuinely pious and religious man, citing his ownership of religious books as proof. He recognized Richard's good work in founding chantries and patronage of Cambridge scholars and denied this was mere hypocrisy, seeing in his foundation statutes for Middleham College a preoccupation with the mutability of human fortune.[57] Ross saw no contradiction between evil deeds and strongly held religious beliefs, but he looked no further at the relationship between them and was sceptical of Richard's sexual morality, which he claimed was used to make political capital by character assassination.[58] Furthermore he saw no point in delving any further into Richard's character and concluding that he was a 'conventional man for his age and station',[59] he denied his fundamental complexity and intelligence: 'We do not know Richard well enough to indulge in such psychological complexities. Any discordancy arises from his behaviour patterns (notably his loyalty to Edward IV and his disloyalty to Edward's sons). He does not appear to have been a complex man. He does not appear to have been a particularly intelligent man.'[60]

This note of scholarly caution regarding Richard's personality and religion has been maintained ever since. Rosemary Horrox, in her *Richard III A study in service*, used the prayer to St Julian the ferryman, which precedes Richard's prayer, to see the king's religion in terms of notions of public duty describing a ruler with a sincere devotion to the common weal who, as his security crumbled, developed the notion of redemption through service.[61] Anthony Pollard in *Richard III and the Princes in the Tower* in 1991 recognized Richard's knowledge of liturgy, devotional practice and his need to find solace in prayer. However, he expresses caution in reading states of mind into such documents as Richard's statutes for Middleham College and his personal prayer, apart from acknowledging that it is 'another sign that Richard was finding it difficult to cope with the stress he was under'.[62] For Pollard, as for most historians, the real difficulty in assessing the religion of one who 'seems to have had few self-doubts and to have been convinced of his own piety' was that such conviction did not sit well 'with some of his deeds'.[63]

The first and only comprehensive study devoted entirely to this subject of Richard's book of hours and his personal prayer is a scholarly survey entitled *The Hours of Richard III*, completed in 1990 by Anne Sutton and Livia Visser-Fuchs, which describes the style and workmanship of Lambeth MS 274 and analyzes its contents.[64] The authors accept that a book of hours can, in the absence of letters, throw light on Richard's private piety and that such a beautiful and unostentatious book could only have been chosen by the king for its prayers. However, they are cautious in their analysis of the king's prayer, pointing out that it occurs in a number of books of hours. They pinpoint three unique features of this prayer – the inclusion of the king's name and title in the text which shows its special significance for him; the unprecedented occurrence of the word *languor* (which they translate as grief); and the inclusion of the collect of St Michael, a saint particularly associated with deliverance, in the text. From this they concluded the prayer reveals mainly sorrow and grief, an entreaty for comfort and help, and that through repetition the prayer could lead to a cathartic cleansing of the mind. The prayer, they argue, is therefore full of hope.[65] The authors are similarly cautious in addressing the general issue of Richard's piety. Accepting his public piety, they repudiate the charge of hypocrisy on the basis that his guilt in relation to his alleged crimes is unproven.

His preoccupation with sexual morality, they maintain, is a public duty of a prince and the promotion of public virtue is no evidence of any personal preoccupation. They furthermore deny that a study of Richard's public piety contributes to an understanding of his personality and conclude it was no different from that of his contemporaries, though his sorrows and cares were greater than most.[66]

Just as Richard's prayer has been ignored until the publication of *The Hours of Richard III*, so too has the study of prayer in general. In 1988 Virginia Renesburg, in a chapter entitled 'Prayer and the Book of Hours', recognized the potential of the study of prayer to reveal the devotional lives of the fifteenth-century laity observing: 'books of hours tell us much about the art and material culture of the world that produced them, but for twentieth century viewers they are also windows into the interior, spiritual lives of ordinary lay people of the Late Middle Ages'. Her view of prayer is that it was essentially consolatory – the book of hours gives a view of peace and serenity through the worshipper's relationships with supernatural beings that replicate kinship and patronage relationships, but its ultimate purpose is salvation.[67]

Recent works on books of hours have endorsed this twofold function of prayer and have attempted to place Richard's prayer in this context. John Bossy defines prayer, which includes the psalms, as pleas to God for relief from distress and tribulation and from the machinations of the enemy. The obvious personal, political potential for the book of hours for rulers is appreciated when he describes the book of hours of Mary of Burgundy (stepdaughter of Mary of York, Richard III's sister). It contains an illumination of Mary sitting in a closet with hands clenched, nervously contemplating the political shambles bequeathed her by her father, Charles the Bold, and turning to the prayers of another beleaguered ruler, David.[68] However, Bossy's main interest in the prayer is as a plea for deliverance from enemies. Elsewhere Bossy has written about the late medieval preoccupation with different forms of social hostility and the function of the sacrament of penance as a means of reconciling penitents isolated from the community by hostile thoughts and impulses towards neighbours with their parishes. The mass he defines as a celebration of social concord within a community, usually the parish, after social hostilities have been resolved by the performance of penance.[69] Prayer he sees as complementing these activities. The owner of the book of hours seeks, through prayer, a resolution of difficulties with friends and neighbours and frequently the devout layman would pray from his book of hours while witnessing the celebration of mass, the ritual of social concord. Richard's prayer is, therefore, seen as an orthodox and predictable prayer by a king asking for peace. After citing Christ's restoration of concord in the universe, the worshipper asks Christ to remove the hatred of the king's enemies and to make peace and concord between them according to the model of making peace between Esau and his brother Jacob. The key, Bossy maintains, to this prayer and its relationship to the social functions of the sacraments is the part which says: 'And you Lord who reconciled the race of man and the Father who purchased with your own precious blood this proscribed inheritance of paradise and who made peace between men and angels, deign to make and keep concord between me and my enemies'. This he says in an echo of the exposition of the mass and the prayer cannot be used as evidence of individual neurosis or persecution mania, of either Richard's innocence or guilt.[70]

Eamon Duffy, in a comprehensive survey of books of hours and devotions in his *The Stripping of the Altars*, similarly sees the individual prayers of laymen operating within the self-referential terms of the institutions and sacraments of the church. Therefore, he believes them to be of little use to the historian who wishes to use them as evidence of any individualistic beliefs and concerns: 'Though the prayers professedly originate from the devotions of a woman, solitary or recluse, there is no sign in them at all of that growing gulf between individual and official religion which some historians have held to be characteristic of the period. They are resolutely churchly in tone and presuppose the church's sacramental, penitential system.'[71] For Duffy, prayers for deliverance from hostility of enemies are pleas for the help of saints against the Devil and his fallen angels, the source of all evils afflicting humanity including enmity between people. Prayers are, therefore, exorcisms or charms and enshrine a world view in which humanity is beleaguered by hostile troops of demons seeking the destruction of body and soul.[72] Such a view implies that there was a narrow dividing line between prayer and magic and that this was something that did not just inhabit the underground of popular religion but was a belief shared by the most sophisticated people. Duffy, therefore, considers

Richard's prayer as an orthodox plea for deliverance from misfortunes and the hostility of others caused by the activity of the Devil and his minions (an intriguing thought considering many of Richard III's contemporaries considered him to be a demonic force). It is certainly true that George, Duke of Clarence and Richard, Duke of Gloucester labelled accusations of witchcraft at their enemies.[73] There are indeed a number of prayers in Richard's book of hours that ask for deliverence from the devil. However, such a comprehensive and learned analysis of primers rests on the assumption that individual prayers were part of an enclosed Catholic tradition which, like the law, had its own common language, with such points of reference as the liturgy, the seven deadly sins, and the ten commandments. Laymen, therefore, when using a primer would be associating themselves with the more specifically liturgical routines of the clergy.[74] Such a professional, enclosed system would indeed have been ripe for toppling by the reformers; but, religion needs to be approached as a way of adapting to life and one's society and acknowledgement needs to be made to human emotions and situations.

The judgements of Sutton, Visser-Fuchs, Bossy and Duffy on the practice of prayer in the fifteenth century, and Richard's prayer in particular, make sense when considering prayer in institutional terms, as referring the individual to the protection of the church which provided salvation, exorcism and social harmony. However, they ignore the potential of the prayers in the books of hours to encourage individualism and to reinforce a sense of isolation from one's community. I attempted to show this in *Pastors and Visionaries: Religion and Secular Life in Late Medieval Yorkshire*, 1988, and that it was encouraged in the late fourteenth and fifteenth centuries through new saints cults and the devotional literature of the north-east which reinforced a strong sense of self, of individual worth and uniqueness.[75] Richard Rolle described his subjective, sensory experiences of *calor, canor* and *dulcedo* (sweetness, warmth and song), which gave him a feeling of regenerative power, because he was convinced they were manifestations of God's love for him that occurred after he invoked the Holy Name (which occurs at the end of Richard III's prayer). In his *Incendium Amoris*, Rolle describes how, after hearing sweet, previously unheard melodies and feeling an unusually pleasant heat, he sees the door of heaven swing open to reveal the face of Our Lord. Such experiences occurred when Rolle was either reading or singing the psalms, and he repeatedly emphasized that they set him apart from the rest of men and that he needed to pursue a solitary life, often facing deep suspicion and hostility, if he was to recapture these experiences. Many of Richard III's northern friends, servants and relatives were direct descendants of the first patrons of Rolle and his anchoress disciples and first readers of the hermit of Hampole's works.

Henry of Grosmont, the first Duke of Lancaster and a northerner in an especial sense, composed an autobiography in which he revealed the way his religion encouraged a richly associative inner life where the smells of scarlet cloth, the sounds and colours of a market-place, the bandaging of wounds of the battlefield, the rooting out of foxes and the longing at sea for the shore were all used to describe his various spiritual experiences of sin, confession and repentance. Julian of Norwich described vivid visions of Christ in which Christ's wounds bled freely like rain down the eaves of a cottage and Margery Kempe held conversations with Christ and his mother.

The cults of the new northern saints, who were worshipped in many fifteenth-century books of hours, similarly were less concerned with the traditional miracle performing and exorcising functions of the long-established saints and were encouraging a more personal, emotional and mysterious relationship with the supernatural. Holy men such as Robert of Knaresborough, Richard Rolle, St John of Bridlington and John of London occupied an important position in the imagination of laymen and women. The many pilgrims to Hampole experienced dreams and visions of the hermit who they described as a heavenly inspiration. In books of hours such as the Bolton hours, illuminated between 1420 and 1430 and owned by John Bolton, the Mayor of York and his wife (who were members of the York Corpus Christi Guild which Richard and Anne Neville were to join), contained prayers to the Holy Name of Jesus and a full page illumination of St John of Bridlington in the pastoral raiment he wore when appearing to distressed sailors at sea.[76] In another northern prayer book the martyred Archbishop Scrope is invoked *O gemma lucis* and the owners are depicted praying to the Virgin, who appears as a celestial blue apparition surrounded by golden rays. On another page is a bleeding heart on a heavenly blue sky.[77] These new saints were also being worshipped in an increasingly private, nostalgic and sentimental way and were regarded as friends who left behind them memories and precious personal momentoes, such as Archbishop Scrope's missal and St John of Bridlington's cap. Hagiographic accounts of the lives of Richard Scrope and St John of Bridlington emphasized not their power as magicians, but their personal charisma and such saints could be prayed to as friends and engaged in dialogue. Holiness was increasingly being seen in contemplative literature, prayers, saints' cults and in books of hours as a purely individual quality related to the personality, a person's thoughts feelings and individual gestures. Popular religion was not so much a case of a coming together of ordinary layfolk and sophisticated clergy and laymen in an acquiescence to the ritualistic, magic-working properties of the church as Duffy implies. It was more a shared experience of the individualistic, emotive concept of holiness based not so much on the curative power of prayers and relics as their ability to foster an increasing sense of inner richness and worth.

The significance of this for a study of the importance of the psalms and other devotions in the fifteenth century, especially for Richard III, is that this trend in the late fourteenth and fifteenth centuries, in both the more sophisticated devotional literature and the saints' cults and devotions of the layfolk, tended to emphasize that individual experience and occurred at the expense of the more traditional social functions of the church. Indeed in many cases it mitigated against the concept of social harmony. The lives of recent Yorkshire saints such as Richard Rolle and St John of Bridlington, in emphasizing their individual holiness, suggested this was a quality frequently misunderstood and opposed by the rest of society. Their asceticism and compassion set them apart from other men and what was seen as miraculous was their ability to live in the world and to communicate while remaining detached. Saints in fact were beginning to be seen as sages that existed on the fringes of society – the martyred Archbishop Scrope appeared in people's dreams acting as an alternative confessor to those reluctant to take confessions to the parish priest. They served as a focus for political opposition – support for the Scrope cult at the beginning of the fifteenth century became a way of expressing disillusionment with the Lancastrian regime.[78] The leaders of the church in the north, members of Thomas Arundel's circle who included Richard Scrope, were sympathetic to this trend towards a more individualistic religion. In the writings of Walter

Hilton and Nicholas Love there is a recognition that the devout person may have very different values from the rest of the parish community and this conflict could surface during compulsory parish confession. Some, according to Hilton, no matter how often they confessed and performed penances, still felt the biting and fretting of conscience. He expressed his sympathy with such people when, during annual confession, they were judged in terms of their relationship with their parish neighbours. Hilton taught the devout to regard conformity to sacramental rituals with detachment, as tribulations in their days of exile as strangers and pilgrims: 'thou woulds't be well paid for to be trodden and spurned under every man's feet as a thing which is outcast'. He defined the first mystical yearnings as the moment when 'thee thinketh that all creatures rise against thee and all thing which thou haddest delight in before turneth thee to pain'.[79] Nicholas Love, in *Mirror of the Life of Christ* (a favourite book of Richard III's mother, Cicely Neville), uses Christ as the model of the rejected outcast for all devout pilgrims and has him saying: 'if the world hate yow, witeth wele that it hated me firste byfore yowe', and in declaring 'In my confusion, dejection contempt and affliction inflicted upon me, either by myself or others I will rejoice'.[80] By recognizing the redemptive power of affective memory, of a mystical perception of reality as a penitential separation from Christ, these writers were calling attention to the repressive, stifling elements in communal religion. No writer expressed this more forcefully than Thomas Kempis in *De Imitatione Christi*, which was written between 1424 and 1427 and translated into English by a fellow of Pembroke, William Atkynson, and Margaret Beaufort, the mother of Richard III's supplanter, Henry Tudor, and the inheritor of Richard's book of hours and personal prayer. Kempis' sympathies were with those who were condemned and oppressed by others: 'In the Last Judgement they shall judge the oppressors: Than schul rigtwise men stonde in gret constaunce ayenst hem that haue anguysshed hem and oppressed hem; then schal he sitte to deme, that now subduith hem mekely to the iugementes of men'.[81] He gave sin an interior emphasis, regarding it not so much as the breaking of laws or offending a community, but as an inner disharmony. The contemplative man must separate himself from society. According to Kempis, a life spent relating with people, depending on them for comfort, can only be an unstable one. Peace rests not in one's relationships with others, but in one's friendship with God.

Human companionship should be avoided, and affections felt for others should mortify one. The further one withdraws from the consolations of the world into the self, the closer one gets to God: 'Sonne if thou sette thy pes with eny persone for thin owne felynge and lyvynge togidres, thou shalt be unstable and unpesed'.[82] No joy is envisaged in the company of others nor in a social well-being defined in terms of success, prosperity and stability. The outside world is seen as a hostile, alien, sterile place, offering nothing but unhappiness: 'Oure Lorde saith that the reume of God is within youe. Turn thiself to God with all thin herte and forsake this wrecchid worlde, and thy soul shall finde rest'.[83] The object of living a contemplative life is to become independent of the comforts of human society so one does not depend on other people when one is troubled: 'Whan there cometh a litel adversite, we bith anon throwen down and turne us to seke mannes comfort'. Suffering, for the introspective man, is good because 'Hit is good to us that we haue som tyme greuaunces and contrarietes for ofte tymes thei calle a man into himself, that he moue knowe himself to be in an exile, and that he put not his trust in eny erthely thynge'.[84]

There was, therefore, occurring among the sophisticated readers of contemplative literature and among enthusiastic followers of the teachings of Rolle and among worshippers of the new saints, a desire for a more personal relationship with God. They sought a more individualistic notion of sin and repentance and a belief that one's spirituality and closeness with God could be gauged in terms of the hostility and misunderstanding one received from others. It is time that the psalms and individual prayers in books of hours were assessed to consider their likely contribution to these trends. It is in this context that the devotions and prayers in Richard III's book of hours should be studied, to show how they could be used to reinforce values opposed by the rest of his society and to reinforce a grandiose self-image defined in terms of hostility, misunderstanding and rejection.

A cue to the methodology employed in this study of Richard III's religion and personality is provided in John Carey's biography of one of the most baffling and self-contradictory of English churchmen, the soldier, and womanizer who became Dean of St Paul's, the English poet John Donne: 'This critical procedure will, admittedly entail regarding doctrine to which Donne attaches himself not as elements of religious truth but, rather, as imaginative choices. But then, this is what religious doctrines are. For their ultimate truth or falsehood cannot be tested, and all the available evidence – such as that of scripture – is so diversely interpretable that individual decisions in the matter are based in the end to rest on the psychological preferences of the believer (or unbeliever): that is to say on the structure of his personality or imagination. Viewed in this way a writer's (*or anyone else's*) religious beliefs provide an invaluable guide to the workings of his fancy.'[85]

I shall try to show the workings of Richard III's imagination through his religious practices. Some aspects of this study (such as the austere code of chivalric ethics practised by the king) show him to be relatively conventional in some areas and should arouse little controversy. Some may think I am uncritical and accept what Richard says and does at face value, especially his pronouncements on sexual morality and his public religious benefactions. My answer would be that this is my intention. No one has really accepted his religious behaviour at face value – even Ricardians believe he was no more than conventionally pious. I shall be approaching Richard's religion with no preconceptions about his innocence or his cynicism, basing my argument on the acceptance of his complex, religious personality. I suspect my findings on the king's private religion, as revealed in his book of hours, will doubtless arouse most controversy. It should be clear from what I have said already that I will be relating the prayers in Richard's book of hours, and especially those included for him, to what I see as his sense of mission, his belief in his destiny to rule. I will be suggesting that they gave him the strength to pursue a course of action opposed to the values of his contemporaries and that they enabled him to make sense of the hostility he felt. Some will no doubt object to this yoking together of Richard's crimes and his religion. Anthony Storr, in a recent book, *Feet of Clay: a Study of Gurus*, shows that many self-appointed leaders, such as Jim Jones and David Koresh, are fortified by delusional religious beliefs that convince them of their messianic status. They consider that judgement of their actual behaviour by ordinary human standards is irrelevant and that the world is divided into black and white, their supporters and their opponents, who are usually dismissed with the appellation of labels such as communist, or some similar appellation. These gurus frequently see themselves as reincarnations of Old Testament prophets and grandiosity and isolation march hand in hand for such people.[86] It will be argued that Richard III exhibited all these traits. He can be considered a guru in the sense that he was a self-appointed ruler who commanded devoted loyalty in his lifetime, especially in the north, and great hostility and suspicion. Perhaps his guru status is most enhanced by his posthumous reputation and the devoted support he has received during his rehabilitation during the last 500 years, especially in recent times in the Fellowship of the White Boar and the Richard III Society.

Disagreement and criticism will emerge from quarters beyond the Richard III Society. It will be argued, with some justification by some scholars, that it is not scholarly procedure to make assumptions on the basis of what a person may or may not have read. That is a reasonable point of view, though not one I share. In the absence of any letters or diaries one should turn to Richard's books, especially one he would have turned to every day of his life. It will of course be suggested that my analysis of Richard's book of hours is too speculative and naïve and that the contents of prayer books are standardized and cannot therefore yield personal information. This, however, is one of the purposes of this book, to demonstrate that books of hours can be read with fresh enthusiasm and seen in less institutional, self-referential terms and used for their relevence to the lives of the nobility. It is because these sources are so traditional and commonplace that they have not been analyzed in the same way as the more individual productions of the late middle ages, such as devotional texts and Lollard literature, and, therefore, an essential source for an understanding of late medieval piety and Richard III has been neglected. Such sources will enable us to understand Richard III in late medieval terms. The king who will emerge from this study will, therefore, be closest to the Richard III of Sir Thomas More and William Shakespeare.

More showed how spiritual pride made Richard III into an isolated, harsh and deluded figure. Shakespeare, after omitting the religious dimension to the king's character, showed him to be a similarly contemptuous figure, isolated from the rest of humanity. Recent fair-minded historians, such as Michael Hicks and Rosemary Horrox, have chosen to consider Richard III as a man of his time, sharing the political values of his fellow high-ranking noblemen, neither good nor evil, but as one who responded in a conventional way to the political pressures of his day. The difficulty with such an approach is that to eliminate the political above the religious is a modern judgement. Hicks describes Richard as a skilful propagandist, the master of the public statement and press conference: 'in modern parlance Richard had good intrapersonal skills'.[87] These historians also rob him of any real personality and individuality, something that Shakespeare, who remains truest to the individualistic spirit of the real Richard III, gives him. This book attempts to focus on the moral and intellectual influences on this king. Most were mediated through the north and his mother, Cicely Neville, but some were from the court of his father, Richard, Duke of York. These very conflicting influences shaped Richard III's character and made him in part a conventional figure of his time, but also a very unusual, little-understood man, every bit as compelling and even more complex than Shakespeare's mythical anti-hero.

2

THE CHIVALRIC ETHICS OF
RICHARD III

Richard III was in some ways a conventional nobleman who adhered to a code of chivalric ethics that was shared by much of the ruling class in the second half of the fifteenth century. This code was shaped by intellectuals at his father and brother's court and by the influence of conventional lineage values of the English aristocracy. It was also determined by the impact of translations of the ethical writings of antiquity into English by writers patronized by Richard, Duke of York, Edward IV, George, Duke of Clarence and Richard III himself.

Richard Plantagenet was born in Fotheringay in the East Midlands on 2 October 1452, the eleventh child of Richard, Duke of York and Cicely Neville. In his early life he would have been subjected to influences at the Yorkist court. He divided his time between his father's principal residences of Fotheringay, Ludlow in the Welsh marches, Sandal in Yorkshire and the town house of Baynard's Castle in London. In the 1440s and 1450s his father, whose claim to the throne lay with Richard II's nominated Mortimer line, became a focus for noblemen including writers and patrons of the arts, who opposed Henry VI's government and its policies of appeasement in France. As a child and adolescent, Richard was exposed to these influences. In 1461, after their father's death at the Battle of Wakefield, Richard and George were sent to the Netherlands for their safety in the care of Duke Philip the Good of Burgundy, where they were entertained at the ducal palace at Bruges. The English merchant adventurer, William Caxton, had, since 1453, a close relationship with the court of Burgundy, and in 1462 he became governor of the English merchants at Bruges. Richard returned to England in 1461 when Edward was safely installed as king and spent some time in Greenwich palace.[1]

The marriage of Edward IV to Elizabeth Woodville in May 1464 brought Richard into contact with her family of two sons by her first marriage and five brothers. His association with the traveller, jouster, translator and poet, Anthony

Woodville, a man of varied active and contemplative interests and wide curiosity began at this time. In 1465 Richard was sent to the household of his cousin and possible godfather, Richard Neville, the Earl of Warwick, to complete his education. Until 1468 most of Richard's time was now spent in Middleham in Yorkshire. However, he began to play an active role in the court and developed associations with noblemen who were playing a key role in transmitting the teachings of antiquity from Europe into England. Together with Anthony Woodville and William, Lord Hastings, he was involved in preparations for the marriage of his sister, Margaret, to Charles the Bold, the Duke of Burgundy. He was at a Garter ceremony on 13 May 1469, when the Order of Garter was conferred on Charles, Duke of Burgundy, and he accompanied Edward IV, Richard Woodville the Earl of Rivers, Anthony Woodville, Lord Scales and other Woodvilles on a pilgrimage to Bury St Edmunds.[2] In the same year he was made Constable of England, a post that had been held by Richard, Earl Rivers and John Tiptoft, Earl of Worcester (another important patron of humanist writers in Italy and collector of the writings of antiquity) and he replaced William, Lord Hastings as Chief Justice of North Wales. His association with Hastings and Anthony Woodville was strengthened when they all supported Edward IV against the Earl of Warwick and George, Duke of Clarence. When they fled together in October 1470 to the Low Countries, where they were sheltered by Lord Louis of Gruuthuyse, Governor of Holland, in his palace at Bruges, they encountered Gruuythuse's collection. This was one of Europe's finest libraries which subsequently became the core of the library of Louis XII, King of France.[3] It is possible that at this time Edward IV and Richard met William Caxton, who was in the service of Margaret, Duchess of Burgundy as librarian, secretary and translator. With the re-establishment of Edward IV's monarchy in 1471 Richard attained a new importance in the court and he is depicted in particular paintings as being present at some of the cultural events of the period. In an illustration of the presentation of Waurin's chronicles to Edward IV, Richard is shown wearing his Garter, and he is similarly depicted standing in the background behind Anthony Woodville and William Caxton at Anthony Woodville's presentation to Edward IV in 1477 of his *Dicts and Sayings of the Philosophers*.[4] This was the first printed book to emerge in England from Caxton's printing press, which was established at Westminster Abbey in 1476.[5]

Anthony Woodville, Earl Rivers presenting his *Dicts and Sayings of the Philosophers* to Edward IV. Richard, Duke of Gloucester is in the background. (BL MS. 265 fo. 6)

The courtiers of Edward IV (of whom William Caxton was probably one) also drew on Roman history for examples of an austere and manly code of chivalry. Anthony Woodville, Edward IV's brother-in-law, lived an active life as a jouster, courtier, crusader and traveller. He was also a scholar with a sense of mission who translated the works of Christine de Pisan and writers of antiquity from French into English. Caxton, in his epilogue to River's translation of the *Cordyale* or *The Four Last Things*, said of Woodville: 'notwithstanding the labours that he has had in the service of the king of my lord prince of Wales and in England which have been of no little thought, and business both in spirit and in body and to enrich his virtuous disposition he has put him in endeavour at all times when he have leisure which was infrequent to translate diverse books out of French into English'.[6] Woodville was in an especially fortunate position to do so as grandson of the Duchess of Bedford and he probably received many of his books at first hand from the library of Charles VI (he gave a copy of a work of Christine de Pisan, which he received from his mother, to Louis of Bruges).[7] King Charles V commissioned French translations of Livy, Valerius Maximus and of the *Ethics* and *Politics* of Aristotle. In 1405 Laurent Premierfait translated Cicero's *De Senectute* into French for Louis, Duke of Bourbon and completed a translation of *De Amicitia* in 1416. Aeneas Sylvius, secretary of the Duke of Berry, made French versions of the works of Seneca and Aristotle and recommended Cicero's *De Amicitia* for the study of princes. These translations formed the nucleus of the royal library at the Louvre which was praised by Christine as her favourite library in her biography of Charles V. This library also provided her with reference books when she wrote her textbooks of military theory and moral philosophy which were to have such influence in England in the fifteenth century. Woodville's reputation was such that he was entrusted with the welfare of Edward, the Prince of Wales, and he received ordinances from the king telling him to have stories read to the prince communicating honour, cunning, wisdom and deeds of worship. Woodville responded by translating Christine de Pisan's *Livre du Corps de Policie*, a mirror for princes drawn largely from Roman history in which the 'glorious tyme of the Romayns'[8] is upheld as the embodiment of martial self-discipline. In this work it is maintained that at Rome the 'corage of men and women was right vigorous'.[9] They maintained the schools of knighthood that produced 'the cesares'.[10] The authors expressed their admiration for Roman civilization and maintained that its empire was the product of an advanced civilization for whom military and intellectual discipline was synonymous: 'for it is no doubte the exercise of arms and of wisdom togeder helped them gretly in their conquests' and for this reason 'may wele thence that the Romayns wer better men and mor worthy than othre'.[11] Using Vegetius, the author warned Edward IV that the wars of Rome profited the city more than its idleness. Like William Worcester, Woodville saw a cyclical decline occurring in civilizations when masculine, military virtues were eroded. In the case of Rome's decline he maintained that 'while befor tyme were manly and worchippful in arms wexed softe and delicate as women. And so by delycasye and ydelness they wer conquered'.[12]

By 1445 the crisis that occurred in the Roman empire in AD 400, during the minority of Honorius, was being used to mirror the collapse of royal authority under Henry VI. The Duke of York was becoming the focus for hopes of a renewal of English imperial ambitions along Roman lines. In 1436 as Lieutenant of France he helped re-establish the English military position in Normandy and control over the Pays de Caux. During his second term as lieutenant between 1440 and 1445 he ensured that the French would have to fight to take Normandy. This restored effective authority to a province all but lost to rebellion and sustained business confidence in a continued English presence. Despite these achievements Henry VI was determined to pursue a peace policy, and York came to be regarded as a saviour of England's imperial heritage, following the precepts of the Roman general Stilicho. In 1445 an English translation was made of a letter of Claudian addressed to General Stilicho in AD 400 requesting him to come to Rome to accept the honour of consul at a time when the Roman empire, due to weak leadership, was in peril. The translator was possibly Osbern Bockenham, an Augustinian friar of Clare, who travelled to Italy twice and wrote a life of female saints for Richard, Duke of York's, sister, Isabella, Countess of Essex, and perhaps translated the *Golden Legend*, which was printed by Caxton. Stilicho, who represented all the classical virtues of patience, temperance, prudence and chastity celebrated in such works as Scrope's *Epistle of Othea* was a powerful symbol for the Duke of York and his followers, the last great Roman before the collapse of the empire.

The experience of the victories in Normandy under Henry V and the Duke of Bedford and the subsequent setbacks shaped the attitudes of a generation. By the mid-fifteenth century there existed within the English court, and especially in the circle of Richard, Duke of York, a belief in the pre-eminence of Roman civilization and a sense that for a brief period (from 1415 to the death of Bedford in 1435, or possibly until the recall of the Duke of York from Normandy in 1444) England had been involved in an epic of Roman proportions. Worcester in his *Boke of Noblesse*, when he urges Henry VI to conquer his rightful heritage, asks the English nation to remember that they are descended from 'the noble Brutus bloode of Troy'.[13] This story was retold in the *Eneydos* printed in about 1490 by Caxton. London in the fifteenth century was commonly known as New Troy. It is significant that the first book printed by Caxton in the English language, and commissioned by Richard III's sister, Margaret of Burgundy, was *The Recuyell of the Historyes of Troye* by Raoul le Fèure, chaplain of Philip, Duke of Burgundy. It was printed in Bruges in 1474.[14] English failures in colonial administration were accompanied by a search for reasons that forced the English aristocracy to compare the respective values of Roman and English civilizations. It was believed that both were sustained by a sense of natural justice and purpose that was defined as the common weal. Failures to apply this principle in Normandy would inevitably lead to ramifications for England itself and as England slid towards civil war in the 1450s the educated classes were aware of uncomfortable parallels in Roman history where failings in imperial administration had internal consequences. The significance of the *Letter of Stilicho* for the Duke of York lay in its stress on the common weal as a prescription for rule, with the parliamentary peers, like the Roman senate, expressing the *vox populi*, for both legitimized the rule of Stilicho and the Duke of York. Stilicho is taught the lesson of justice, to follow the 'commoun lawys', a phrase that conveys the principle of obedience to English laws made with the consent of people and which were defended by custom and which also bore the sense of the common weal.[15] Stilicho accepted the people's offer of the consulate because he had a dynastic connection with the royal house; because the people called on him to do so; and because in an emergency he had the interests of the common weal at heart. If one accepts the 1445 date of the letter in the manuscript it coincides with the recall of York from Normandy and his popular image as the military leader committed in the face of the pro-French monarchy to the defence of the empire. By 1455 York would have been able to apply this text to the circumstances of his protectorship – his taking the burdens of kingship, after being petitioned three times, from the child king, Henry VI (who is identified with Honorius), in the face of opposition pretenders such as Somerset (Rufinus). On 17 November York presented articles explaining his assumption of the protectorship that were closely in accord with the *Letter of Stilicho*, drawing attention to the intended benefits of the protectorate sanctioned by parliament: 'the welfare and honour of the king the politique and restful rule and governance of this his land and the entreating of his laws and peace wherein rests his joy, consolation and surety of years and all his liege people and of my self especially the fruits of government'.[16] This translation of Claudian's letter is an eloquent testimony to the impact of classical history on the political and intellectual life of the fifteenth century.

The house of York continued through the reign of Edward IV to be linked with the production of works of antiquity associated with the education of the aristocracy and the application of such learning to common weal ideals. Benedict Burgh, chaplain to Edward IV in 1470 and a friend of Lydgate, translated Cato's distichs into English verse for Henry, Earl of Essex, the son of Lady Isabel Bourchier, Countess of Eu, and sister of Richard, Duke of York. Burgh and this family were connected to the Woodvilles as Henry's son, Sir William Bourchier, married Anne, sister of Elizabeth the wife of Edward IV.[17] William Caxton printed this work under the title *Parvus Cato and Magnus Cato* about 1477. In the prologue he explained that he had done so in order that the young of the city of London could live profitable lives augmenting the prosperity of their parents and the city as citizens in other European cities he had travelled to managed to do and above all as the ancient Romans had done: 'O whan I remember the noble Romayns/ that for the comyn wele of the Cite of Rome/ they spente not only theyr moeuable goodes/ but they put theyr bodyes lyues in iopardy to the deth'.[18] Edward IV himself owned a glossed version of *Secreta Secretorum* and Pietro Carmeliano presented to him a copy of Cicero's *De Oratore*, probably a copy of the edition printed in Vienna in 1478.[19] In 1475 Caxton, in his prologue to the first edition of *The Game of the Play of*

Chess, which he dedicated to George, Duke of Clarence, said: 'As I understand and know you are inclined unto the common weal of kings, nobles, lords and common people of the realm of England and you saw gladly the inhabitants of the same informed on good virtues, profitable and honest manners which your noble person with guidance of your house have in abundance has caused me to translate the book out of French into English which I have found the authorities, sayings and stories of ancient doctors philosophers poets and wise men applied to public weal of nobles and common weal after the name of chess'.[20]

Richard III was an important beneficiary of many of the imperial assumptions and ambitions discussed above. In one of Bishop John Russel's preliminary drafts for a sermon prepared for the first parliament of Edward V he likened Richard, Duke of Gloucester, to Marcus Lepidus the tried and trusted third sharer in the Yorkist family's inheritance, the kingdom's stand-in between Edward IV and Edward V.[21] Archbishop Whitelaw, in his address to Richard III advocating the strengthening of peaceful ties between the English and the Scots in September 1484, expressed the same admiration for the Augustan age as Fortesque. Citing Cicero's eulogy of Pompey, Whitelaw describes Richard as an embodiment of military skill, prowess (*virtus*), good fortune and authority who must now exercise self-control, intelligence and humanity to bring about peace. For it was during the time of 'the peace that reigned when Augustus Caesar having defeated Mark Antony by land and sea and routed Cleopatra, Queen of Egypt, that Augustus and Rome held the whole world in tranquillity as a result of his prowess in war.' Noting that it was in this time of peace that Christ was born, Whitelaw pointed out that the Romans built a temple to peace and Cicero 'that master of Roman rhetoric and wisdom declared that peace and concord were the foundations of all ordered government'. He also quoted from the great epic of the age of Augustus, Virgil's *Aeneid*, to show how the Romans in this period used the empire to advance the cause of peace: 'Romans, remember that it is your destiny to rule the people of the world with your command; your skill will be to impose the habit of peace, to spare the conquered, but to defeat in war those who prove intransigent'.[22] On such foundations, Whitelaw points out, rest justice, law and order and the achievements of civilization.

Richard, Duke of Gloucester's upbringing in the household of York took place in an environment where there was a professed commitment to the concept of the common weal as a basis for taking and exerting political power. When Richard, Duke of York was killed at Wakefield in 1460 his namesake and youngest son, Richard, was only eight. As he grew to resemble his father physically, so he attempted to adopt many of the principles held by the Duke of York and his followers among the circle of Sir John Fastolf, the ex-soldiers who were disillusioned by the defeats in Normandy. After his father's death, Richard was brought up by his mother with her other, younger children in Fastolf's London house in Southwark. He read the sort of chivalric manuals and histories that encapsulated the virtues his father stood for – empathy with the common soldier and commitment to justice and the common weal. Among his books was a northern manuscript containing Vegetius's *De re militari*, a copy of which was also in Fastolf's library.[23] Richard established his military reputation by helping his brother regain the throne at the battles of Barnet and Tewkesbury, which earned him comparison with one of the nine worthies, Hector of Troy.[24] He also seems to have shared the same imperial ambitions as members of the Yorkist circle, which, as we have seen, were not confined to northern France. The moral superiority claimed by James Butler, the Earl of Ormond and lieutenant of Ireland, who received a translation of the *Secreta Secretorum* from James Yonge extolling the English civilizing mission in that colony,[25] was shown by Richard, Duke of Gloucester in Scotland. He was a reluctant executant of the Treaty of Edinburgh in 1474, and the crumbling of the peace in 1479 was partly due to Gloucester's lack of enthusiasm – when war broke out he was twice the king's appointed Lieutenant General in 1480–2. From the point of view of northern England his campaigns were a triumph – he contained all Scottish raids within a few miles of the border and raided deep into Scotland. These raids culminated in 1482 in an unopposed march on Edinburgh and the recapture of Berwick,[26] the first triumph over a foreign country since the days of his father's campaigns in Normandy in 1441–4. Richard attempted to install a younger brother of James III, Alexander, as King of the Scots and he probably saw his palatinate of Cumberland as a base for the eventual subjugation and conquest of Scotland. That his campaigns were driven by a degree of moral fervour is indicated by his enthusiasm for the cult of St Ninian (the Briton who converted the Picts to Christianity), the patron saint of the western march towards Scotland where Richard was warden. Ninian was worshipped at Richard's chantry foundation at Middleham and was to be worshipped at his proposed foundations of York and Barnard Castle; at Queen's he endowed four priests to say a collect of St Ninian every day with the prayer 'O God you who has converted the peoples of the Britons and Picts by the teaching of St Ninian your confessor to knowledge of your faith asks intercession to the joys of heaven'. The moral and even religious enthusiasm shown by some of those partaking in Richard's Scottish campaigns is demonstrated by Sir Hugh Hastings (brother of Richard's steward of the manorial lordship of Pickering), who made his will in 1482 before joining the Scottish expedition. Hastings left a wax taper burning with the friars of Tickhill in honour of St Ninian, and stated his intent and purpose 'under the protection and grace of Almighty God to passe towardes the Scottis, the kingis enemyes'.[27] Sir John Constable also began his will stating that by the grace of God he proposed 'to go in viage into Scotland'.[28] His fellow northerners shared his enthusiasm for the saint, a retainer of Gloucester's. Thomas Merkenfield of Merkenfield near Ripon called his son and heir Ninean[29] and in 1466 Margaret Aske willed that some man be appointed to go on pilgrimage to St Ninian's. William Eccop, rector of Hesleton, sponsored a pilgrim to St Ninian's shrine in Whitehorn in 1472[30] and in 1491 Margery Salvin left one of the saint's bones to the Grey friars of York.[31] Richard's ambitions in Scotland were part of his policy of consolidating power in the north, which culminated in February 1483 in the creation of a county palatine comprising Cumberland and a large stretch of south-west Scotland, which it was his declared intention to conquer. At this time Richard was set to become a duke of a semi-autonomous duchy in the north-west akin to Burgundy, ruled by his chivalric brother-in-law, Charles the Bold.[32]

It was in his attitudes towards England's imperial destiny in France that Richard of Gloucester showed himself to be his father's son. His eldest brother, Edward, Earl of March, became, after the Battle of Wakefield, the first Yorkist king and the natural focus for the imperial hopes of William Worcester and his circle. Worcester rededicated and adapted his *Boke of Noblesse* to Edward IV in 1473 to coincide with his invasion of France in 1475. However, Edward, after his successful campaigns in 1471, failed to live up to these expectations and as his corpulence increased with his reputation for womanizing, Richard, Duke of Gloucester's austere code of chivalry began to run counter to the policies of his brother. Edward's invasion of France in 1475, in alliance with Burgundy, gave Gloucester the chance to emulate the achievements of Henry V (there were two days of military activity at Agincourt). But Edward IV agreed to withdraw at the Treaty of Picquigny in return for a pension and the betrothal of his daughter, Elizabeth, to the Dauphin. Gloucester was reported to be very displeased at this (he was an absentee at the treaty) and it was likely that his opposition was based on the conviction that the settlement was dishonourable. According to Commynes, at the meeting between Edward IV and Louis XI at Picquigny Bridge with Clarence, Hastings, and possibly Richard, the French king suggested Edward come to Paris to dine with the ladies and he would give him my Lord Cardinal of Boubon as confessor, since he would willingly absolve him from sin as he was a jolly good fellow. One cannot imagine Gloucester approving of this remark which he must have heard, nor of the free wine given to the English troops that night at Amien.[33] His military ambitions in France were consistent with those of his father and writers such as William Worcester and based on the sort of high-minded principles of chivalry espoused by Henry V and his court. It has been suggested that if 1475 had seen a second Battle of Agincourt the power struggle and usurpation may have been avoided – war with France would have clarified such issues as service to one's prince and Gloucester may have found a sphere to occupy his restless energies.[34] This incident marked the growing estrangement of the more austere Richard from the brother he idolized and the Woodvilles' domination of the court, and he would have seen the treaty as a betrayal of all his father had stood for in Normandy. In the following year, 1476, he played a part in the reburial of his father at Fotheringay, and as Constable of England he encouraged the heralds to pay tribute to York's martial prowess at the end of the Hundred Year's War. During York's governorship of Normandy it was recalled how 'he passed the river at Pontoise and drove away the French king'. The campaign Richard was referring to, which occurred on the Seine and Oise in the Summer of 1441, represented the last chance of turning the tables on Charles VII, for the Duke of York's army came close to capturing the

enemy monarch, an achievement Richard held in high esteem.[35] When
Edward IV failed to support Richard's sister, Margaret, Duchess of Burgundy
(who by 1481 was widowed and in charge of the infant heir to Burgundy),
Gloucester became the focus for Burgundian hopes of English intervention.
Margaret and the regent of Burgundy, the future emperor Maximilian, became
tacit supporters of Gloucester's usurpation and continued to identify him with
the Yorkist cause.

The circumstances of Richard of Gloucester's seizure of power suggest that
he intended to emphasize the physical and moral bond between himself and his
father. When Dr Shaw delivered his sermon on the bastardy of Edward IV's
children at St Paul's Cross on 22 June 1483 he spoke of the adultery of the
Duchess of York. He claimed that Edward IV and George, Duke of Clarence
(who were both tall and did not resemble Richard, Duke of York) were not
Richard of York's children and that Richard, Duke of Gloucester was the Duke
of York's only legitimate son, his father's image and likeness. According to
Thomas More, at this point Richard was supposed to appear on a balcony.[36]
This biblical rivalry between the brothers will be referred to later. What is likely
is that Gloucester regarded his assumption of the throne and disinheriting his
nephews as a military usurpation in which he was following in the footsteps of
his father, who made his bid for the throne with the encouragement of the
soldiers who had served him in France. Gloucester summoned his northern
supporters on 10 June 1483 and a small army bore down on the capital, where
he was proclaimed king sixteen days later. The chroniclers stress Richard's
personal inspection and leadership of these troops: 'to be sure of all his enemies
he sent for . . . men of the north agaynst his coronacion, which came up and
shewed themselves in Finsbury fielde, where king Richard received them, and
rode with them throughe Chepe to Barnardes Castle'.[37] His strike against the
Woodvilles was also intended to be seen in military terms – the Earl Rivers was
beheaded at Pontefract after being tried by a military commission drawn from
Richard's own northern army. The tone of his short reign was set by his
aggressive policies towards France. According to Henry Tudor's spy, Richard III
intended to mark his reign with a new invasion of France. The continuity with
his father's policies was symbolized when William Worcester's son rededicated
The Boke of Noblesse to Richard III. The heroes of this work were the Duke of

York, Fastolf and Henry V, and there is an exhortation to follow the example of the boar and advise courageous hearts to war, and by implication the Duke of York's cause.[38] Like the boar who forgets its own strength until it sees its own blood, Richard is advised to put himself to war to revive strength and courage against these nations that put him from his rightful inheritance.

There was an ethical dimension to Richard's military ambitions consistent with the sort of literature read in his father's court which was inspired by ancient history. In his formative years Richard acquired *The Siege of Thebes*. Three other works bearing his signature are the *Grandes Chroniques*,[39] *Tristram*, and Giles of Rome's *De regimine principum*. The latter was composed between 1277 and 1279 for the future Philip IV of France and deals with the practical, ethical problems facing a prince who has to learn to govern himself before he can govern others.[40] When he was king, Richard acquired the *Historia Destructionis Troiae* and *Historia Regum Britanniae*, both signed *Ricardus Rex* and the *De re militari*, which is decorated with crowned arms.[41] In the same year as Worcester's son rededicated *The Boke of Noblesse* to Richard III, William Caxton dedicated his translation of Lull's *Order of Chivalry* to Richard III. He laments, in a manner reminiscent of Worcester, the decline of chivalry from the time of the knights of the round table and urges the king to institute a programme of uplifting education and tournaments to lure corrupt youth away from the brothels and gambling dens of London. Knights, he said, now go to baths and play at dice rather than reading Lancelot and Gawain. How many knights, he asks, now use and exercise a horse? He suggests that the king call jousts of peace two or three times a year, and desires that his book be read by all noble men, and to this end he asks the king to order it to be read to young knights and gentlemen.[42] This recalls the praise given in *De re militari* (owned by Richard III) to the Athenians for commanding the masters of chivalry to teach and read to young warriors books of chivalric conduct.[43]

Richard of course did not have the opportunity to invade France, preoccupied as he was with internal rebellions, but, like his father before him, he employed a patriotic rhetoric against his political opponents and proclaimed his hatred of the French. In calling for support against the Marquis of Dorset, Jasper Tudor and Sir Edward Woodville, Richard, like his father before him, appealed to Englishmen's patriotism and their hatred of the French, making much of the fact that he was the only King of England to be born in that country. In a proclamation from Westminster entrusted to his chancellor, the Bishop of Lincoln, to be delivered to the sheriffs of all counties of the realm on 7 December 1484, he revealed that the rebels had forsaken their natural country for Brittany and had sought the support of the ancient enemy, the King of France. They had, in return for the king's support, promised to give up all claims to the crown of France, the duchies of Normandy and Gascony, and called on true Englishmen to defend themselves against the conspiracies of the ancient enemy: 'and our sovereign lord as a well willed, diligent and courageous prince wol put his royal person in defence of the enemy'.[44]

Continuity with the ideals of Richard, Duke of York and his circle can also be seen in the rhetoric Richard, Duke of Gloucester used when he assumed power. The establishment and maintenance of political authority in fifteenth-century England involved leaders at least pledging their pursuit of principles concerned with strong government in the interest of the common good and continuity.[45] His father, as we have seen, established the precedent of an assumption of power based on the will of the people and the common good in the parliament of 1455, during which Humphrey, Duke of Gloucester was rehabilitated and praised for having ruled for the benefit of the common weal on behalf of an impotent king. Richard, Duke of Gloucester may in 1483 have identified with his namesake Humphrey (who had been arrested by his nephew Henry VI) and saw himself as a defender of the common good who was in a similarly vulnerable position regarding his nephew Edward, Prince of Wales. In the sermon delivered by Bishop Russell during Gloucester's protectorate, classical precedents were used to justify Richard's extreme actions. Russell used the example of Marcus Emilius who, after the death of Ptolemy, was given custody of the heir and his realm by the senate.[46] The circumstances of his assumption of the throne in August 1483 closely followed those of his father's protectorate in 1455. A petition from the citizens of London (or New Troy) was stage-managed by Buckingham, and Richard twice rejected the offer before accepting the crown. This of course followed the pattern of the well-known drama staged by Mark Antony for Julius Caesar, who was also offered the crown by the citizens of Rome three times.

In Yorkist circles, including those of Sir John Fastolf and William Worcester, concern for the common weal was expressed in terms of opposition to corruption and intimidation on the part of Henry VI's ministers, and during his short reign Richard III upheld the tradition more vigorously than his brother Edward IV.[47] At his coronation oath, given in English for the first time, he swore to maintain the church, administer justice, uphold the laws of England and defend his subjects.[48] He later referred to his oath in a letter to the Earl Desmond which summarized his objectives of establishing good government and maintaining the common weal. One of his proclamations begins: 'The king's grace willeth that for the love that he hath for the ministration and execution of justice for the common wealth of this realm, the which he most tendereth'.[49] He was specially concerned with his reputation as a man of justice and frequently referred to the profession of justice made at his coronation oath and encouraged the clerk of his council, John Harrington, to discriminate positively in favour of petitions from the poor in an initiative which was the first step towards establishing a court of poor requests. The council of the north, which he established at Sandal and Wakefield and which met quarterly at York under the presidency of his heir, Edward of Middleham, and then John de la Pole, had the duty of keeping the peace and punishing law breakers. One of the articles enjoined counsellors not to be swayed by 'favour, affection, hate, malice or meed, nor to speak in the council otherwise than the king's laws and good conscience shall require, but be indifferent and no wise partial'.[50] The legislation of his one parliament also dealt with the administration of the law allowing bail to those suspected of felony and laying down standards of property qualification for jurors and making arbitrary taxes or benevolences illegal.[51] In a letter concerned with the regulation of the cloth trade, Richard described himself as a 'Christian prince above all things earthly intending the common wealth of his realm, the increase of wealth and prosperity of his subjects'.[52] After the collapse of the 1483 rebellion he issued a proclamation in Kent stating his determination to see the administration of justice throughout his realm, to punish and subdue all extortions and oppression, and requesting that on his coming into Kent any person who found himself grieved and oppressed or unlawfully wronged should make a bill of complaint to his highness and he would be heard, for 'his grace is determined all his subjects shall live in rest and quiet and peacefully enjoy their lands'.

CHANGES IN THE CODE OF CHIVALRY: ANTIQUITY AND THE
IMPORTANCE OF THE STATE

Therefore, it is clear that in many respects Richard, Duke of Gloucester was an intellectual heir to many of the ideas circulating in the circles of his father; but he only managed to hold on to his throne for just over two years. This can be attributed to his failure to use the developing code of ethics of the governing class to secure the allegiance of the nobility to create a unified state. The code of chivalry was changing quickly in the fifteenth century due to the impact of Roman philosophy. The family was no longer the only focus for loyalty and the honour of the lineage was ceasing to be the sole dictate of behaviour. These values had been defended as recently as 1383 in the north of England in an armorial dispute in the court of chivalry between a Cheshire and a Yorkshire family, the Grosvenors and the Scropes, over the right to bear the Azure Bend Or arms. In this dispute the nobility of England unanimously voiced their approval of the rights of a noble family to assert themselves aggressively and unquestioningly in defence of family pride and honour. For these families and their deponents the right to bear a coat of arms, and the sense of timelessness they felt in belonging to a family in which honour could be inherited and transmitted down the lineage, acquired an almost religious significance. By the fifteenth century, as hereditary class barriers hardened because of economic competition from prosperous peasants, the claims of blood over virtue were being advanced and backed up by a hardening of lineage into a legal doctrine. This was further supplemented by increasingly sophisticated knowledge of the past employed in the service of family pedigrees and histories in such works as William Worcester's lost genealogy of Norfolk families and John Rous' history of the Earls of Warwick. Indigenous traditions in the form of Arthurian myths reinforced the individualistic pursuit of private rights and honour and Arthurian pageants, tournaments and the Order of the Garter gave weight to Edward III's 'just quarrel', his campaigns against the French between 1342 and 1367. But such claims for the lineage were being made against an increasing weight of opinion asserting the claims of virtue over blood and the community of nation. This had been started by Dante and had attained the status of a full-bodied debate by the mid-fifteenth century which was to continue and to receive expression in the works of Shakespeare. Virtue was defined largely in terms of service to the common good, and the intellectual basis for such a definition of nobility was not native myths but Roman history and philosophy. There was nothing new in this. Renewed interest in antiquity in the twelfth-century schools was reflected in the court of Henry II of England in such chivalric literature as the *Faits des Romains*, a translation from Lucan's and Caesar's commentaries. Experts on Roman Law, such as Bartolus of Sassoferrato, also wrote on war and the duties of the soldier in terms of public service. By the fourteenth century theoretical treatises on chivalry in Europe, such as Bonet's *Tree of Battles*, defined knightly duty in terms of definite obligations to the state. This recalled the example of ancient Rome and depicted service to the prince as the embodiment of the common weal and the proper way for aspiration to nobility. The virtues that guaranteed such nobility were the four cardinal virtues which were demonstrated in classical mythology and retold by Christine de Pisan in her *Epistle of Othea* and the translation of Stephen Scrope. The heroes of chivalry were Hector, Alexander and Scipio. In one text commonly copied in heraldic collections there was a debate between these three princes to find out who was the greatest knight and the judge, Minos, pronounced in favour of Scipio because he: 'set about it all in the will to maintain forever the dignity of the name of Roman'. By the end of the fifteenth century there was a hardening of attitudes on both sides of the debate between inherited virtue and nobility through service. The successful reign of Henry V, the conquest of Normandy and the disintegration of his achievements during the Wars of the Roses sharpened the focus of those writers who were discussing the concept of service to the state following the Roman model.

The first work in England to reproduce the heroic ideal found in antiquity of sacrifice for the state was Lydgate's *Fall of Princes*, translated from Boccaccio's *De Casibus Virorum illustrium*. The conventional inflexibility of the man of honour is questioned in this work in which it is suggested that all the blows dealt great men by fortune are the result of pride and ambition. This work was intended as a mirror for princes to teach wisdom and moderation and Lydgate, using classical sources from Humphrey, Duke of Gloucester's library such as Ovid's *Metamorphoses*, made ancient Roman history and figures such as Hannibal and Caesar central to his study of heroic self-sacrifice for the good of the state. The

The castle of the Scropes of Bolton in Wensleydale, built in the second half of the fourteenth century. (A.D. Worsnop)

concept of an educated aristocracy serving the state was further expounded by Peter Idley, a bailiff of the honour of Wallingford who was closely associated with William de la Pole, the Earl of Suffolk. Idley was a falconer and under keeper of the royal mews in 1453 and controller of the king's works in 1456. Before he lost office, when Edward came to power in 1461, he compiled a series of instructions for his son, Thomas, which through his source, Arnold of Brescia, and his own researches provided precepts of Seneca, Cicero and Aristotle on self-discipline and service to the common weal.[53] Idley reflected a growing sense that nationalism was stronger than family loyalty when he qualified the commandment to honour parents by saying first love and fear God and then the king and do not obey parents against God and king. In a section original to him he condemns the status-conscious gentry and nobility who purchase great buildings and towers and buy up pictures and meadows and hang their walls with tapestries, for their children and not their souls. Such people, he claimed, do not care how they obtain wealth as long as they are trapped in furs to glorify their corpse, and their wives and children are clothed

The gatehouse of Kirkham Priory in the East Riding of Yorkshire, showing the
coats of arms of the leading families of the diocese. (A.D. Worsnop)

expensively. Such narrow focus on one's progeny or lineage could lead to an aristocratic isolation that Idley maintained was increasingly anachronistic. New social skills, especially communication, were necessary, he maintained, if the nobility were to enjoy continued security. There was no use, he observed, in the aristocracy continuing to build towers and castles with high walls, shutting themselves like oxen in a stall, if they could not get on with their neighbours. Only by maintaining good relationships among neighbours could they enjoy freedom from fear of misfortune and have secure walls behind which they could sleep easily at night.[54] Furthermore the pursuit of family vendettas and wars, he warned, could only lead to the impoverishment of the nobility: 'If a man of high estate and mighty possessions persevere in war, strife and debate he will wear a threadbare hood'.[55]

Narrow-minded aristocratic loyalty to the family with its negative implications for national unity was closely scrutinized in Alain of Chartier's *Quadrilogue Invectif*.[56] The original French version, made in 1422, and an anonymous English translation made in the 1470s, focused on the civil wars of France in 1409–22 and England 1450–60. It blamed these on the selfishness of over-mighty barons and contrasted their narrow concern with family honour with the Romans 'our auncient faders'. The authors drew on Vegetius to give examples of their sacrifices for the common weal. According to Chartier and his translator the Roman aristocracy recognized the importance of intellectual skills, especially communication, rather than military prowess 'for the penne and the tongue of oratours enhauncid as moche the glory of Rome as did the feighters', and they made the same claim for their work asking that they be judged in doing this work not for glory but 'for compassion and necessite of the common wele'.[57] In the *Quadrilogue Invectif* there was an implicit condemnation of the aristocratic familial pride of modern knights who had little knowledge of *vertu* (the mental skills Machiavelli was to see as crucial for service to the state) and an exhortation to learn from Livy to put civil obedience before family honour. The society of Romans, according to these authors, was based not on inherited hierarchy but merit, where obedience and skilful service to the state was all that mattered. They illustrated this through examples of dictators and consuls of Rome and great generals who were often taken out of fields and from their labours to serve the state.

It was Christine de Pisan, drawing on French translations of Latin classics in the library of Charles V, who at the end of the fourteenth century first used Cicero to give a broader view of the functions of the governing class as professional civil servants rather than a retained nobility. This is especially apparent in her *Livre de Corps de Policie*, a manuscript of which bears the arms of the Haute Woodville family, probably Sir Richard Haute, son of Joan Woodville, an aunt of Queen Elizabeth.[58] The probable translator of this work was Anthony Woodville the nominated overseer of Richard Haute's will, an ascetic and well-educated man who approached Christine de Pisan's ideal of the austere knight who dedicated himself to the common weal.[59] Woodville's educational ideals can be seen in his will where he bequeathed money to Whittington College.[60] The translation of this work by Woodville at this particular time signifies the increasing importance of the concept of the state, which had been relatively weak at the outbreak of the Wars of the Roses because most of the nobility felt a strong sense of loyalty to their feudal overlords, to whom they were indentured either through lands or retaining fees. 'The right worthy Romayn prynces, seith he, [Aristotle in his *Poetics*] had their hartis so moche in the loue of the common wele and it is maintained that "every man entendid for the proffyte of the common wele and not for his owyn singuler wele"'. Woodville also held up Roman society as a mirror of a less-feudal, lineage-based form of social order based on reason and merit in which the governing classes were trained and educated for respective tasks, knights in warfare, and lawyers in philosophy and law. What Christine de Pisan and Woodville were advocating was the development of a professional civil service where officials were not appointed through favour and the help of lords and friends. Instead they advocated following the example of the Romans, who 'had their hartis so muche in the loue of the common wele' and who governed the city through order and reason with the common weal in mind by changing their officials annually. Woodville, presumably with the triumphant processions of Henry V in mind, even advocated a revival of Roman state processions as a means of encouraging the nobility to serve the state. He anticipated chariot rides, salutes, and the presentation of laurel crowns and jewellery as tokens of deeds of valour in emulation of the triumphs of Caesar and Scipio: 'wherefor and it was pleasyng to our blessed lorde Jhesu I wolde that Englond, which is one of the nobleste realmes of the worlde, wolde use this custome'.[61]

The challenge that such notions of state service represented to conventional lineage values was clearly recognized and forcefully expressed in the *Controversia de Nobilitate* (originally written in 1428 by a Florentine jurist Buonaccorso da Montemagno) and translated by John Tiptoft, the Earl of Worcester, before his death in 1470.[62] In the *Declamacion of Noblesse* the conflict between conventional and modern views of chivalry was expressed as a debate, occurring appropriately enough in the senate, as two rival suitors appeal to a prospective bride with their opposing views on nobility. The first suitor, displaying pride in his ancestry, wealth, estates, houses and household, expresses the sort of feudal insularity that characterized such over-mighty fifteenth-century subjects as Warwick the Kingmaker and such northern barons as the Percys: 'ther is ful lytil difference bytwene the palacys of kyngys and my byldyngs. I have in chempagne, fertyle feldes, ryche possessions and fayr vyllages, which be allee to receyue not only a grete howshold, but a grete hoost.'[63] Tiptoft, in his translation, is aware that Cornelius' refusal to acknowledge that there was any difference between him and a king makes him a potentially unstable force in the state and also hints at the vacuity of the old-fashioned knight when Cornelius boasts to Lucresse that if she marries him she will have chambers fit for a king, servants, pleasant idleness and merriment in dancing, hunting and hawking. The anachronism of such familial chivalry is eloquently demonstrated by expressing these attitudes in a Roman Senate, followed by the suit of the educated Guyus Flammineus, a representative of the new breed of nobleman in the image of Tiptoft himself, and Anthony Woodville. Guyus proclaims that nobility has nothing to do with possessions or inheritance and is not subject to fortune but rests in cunning and *vertu* which is applied to service to the state. A poor man could be noble if he 'left alle theyr own playsyr and prouffytes to doo theyr seruyse for the comyne weale'. He then gives examples of those of humble birth who gave great service to the state, pointing out that their nobility was not transmitted to their sons who had to prove themselves. The best way to advance to noble status, he says, is to devote yourself from earliest years to the study of philosophy. As for himself 'there is no day I spent in idleness and no night without study and learning' until he realized every man with virtue and cunning was bound to serve the 'estate publyque'; and he gave himself to the service of the weal public of this city.[64] In a criticism of the feuding mentality of the feudal aristocracy, he maintained that no man had cause to hate him who was not an enemy of the common weal, which was the sum of all his labours. Here Tiptoft is enunciating the new fashionable concept of the ruling class, those who drink from the well of Greek and Roman learning. It was the start of the concept of the English gentleman, educated in the classics and prepared to serve the state and eventually in the seventeenth century the empire. Such men were more likely to take pleasure in their libraries than their meadows. Guyus promises to take Lucresse back to his lodgings which, though more humble than Cornelius's, are better furnished in *virtu*: 'fyrst I shall take you to my lyberary, wel stuffed with fayr bookes of Greke and Latin wher unto is euery adversyte and my chief resorte for couneyll and comforte'.[65] Among the English aristocracy of this period there were increasing expressions of admiration for the virtue of intelligence and skills in communication, especially in those positions of administrative authority. John Paston III recommended Thomas Boyd, the Earl of Arran and son of the Governor of Scotland, to John Paston II as 'the most courteous wisest knight . . . one of the lightest deliverer best spoken . . . of all knights that I wer was acquainted.'[66] Edward IV said of Sir John Ormond the Earl of Ormond that 'he is the goodliest knight who ever beheld' and 'if good breeding, nurture and liberal qualities were lost in the world they to be found in this earl of Ormond.'

The task of providing accessible translations and adaptations of classical literature to ensure that Yorkist courtiers approached Tiptoft's ideal was undertaken by the printer, translator and entrepreneur, William Caxton. He enjoyed the patronage of Margaret, Duchess of Burgundy from 1468, George, Duke of Clarence, and Edward IV himself. Caxton, as Governor of the English Nation at Bruges, benefited from close contacts with the Burgundian court, which by this time had taken over the role occupied by the Valois court in transmitting the classics into the vernacular. According to David Aubert in his prologue to *Histoire abrege des empereurs*, Philip the Good, Duke of Burgundy, was 'accustomed to having the ancient histories read to him daily', and Louis, Lord of Gruuthuyse, the host of Edward IV, Richard, Duke of Gloucester, Anthony, Earl Rivers and William, Lord Hastings in 1470, had Dutch vernacular translations made of Livy, Caesar, Ovid and Maximus.[67] It was in Burgundy that Caxton, who had entered Margaret, Duchess of Burgundy's service in

1468, began to provide didactic moral treatises based on classical history and ethics for the noble and merchant classes. It is significant that the first book printed in English was his 1474 edition of *The Histories of Troy*, translated from the French *Le Recuil des Histoires de Troye* of Raoul Lefévre, the chaplain and secretary of Philip the Good. Caxton's prologue reveals the almost high Victorian attitude the ruling classes of England had towards reading in this period. He explained that he found himself in no great charge of occupation and knowing that the wise man enschews vice and idleness and having no virtuous occupation he put himself to reading marvellous histories in which he took delight and to pass the time he translated them and was encouraged by the Duchess of Burgundy to continue with this task.[68] This was soon followed by *The Game and Play of Chess Moralized*, which was dedicated to George, Duke of Clarence. In 1476 Caxton, encouraged by Edward IV and his family, returned to England to establish the first printing press in England in the precincts of Westminster Abbey. It is a measure of the significant place that the wisdom of antiquity occupied in Caxton's education purposes that the first book he printed in England in 1477 was Anthony Woodville, Earl River's translation of *The Dicts and Sayings of the Philosophers*. Caxton underlined Tiptoft's identification of the English ruling class with the Roman senatorial class, a class defined not by blood but virtue, which was defined as the application of learning and skills to the service of the state. In his prologue to the English translation of Chartier's *Curiale* he compared the customs of Rome to those of London and described this book as designed to improve the morals of merchants rather than to amuse the nobility.[69] In his activities as a printer and translator Caxton provided improving ethical literature along classical lines for the governing class of England. He was not just a business man, but he believed in the potential of the English language as a medium for transmitting the teachings of antiquity. Through his presses he was creating a unified language that would provide the foundations for England's literary achievements in the sixteenth and seventeenth centuries and serve the interests of an increasingly coherent state. Besides celebrating the achievements of the ancients he was providing the governing class with the ethical and moral teachings that helped them to be servants of the state by making such advice available on printing presses. His educational goals are apparent in his dedication to the city of London in the edition of his translation of a French version of Cato, which he described as 'the beste booke for to be taught to yonge children in scole' to show the young how to govern themselves and to build upon the achievements of their parents.[70] By making such literature available on printing presses he was aiding the development of a professional governing class and ensuring that membership of a hereditary aristocracy no longer guaranteed or required participation in national politics. Those who chose to do so were increasingly educated in classical literature like Anthony Woodville and John Tiptoft. For such men both the monuments and literature of ancient Rome exercised a strong fascination. In 1461 Idley exclaimed 'In Rome, that most noble and roiall cetee'.[71] In the same year Tiptoft went to Rome carrying the king's obedience to Pope Pius II and the Pope said of him (according to Tiptoft's companion, John Free of Bristol) that he 'above all princes of the age was one worthy to be compared in virtue and eloquence with the greatest emperors of Greece and Rome'. According to Vespiano, Tiptoft saw everything that he could in Florence before exploring Rome.[72] He was away from England for four years collecting books from all over Italy including Suetonius's *De Claris Grammaticus Rhetoribusque*, the Tacitus's *Dialogus de Oratoribus Claris* and the proverbs of Seneca and of Lucretius's *De Rerum Natura*. He left a collection of such works to Oxford University worth 500 marks and wrote to the chancellor from Padua referring to the benefits he had obtained from studying at Oxford which he describes as a second Athens.[73] Anthony Woodville undertook his Italian tour in 1475–6 and visited Rome with his companions, John Lord Scrope and John Ormonde, the sixth Earl Butler. A description of his visit, including his being robbed of all his jewels just outside the city, occurs in a letter written in 1476 by John Paston II to his mother, Margaret.[74] Edward IV himself had a large collection of translated works containing the philosophy and myths of antiquity including Wydeville's translation of *The Dicts and Sayings of the Philosophers*, the *Epistle of Othea*, *Histoires de Troiae*, *A Narrative of Hercules*, *A History of Caesar*, *The Boke of Noblesse* and the book of *Valerius Maximus*.[75] Many of these works came from the library of Louis of Bruges, for after France Burgundy was the important source of most classical models in England in the fifteenth century. Sir John Howard of Suffolk, a member of Edward IV's court and a diplomat in the 1470s, could also be considered one of a new breed of classically educated officials. On campaigns to

Scotland in 1481 he took his copy of *The Dicts and Sayings of the Philosophers*. When Woodville, Tiptoft, Scrope and others visited Rome they were anticipating the grand tour that came to be regarded as an essential part of the education of the English gentleman in the eighteenth century. When they visited such ancient sites of Rome as the forum, protected by a bull issued by Pius II, they were observing monuments to a state based on reasoned discourse. Such sites were possibly more important than the pilgrimage shrines which were on these travellers' itineraries. The Italian tour and the works of such writers as Cicero and Seneca, with their emphasis on communication skills and dispassionate state service, were coming to be regarded as the hallmarks of the education of English gentlemen, who would contribute to the administration of a more civilized state and eventually an empire.

There was, therefore, at the time of the accession of Richard III no shortage of advice on how to adopt the conventional code of chivalry of the English aristocratic families to create a unified and strong state. To some extent all the above works looked back to Henry V as the prince who provided the mirror for the code of Roman chivalric discipline. During his nine-year reign he was able to weld together representatives of families who bore grudges towards one another going back to the reign of Richard II and involve them in a co-operative enterprise in northern France. Henry V also staged Roman triumphs after his victories and was beginning to use chivalry as an instrument of the state. Richard III, however, despite his adoption of some of his father's common weal rhetoric and endorsement of his austere military ideals, failed where Henry V was most successful – as a communicator. His chivalry remained essentially old fashioned and egocentric, based firmly on the code of honour of the family. This martial code still dominated the aristocracy of the north of England, especially among the guardians of the marches, the Nevilles and the Percys. At this time Idley and the translator of the *Quadrilogue Invectif* were criticizing noblemen who chose to remain isolated behind castle walls and were condemning the selfishness of those who put family interests above those of the state. The landscape of Yorkshire still bears testimony to the independence and ancestral pride of the aristocracy. Richard, as Duke of Gloucester, spent much of his time in three imposing fortresses, Middleham, Sheriff Hutton and Baynard Castle. His near neighbours at Middleham, the Scropes of Bolton, were living in the imposing fortress of Castle Bolton, built at the end of the fourteenth century, which was too far from the Scottish borders to have any significance other than a symbolic assertion of the lineal pride of the victors in the Scrope-Grosvenor lawsuit. Even lesser gentry such as the Merkenfields, retainers of Richard, Duke of Gloucester, lived in a fortified manor house surrounded by a moat at Merkenfield Hall near Ripon (which is still standing today). Richard himself endorsed many of the older lineal values. He was appointed Constable of the Court of Chivalry of England while still a teenager and he owned two rolls of arms. Ordinances composed by him in 1478 show his interest in heralds urging them to study books of arms and records of ceremonies. Richard also, as Duke of Gloucester, owned heraldic rolls including: the St George's Roll made in about 1285; Thomas Jenkyn's book, a collection of arms made in about 1400, with a Yorkshire bias; and the Salisbury Roll, a pictorial roll of the ancestors of the Earl of Salisbury, made in 1463 glorifying the Nevilles, the ancestors of Warwick the Kingmaker.[76] While he was King Richard's mother-in-law, who was living with him and his wife, or perhaps he himself, commissioned the Beauchamp Pageant, fifty-three monochrome drawings with text illustrating the life of Richard Beauchamp the Earl of Warwick.[77] In 1484, as king, he granted heralds a charter of incorporation and gave them the London house of Cold Harbour for their headquarters. The above works and activities indicate that Richard may have had an interest in secular and biblical history, the origins of Britain and his own family, and in the practical application of chivalric ethics in the exercise of authority. Above all they provided him with a model for aggressive pursuit of his own rights and defence of his honour. For Richard the focus of service and patronage, despite much of his common weal rhetoric, remained the family and its retainers rather than the state, and this more than anything else undermined his kingship. His granting of estates and offices in the south in 1483 to such northern friends and neighbours as Sir Marmaduke Constable of Flamborough, Sir Halneth Mauleverer and Sir Thomas Merkenfield and John, Lord Scrope of Bolton (who actually took up residence in the south) inspired a rebellion among his subjects in the south-east. Richard preferred to rely on traditional concepts of loyalty and service and never mastered the art of rhetoric or communication that was advised in all the mirrors for princes in the fifteenth century. His chivalric gestures were more private, such as his instructions to the priests of his endowed college of Queens' College, Cambridge to pray for a number of his relatively humble servants who had formed part of his retinue and had grouped around his person, under his standard, and had died fighting for him at Barnet and Tewkesbury.[78] His chivalry was essentially introverted – despite his reputation for bravery acquired at Barnet, Tewkesbury and Bosworth, his military aspirations were largely unfulfilled. Throughout most of Edward's reign he was prevented from fighting and tourneying and was not able, like Anthony Woodville, to build up a reputation as a crusader and jouster. He never successfully used chivalry to bring the nobility together through warfare and tournaments as Edward III and Henry V had done. He had a narrower concept of camaderie restricted to a circle of northern friends and retainers. He trusted in the traditional concept of familial loyalty and bore loyalty as his motto. His distribution of white boar badges was reminiscent of the white hart livery by Richard II, a king similarly undone by sentimental loyalty towards his friends. Richard III's concept of chivalry was similarly based on friendship, military service and loyalty. He owned *The Knight's Tale*, which expounded ideals of friendship among brothers in arms and expounded a concept of chivalry recognized by the author, Chaucer, as old fashioned. Also in this manuscript, which he acquired in his youth and which was written in the north of England in about 1420, was an inscribed copy of rules of service for a gentleman that was possibly intended for Richard himself while he was a page in the Earl of Warwick's service.[79] His failure to adapt to the changing code of chivalry contributed to his defeat at Bosworth. Here he was deserted by the Percies and the Stanleys, the latter basing their conduct on more pragmatic and rational principles of loyalty to Henry Tudor as the one who was more likely to prove popular enough to weld together the nobility.

Richard's defeat at Bosworth completed the erosion of many of the old chivalric attitudes that he had stood for. The literature produced between 1460 and 1480 for the Yorkist court reflects a growing desire for stability and strong government. The voice of the intellectuals of the period was heeded and the ruling class put aside narrow self-interests to serve the state in the way that they perceived the Roman senatorial class had done. They did this because they were following their own interests, surrendering political and economic power and privilege so that in the future a stronger state would be able to defend their interests. As Hobbes was to claim in the seventeenth century, reasonable men could always be relied on to hand over to a sovereign whatever power the sovereign thought necessary to prevent a breakdown of society and civilization in which there was 'continuall feare and danger of violent death'.[80] The Wars of the Roses can, therefore, be seen as a conflict fought over a higher principle than mere power struggle and the settling of scores. The principles at stake were justice, strong government and stability.[81] Like all wars fought with passion (and the mortality figures at Towton indicate this) a question of self-identity was at stake – the identity of a new nation state of England. This was appreciated by Shakespeare, who makes Richard III's reign the culmination of a national epic to rank with those of Virgil and Homer. Out of the dynastic feuds, the Hundred Years' War, the Wars of the Roses and the apocalyptic reign of Richard III emerged a more unified and centralized English nation state. In spirit Shakespeare was right. People were fighting in the various dynastic struggles of the fifteenth century that culminated in the Wars of the Roses over the future identity of England, whether it was to be a centralized modern state that incorporated the various national minorities and feudal dynasties. As in all great civil wars there were casualties and the casualties of the conflicts of the fifteenth century were the individualistic northern families and the separate identities of particular regions, such as Yorkshire and the Welsh marches, captured so poignantly in *Henry IV Part I* in the characters of Hotspur and Glendower. Richard III (though not Shakespeare's Richard) was, along with his brother, George, Duke of Clarence and his cousin the Earl of Warwick another such individualistic anachronism. It is perhaps because Richard III represents the feudal dynastic independence of the northern families that he remains, in the north, a potent symbol of northern independence in the face of continuing domination by the south and London.

If Richard III can be considered in chivalric terms to be an old-fashioned and introverted dreamer who unsuccessfully communicated his chivalric enthusiasm to others and failed to make political use of it, the same judgement can be applied to his religious outlook, and this places him even more firmly within the intellectual, cultural traditions of the north of England.

RICHARD III AND THE CHURCH

The changing code of chivalry under the impact of writings of antiquity elevated the state at the expense of the family, the traditional focus of chivalric values. If Richard III was reasonably conventional in his adherence to the code of chivalry, he was more focused on the traditional family and household loyalties that were stronger in the north. The growth of the notion of a secular state also challenged the independence and autonomy of the church and Richard in his support and defence of the church was a much more individualistic figure. A defining characteristic of the governing classes of fourteenth-century England (who were mainly the clergy educated in canon law) was an interest in mysticism and the solitary life of the recluse and the emotional subjective experiences that were the reward of full- or part-time practice in the devotional arts. The religion articulated by this class had a decidedly other-worldly outlook, with an emphasis on the afterlife, intimations of which were described by such fashionable northern writers as Richard Rolle. The dominant buildings of this period, apart from the castles that proclaimed the importance of family codes of honour, were the religious houses and chantries which symbolized this rejection of the world and aspirations concerning Purgatory and Heaven. By the mid-fifteenth century a sea change was occurring in the religious outlook of the governing classes of England, among whom educated laymen were playing an increasingly significant role. The fashionable authors were no longer canon lawyers and clergy of the fourteenth century, such as William Nassington, Walter Hilton and Nicholas Love, members of the governing class who provided guides to moral and intellectual life which emphasized their belief in detachment, their faith in the future and even in intimations of another world. They were laymen and women who were translating and disseminating the philosophy of Cicero and other Roman writers, such as Seneca, through the circles of Sir John Fastolf, Richard, Duke of York and the court of his son, Edward IV. Anthony Woodville, in his independent translation of *The Dicts and Sayings of the Philosophers*, popularized classical philosophy by providing succinct biographies of leading Greek and Roman statesmen and philosophers including Socrates, Plato and Cicero; and sayings attributed to them that provided guidance on how to live according to the dictates of reason to achieve mastery of self and one's fate. Hermes claimed 'the noblist thinge that God hathe maad in this world is man, and the noblist thyng that is in this worlde is reeson'. Aristotle said of reason 'this prerogative that God hath yeueven to men to regard of other beestes' and described the purpose of life as the acquisition of wisdom and knowledge: 'konnyng is lif and ignorance is dethe; therefore he that knowithe is lif, for he undrestandithe whate he dothe, and he that knowithe not is dethe, for he undrestandithe noo thing that he doth'.[1]

In Cato's *Distichs*, translated by Burgh and printed by Caxton, there is an emphatic denial of the validity of using the certainty of death for any moral educational purpose: 'drede not deth with ouer besy cure./ To lyue on erthe is but a jape,/ Yf thou shalt alway after deth so gape'.[2] The young recipient of this educational treatise is reassured that he need not fear death even if he has led a life wicked to man and God because death 'maketh an end bothe of bad and able'.[3] Such a pragmatic approach contrasts to that of the writers of the fourteenth-century religious manuals, such as the author of *The Prick of Conscience*, who regarded the afterlife and its terrors and pains as a tangible reality that had to be meditated on constantly. There is in such meditations on death a tranquillity and detachment that was far removed from the sort of detachment advocated by fourteenth-century mystical writers, such as Hilton and the author of *The Cloud of Unknowing*, which depended on attaining experiences that defied the physical and emotional limitations under which people lived.

The emphasis on the survival of the achievements of a soul in posterity places a reliance on reputation and fame, military deeds, the begetting of children and art as guarantors of a sort of immortality. This is demonstrated in *The Dicts and Sayings of the Philosophers*, where the reader is urged 'lete alle your desires be to gete a good name'.[4] Skepticism about the next world results in a concern with the social skills that ensure the individual soul is not forgotten: 'there abideth not bot good name and loue, the which passeth the good dedis of aunsient peple abiden in the hertis of theire successors; strengthe you then to gete a good name, the whiche failithe no tyme; and bi this good name thi noblesse shalle endure'.[5] In one of Christine de Pisan's *Moral Proverbs*, which were translated by Anthony Woodville, probably for the Prince of Wales, and printed by Caxton, it is maintained that 'It is better to love honour and good name than rich treasure and their fame shall endure longer'. In another proverb she says 'In great estate lies not glory but in vertu whose worth is memory.'[6] Caxton's activities as a printer played a significant part in enabling the aristocracy of the latter half of the fifteenth century to leave behind some record of their achievements and their personalities, because he gave writers the potential for reaching far greater numbers of people than through manuscripts. Such a preoccupation with posterity and human achievement anticipates the philosophy of Shakespeare's sonnets and implies a weakening of belief in purgatory and a dependence on intercessory masses and prayers.

In the literature of these circles there can also be seen an increasingly secular attitude towards the uncertainties of life which instead of being propitiated with prayers and masses are to be confronted with a rational detachment. Anthony Woodville's translation of *The Dicts and Sayings of the Philosophers* provided guidance on how to attain self-mastery and overcome unhappiness and the vagaries of fortune. Life, it was claimed, was the end product of sensuality and lust, whereas peace was the product of a soul subject to discipline, a discipline acquired by rejecting vices which seem sweet but turn bitter, and developing virtues that are initially sharp and bitter but turn out pleasant.[7] Such self-mastery resulted in esteem of self and others: 'how shulde one loue another that can not loue himself . . . a man may not haue felicite in himself if he do not wele to other.' This was a happiness or detachment that could not be negated by misfortune or grief and, as Boethius expressed it, 'Who-so is quietede is saued'.[8] A key text was Boccaccio's *De Casibus virorum illustrium*, which was translated into French by Premierfait. One copy of this French version was executed in Bruges for Edward IV's library. In the fifteenth century Boccaccio was a moralist compared to Seneca and Boethius, and Chastellain described him as a doctor of patience in adversity.[9] Humphrey, Duke of Gloucester, commissioned Lydgate to translate Boccacio's *De Laudibus virorum* into *The Fall of Princes* while he was suffering the fluctuating fortunes of war as lieutenant in France in 1430 to 1432.

In this work the heroes of classical legend and history are shown suffering with dignity and without any application to the principles of Christian chivalry. When Scipio or Hannibal bring about the buffetings of fate because of their pride and egoism an attempt is made to teach princes moderation, wisdom and detachment in the face of fortune. This was no doubt how Worcester regarded the work – he studied it in the original Latin and took notes from Boccacio's original text.[10] Charles of Orleans turned to it for consolation during his long years in English captivity and called for a manuscript to be sent to his prison. He approached such sufferings as the death of his wife, Isabella, in childbirth, his long imprisonment and exile from his homeland, and the death of his daughter in a spirit of Greek fatalism. He saw his life of troubles as his fatal destiny against which rationalizations of reason were powerless and which had to be accepted and endured stoically with the assistance of Plato, Cicero, Ovid, Virgil and Boethius. Chastellian's version of Boccaccio's work, *Le Tempe de Bocace*, was written for the consolation of Queen Margaret of Anjou after her flight from England. Copies of *De Casibus virorum illustrium* were also owned by English public figures who were prominent in the period of political upheaval in the 1470s and 1480s, such as John Russell and John Tiptoft, the Earl of Worcester who owned Lydgate's *The Fall of Princes* in a manuscript containing Seneca's *Proverbs*.[11] Such teachings were increasingly required to confront the political uncertainties of the period known as the Wars of the Roses. William Caxton, when he printed Chaucer's translation of Boethius' *Consolations of Philosophy*, in his prologue praised the translator who, he said, 'can see what this transitory, mutable world is and where every man is going' and he printed it in the hope that it would 'profit people for the wele of their souls and have better patience in adversity'. Interestingly for Caxton it was not Boethius' Christianity and martyrdom that was of interest but the fact that in exile he worked for the common weal and that 'our excellent author had been a senator in that noble and famous city Rome'.[12]

A work which powerfully evoked the fluctuations of fortune and the attractions of a classical ideal of contemplative detachment and which placed them within the political context of the Yorkist court was William Caxton's translation of Alain Chartier's *Curiale*. Caxton printed this work in 1484 and addressed it to a noble and victorious earl (probably Anthony Woodville, Earl

Rivers).[13] The court, watched over by Dame Fortune laughing at the vagaries of great lords' fates, is described as an assemblage of mutual deceivers who buy and sell one another, and any one who enters it loses the rule of himself.[14] Classical authors are used to comment on the cruelty of the court. Seneca, in his tragedies, says age comes too late to people of 'smale howses who live in sufficiance but among we courtiers servants to fortune we live disordinantly and grow old by force of changes rather than years. Courtiers grow weary of life and haste to their death losing their honour as they turn idlers and place hunters lodging in other's houses eating and sleeping at another's well.'[15] Caxton, in his translation, reveals the court to be a dangerous place encouraging paranoid states of mind: 'The halle of a grete prynce is counely Infecte and eschaufed of the breeth of the peple', no one is certain all are in danger and no one is safe in his situation. Cato, who desired just to serve the common weal, was an exception – most desire honours although they know they are not worthy of them.[16] The unhappy Chartier advises his brother not to follow him into a situation where he is surrounded by traitors who watch every word; the court, he says, breeds men who study to entrap you into talk by which they can disclose and get favour with the great. The only way you can keep from being replaced by another is through the payment of bribes.[17] By translating the work in 1483, Caxton was encapsulating the insecurity felt by those who were close to the throne of Edward IV such as Anthony Woodville and his in-laws, George, Duke of Clarence, before his death, and Richard, Duke of Gloucester. He was urging such courtiers to react with a stoical philosophical detachment by ignoring fortune and fleeing to the river bank to watch others drown. Idealistically evoking the classical concept of *Otium*, he advises the reader to withdraw into a private house where he can become a king and return to himself to learn the happiness of private life.[18]

This longing for sanctuary from the dangerous world of the court has strong echoes of Seneca's tragedies and many in this period, like Shakespeare's Mark Antony, found it impossible to live as a private citizen after high office. Such insecurity probably explains Richard of Gloucester's decision to seize the throne rather than to trust in the friendship and cooperation of his nephew's uncles on the Woodville side of the family. The turbulent career of Anthony Woodville himself eloquently illustrates the fickleness of fortune and explains why Caxton decided to dedicate the work to him. Woodville's fortunes rose with the marriage of his sister to Edward IV in 1464, when he became Edward IV's leading courtier. His fortunes fell as dramatically when his father and brother were killed at the Battle of Edgecote in July 1469 fighting for Edward IV against the Neville uprising and he was forced to join Edward IV and Richard, Duke of Gloucester in exile in Burgundy. His luck turned again the following year when he assisted Edward and the Duke of Gloucester in recapturing the throne for the house of York. But, in 1473 his wife died while he was on a pilgrimage to Compostella and in 1476 he was robbed of his jewellery and plate 12 miles outside Rome. On Edward IV's death in April 1483 he was at the height of his power as guardian to the young Edward V when he was arrested by the Duke of Gloucester and imprisoned and executed in Pontefract Castle. Caxton, in his epilogue to his printed edition of Woodville's translation of the *Cordiale* or *The Four Last Things*, described the Earl Rivers as a model nobleman, scholarly, rational and detached in the face of misfortune. Since 'his great tribulation and adversity' Woodville, Caxton informs the reader, has occupied himself in pilgrimages to Rome, and 'conceiving the mutability and unstableness of this present life' he has translated the *Cordiale* so that his readers 'sholde know their selfe here after the better and amende their lyuyng'. Caxton, judging the translation to be a noble and meritorious deed, pledges to accomplish Woodville's desire in printing the work and prays to God to maintain him in his noble and joyous desires in the world and that after 'this dangerous and transitory life to have everlasting bliss'.[19] Woodville himself, in the prologue to his translation of *The Dicts and Sayings of the Philosophers*, expressed his awareness of the precariousness of his position as a courtier when he says every creature born is ordained to be subject to the storms of fortune and so 'in diverse many sondry wyses man is perplexid with worldly adversitees'. Woodville goes on to add that he has had his fair share of worldly adversity and the lord has given him grace to 'sette a parte all ingratitude/ and drove me by reson and conscience as far as my wrecchednes would suffyse to give therefore synguler lyf to his seruyce in folowing his lawes and commandements'.[20] Pious and orthodox Christian that he was, and this is how others perceived him, there was in River's piety an impassioned, classical notion of the deity. In this prologue, describing his sufferings, he says he turned to the wisdom and the sayings of ancient philosophers 'because of the wholesome and sweet sayings of the pagans, which is a glorious fair mirror to all good Christian people to behold and understand . . . a great comfort to every well disposed soul'. Although he had no opportunity to read this book on his sea voyage (which in itself was a pilgrimage of thanksgiving for his deliverance from exile in Flanders) the book, he says, filled him with excitement because it was full of wisdom and history-giving example and doctrine to princes, kings and people of all estates, and he resolved to get better acquainted with it at the first opportunity. This practice of regarding books as friends recalls something of Petrarch's attitude to his favourite ancient authors.

The tone of Woodville's piety, in which he shows rational detachment towards the vagaries of fortune and sees a reasoned pattern in life, is in accord with the Christian stoicism of Boethius. This emerges in the ballad he wrote at the time of his imprisonment at the hands of Richard III which passed into the hands of John Rous (d. 1491), the author of the chronicle of the Earls of Warwick. Musing on the unsteadfastness of this world, unfeeling and contrary to expectations which fills him full of fear, Woodville resolves 'to cease my woful dance'. As unkindness has advanced his grievances without any hope of remedy he is now at a state when 'such is my dance willing to die methinks truly bound am I and that greatly to be content seeing plainly fortune turn all contrary to my intent. My life was lent to one intent. It is nigh spent, welcome fortune'. He concludes his poem with the reflection that he never wanted things to turn out the way they had but such is fortune's desire.[21]

The concept of detachment outlined in the above work was purely secular and bears little relation to the fourteenth-century ideal of religious detachment outlined by such writers as Walter Hilton and the author of *The Cloud of Unknowing*. It also contrasts markedly with the religion of Richard III, shaped as it was by northern influences, in which prayer and introspection were tools not designed to achieve a state of detachment and reconciliation with fortune, but to convince the worshipper of his special relationship with a divinity that would actively intervene to fulfil his individual destiny. In the Christian stoicism of the court of Edward IV one can see how the increasing use of the classics led to the development of a secular moral code. This code rendered Christianity an increasingly anodyne forerunner of the Senecan stoicism of Montaigne and

Shakespeare, where the educated man contemplated an agnostic universe and looked courageously at life as it is. This was as important and challenging a notion to the late medieval church as the Protestant Reformation.

It is significant that on a general level the symbol of intellectual and moral authority in the fifteenth century was increasingly becoming not papal Rome, but imperial Rome. The increasingly secular outlook also manifested itself in an increasing dependence on classical philosophy and myths for the sort of moral teaching that was once supplied in the penitential manuals of the fourteenth century. A different sort of Christian teaching was transmitted. The Yorkshire religious writers of the fourteenth century such as Rolle, the author of *The Prick of Conscience*, and Walter Hilton evoked in varying degrees the pain and misery of the world, the individual's significance in the face of death, the fallibility of the human will, the dependence of the individual on God's grace and the attractions of the eremitic life. Woodville used classical literature to give a new emphasis to free will and a rational approach to such questions as guilt and death and a confidence in the individual's capacity to triumph over fortune through the use of reason. In *The Boke of Noblesse* William Worcester asserted that prophecies derived from heavenly constellations were contingent rather than of necessity and could be interpreted as heavenly warnings that a change of direction and disposition was necessary to avoid a certain fate. If such warnings were heeded men could be 'sovereign over the stars'.[22]

The increasingly secular perspective adopted in Yorkist circles had important political implications. William Worcester, in his analysis of the recent failures in France, showed a strong sense of historical perspective when comparing the reigns of Henry VI to those of the more successful Henry V and Edward III, and this perspective was also applied to the question of national identity and political power. Rather than being considered within the the context of biblical history, the state was now beginning to be considered as a purely human institution which reached its apotheosis in ancient Rome; and the role of Christianity in such a state was no longer considered to be central. The commissioning of works such as Claudian's *Letter to Stilicho* shows the ways in which the fifteenth-century ruling class of England was interested in fourth-century Rome. Members of this class were not interested in the rise of Christianity and such architects of the institutions of the secular church and the monasteries of St Augustine and St Jerome, but secular Rome in its decline and its cardinal virtues of prudence, patience, justice, temperance and chastity. Therefore the defenders of this secular state who demonstrated these virtues, such as Stilicho, the last defender of the Roman empire against the Christian Goths, and the generals of Rome during the height of its power, such as Caesar, and Scipio were admired.

This admiration for the Roman secular state was accompanied by a weakening of the concept of a universal Catholic church. The Hundred Years' War contributed to a hardening of national divisions between England and France and intellectual justifications for this were provided in both countries. Alain of Chartier, in his *Le Quadrilogue Invectif*, has a dream vision of France upbraiding her children for not defending her, which in the English translation of the 1470s could be equally applied to Edward's court: 'aftir the bonde of the feith Catholike, nature byndyth yow to fortefye the comon wele of the londe wherin ye wer borne and to defende the lordeship undyr the which God hath lent the grace to be born unto and haue lyf'.[23] Such a statement illustrates the growing sense of conflict between the ideal of the universal church and the Aristotelian notion of natural law in which people share with animals a natural desire to defend their home territory. If the crusade was weakening as a practical ideal it was being replaced by this sense of a compelling urge to defend one's birthplace 'suche people ben unnaturall that woll not enforce themself for the sustentation of the comon wele and levir suffir themself to be lost with the comon wele thanne dispose themself to perile for the same'.[24] This love of and interest in one's native land is expressed in Worcester's travels and his minute observations of England's towns and countryside. It can also be seen in Richard III's boast that he was the only King of England to be born in England.

With the secular concept of the state there came a reassessment of the Church's significance in such a state. Increasingly educated laymen were being employed in government instead of clergy and employed not for their chivalric pedigrees but their educational skills or *virtu*, the quality emphasized in the works of Lydgate, the *Secreta Secretorum*, the translations of Christine de Pisan, Stephen Scrope, William Worcester and Anthony Woodville. The nobility who were reading such adaptations of classical philosophy and history were a high-minded ruling class, but their Christianity was becoming of an increasingly anodyne nature and was expressed in Woodville's translation of Christine de Pisan's *Book of Policy*. Knights were bound to serve the common weal as well as to love and fear God and the two things were interdependent. Christine de Pisan unfavourably compared contemporary Christian practice with the zealous religious observances of the pagans, who believed they acquired their empire by serving their gods: 'The noble Romayns whiche wer paynemys and mysbeleuers, yet they gouerned theim so well that it ought to be example to us, Valere seith'.[25] Religion, in the minds of members of the ruling class of England, was becoming a tool of the state (anticipating the attitude of Machiavelli). Once again it was Henry V who was the pioneer by harnessing devotional enthusiasms aroused by the Yorkshire religious writers into a more public, ceremonial religion based on national saints like St George and St John of Beverley and liturgical innovations that made religion into a social cement.

Ancient Rome gave the highest value to participation in the political and social life of cities and gave power not to priests and warriors but a widely based citizen class which controlled and participated in priestly functions. In fifteenth-century Italy there was a conscious emulation of such a system and a growing subservience of religion to the classical ideal of the overriding importance of the state, which involved a willingness to sacrifice one's life and if necessary one's Christian morality for one's country. Plato's *Republic* and Aristotle's *Ethics* encouraged such flexible attitudes to politics and Christian morality in the interests of the ideal of the commonwealth and translations of these works were commissioned by Humphrey, Duke of Gloucester. However, as the fate of John Tiptoft the Earl of Worcester shows, to submit all to the interests of reason and service of the state could prove unpopular. Tiptoft's classical education and wide travels in Italy seem to have encouraged the suspicion that he was impelled by a different morality than his countrymen, and he acquired a reputation for ruthless brutality as Constable of England in the 1460s.[26] Edward IV had broadened the constable's jurisdiction to cover all forms of treason and disaffection. One of Tiptoft's most ruthless acts was the arrest and murder of Thomas Fitzgerald, the seventh Earl of Desmond, on frivolous charges (Desmond had criticized Edward's marriage to Elizabeth Woodville) and the murder of his two young children in prison. Richard III was to imply in a letter to the Earl of Desmond that the same people were behind the murder of his brother Clarence (who was probably prepared to use rumours about the invalidity of Edward IV's marriage for his own political lends). When he was captured by the Lancastrian army in September 1469, Tiptoft awaited his execution with stoic patience and said of his cruel judgments that he had done all for the good of the state. His calmness and bravery made an impression on Caxton who said, ten years later, that it was a model for others. It is also true that his unpopularity and reputation as a butcher also rested on this same dispassionate service to the state which was based on classical principles alien to many ordinary people. Tiptoft was at Padua in 1458, probably studying civil law, and chroniclers charged him with bringing an unfamiliar morality into England: 'the people, as they are wont to do, all clamoured for his death, the chief reason being that he had revived certain laws, which he had brought back from Italy, against the people's will; and for this reason he was condemned to death . . . And when he went to die, the people, like most of those who flock to the winning side, rejoiced greatly and shouted that he must die because he had brought back from Italy the laws which are called the laws of Padua, and are against the people'.[27] In the same way a classics don, Kenneth Dover, the head of Corpus Christi College, Oxford, was attacked in the press in 1995 for claiming to have orchestrated the suicide of a colleague. He defended his actions by claiming he felt no remorse because he believed he was serving the larger interests of the college community and thereby following the principles of writers such as Seneca.[28] Later we will consider another infamous incident involving the mistreatment of young children – the disappearance of the princes in the Tower, and we shall attempt to show that there were principles underlying this, although they were of a more irrational and religious nature. Increasingly knowledge of Roman principles of government also entailed awareness of the tyrannical power of the state. In Chartier's treatise on hope, translated into English at the same time as *Le Quadrilogue Invectif*, there is a note expressing an awareness that all the great expounders of service to the common weal died at the hands of tyrants – Seneca, for all his great doctrine and service to Nero, died bleeding in the bath; Cicero's reward for his offices in the city of Rome was cruel beheading by Mark Antony; and Boethius was imprisoned and tortured for his defence of the common weal.[29]

This increase in lay literacy and in a more secular outlook and the growth in the power of the state posed a considerable challenge to the church. This challenge was as formidable as that met in the middle of the fourteenth century by Thoresby and his York clergy, who had combated lay and clerical ignorance by extending the scope of pastoral care. It might also be compared with the strength of the challenge met by Thomas Arundel and his northern clergy, who combated the spread of Lollard heresy and lay piety and devotional enthusiasms by formulating pastoral policies that met people's spiritual needs while reinforcing the authority of the church and the structures of society. The northern clergy who were the successors of these pioneers in pastoral reform and who were prominent during the reign of Richard III, should be examined as they had to face a challenge from outside the church, from the culture of ancient Rome and an increasingly secular state, hostile to the power and privileges of the church. One of the most striking things about the northerners who were to become the intellectual leaders of the church in the second half of the fifteenth century was that their careers followed similar patterns to their predecessors, the protégés of Thomas Arundel, with Cambridge as the focus of their lives. The churchman most reminiscent of Arundel himself was John Alcock, the son of William Alcock, a burgess of Kingston-on-Hull, who was born in 1430 in Beverley and who died in 1500. Alcock, like Arundel, was closely connected with Peterhouse, where he was a fellow, and he too was Bishop of Ely in 1485. He was also a prominent statesman, a key figure in Edward IV's government, a keeper of the Great Seal in 1472, tutor to Edward, Prince of Wales (until removed from the post by Richard, Duke of Gloucester), president of his council in 1473, and a commissioner of Richard III in negotiations with the Scots in 1484.[30] The most influential figure to return to the diocese of York was Thomas Rotherham from Rotherham in Yorkshire. Rotherham was a fellow of King's Hall, 1446–60, Chancellor of the University of Cambridge, 1469–71 and Archbishop of York 1480–1500. He too was a prominent servant of Edward IV in the 1470s and Chancellor of England in 1474.[31] William Melton of the diocese of York was a prominent fellow at Michaelhouse from 1485 and a chancellor of York Cathedral in 1495.[32] His pupil at Michaelhouse was John Fisher, a mercer's son from Beverley who was ordained by Archbishop Rotherham. Fisher was a pensioner of Michaelhouse and a fellow in 1491 and Vice-Chancellor of Cambridge at the end of the century. He too moved in court circles and was chaplain to Margaret Beaufort.[33]

These clergy addressed the challenge of the growth of lay piety and literacy by trying to encourage spiritual reform within the church. Unlike the fourteenth-century clergy, who stressed the importance of confession as a means of religious instruction and the importance of the mass as a focus of communal religion, these northerners were concerned to establish the reputation of the clergy as scholars and preachers. These men were the intellectual, spiritual heirs of the northern Cambridge writers of the end of the fourteenth century. The challenges facing them were different. Thomas Arundel and his clerks, John Newton, Richard Scrope and Walter Hilton, had established a pastorally acceptable structure for the piety of clergy and laymen in the face of heresy and devotional novelties. By 1470 the increasing sophistication and independence of the laity in religious matters and their increasingly secular outlook posed an indirect threat to the prestige and sanctity of secular clergy and the religious orders. The northern, Cambridge-educated clergy of the second half of the fifteenth century reacted with as much energy as their predecessors to meeet the challenge of lay piety and to restore the reputation of clergy by infusing greater spirituality into the lives of priests and monks. One of the ways this was attempted was through educational reform – the provision of education in grammar in new schools for young men training to be priests; the foundation of colleges in Cambridge with a new emphasis on theology rather than canon law, that would provide a training for pastoral service and encourage greater spirituality. In 1479 John Alcock founded, at the home of his parents in Hull, a free school teaching grammar and song which would also provide for the founder's soul.[34] Rotherham, a fellow Yorkist diplomat, founded a grammar school in Rotherham called Jesus College. Its purpose was to preach the word of God in the parish and diocese of York and to raise the standards of the clergy by teaching the rules of grammar and song to scholars from all parts of England but particularly the diocese of York.[35] However, it was in the universities, especially Cambridge, that they directed most of their efforts. Between 1496 and 1525 six new colleges were founded in Oxford and Cambridge and five of them were northern foundations. Between 1470 and 1473 Thomas Rotherham built the eastern front of the Cambridge library, to which he contributed over 200 volumes and he contributed to the restoration of Great St Mary's.[36] During this period Michaelhouse became a centre for the study of Theology – 83% of graduate degrees were taken in this subject and prominent men were William

Melton and his pupil John Fisher, who recounted his teacher's exacting standards.[37] In 1496 Alcock suppressed the Benedictine nunnery of St Radegund and founded the college of Jesus in its place; its first master was a Yorkshireman, William Chubbes.[38] Alcock envisaged it consisting of a master and six fellows and six boys studying grammar, reflecting the interest he showed in his chantry school at Hull, and echoing Rotherham's Jesus College. Alcock took the same close interest in the architecture of his educational institutions as he did in the printing of his sermons (like the Roman pontiffs of this period) and he supervised the design of Jesus College, placing various images of cocks and globes to symbolize his name. Bishop Fisher was involved in establishing Jesus College's identity – he was senior proctor in 1494 and wrote the foundation charter in 1496. The college acquired the lectureships that characterized the new learning and was committed to the study of theology in which a lectureship was endowed in 1506. The college was committed to the spiritual life and among its fellows was William Atkynson of Pembroke who, at Lady Margaret Beaufort's request translated the *Imitatio Christi* from French into English.[39] Fisher himself in 1506 converted God's House, a struggling college for schoolmasters into Christ's College, a community of twelve fellow scholars and forty-seven pupil scholars. The purpose of the college foundation was to produce an improved clergy and preference in the election of fellows was given to natives of the northern counties. Two of the leading figures working on the establishment of the new college were northerners and members of Margaret Beaufort's household – John Fothede, Master of Michaelhouse in 1493 and a university preacher and Robert Bekynson, fellow of Michaelhouse and Fisher's successor as president of Queens'. In 1505 Fisher and Lady Margaret discussed a plan to suppress the Hospital of St John and found a College of St John, a task completed by Fisher after her death in 1507. The statutes, finally completed in 1516, specified a master of arts who was a theologian, twenty-seven senior fellows, two deans and twenty-eight foundation fellows studying philosophy and theology and thirty undergraduates scholars. In electing fellows preference was again given to northerners. The college was intended to be for priests and those planning to become priests. These northern clergy, in their activities as founders and patrons of Cambridge, in their preferential patronage of northerners and in their dedication to the ideals of clerical education and to the study of theology and devotional literature were continuing the traditions established by those northerners who established Cambridge's identity as a bastion of orthodoxy, pastoral reform and correct religious enthusiasm at the outset of the century.

One of the ways these clerks attempted to raise the spirituality and education of clergy was through sermons. Apart from sharing in close common links with Cambridge, these northerners were all distinguished scholars and preachers. Alcock wrote four collections of sermons in English, all printed by de Worde,[40] and a Latin sermon[41] printed by Pynson. Alcock was also interested in the printing of his works and the designs of the accompanying woodcuts. Rotherham preached a 'noble sermon' at the reinterment of Richard, Duke of York in Fotheringay in 1476[42] and bequeathed a large library to Cambridge University.[43] Melton was the author of the *Continuation of the Lives of the Archbishops of York from Alexander Neville to Thomas Wolsey* and an exhortative sermon to those who seek to be promoted to holy orders.[44] A specific purpose of Rotherham's school in Hull was the preaching of the word of God in the parish and diocese of York. Alcock frequently sponsored preachers in his diocese of Ely and once preached a '*bonum et blandum sermonem*' in Great St Mary's, Cambridge in Lent from 1 p.m. to after 3 p.m.[45] Fisher and Lady Margaret Beaufort planned to establish a university preachership in 1504 for a college fellow to preach six times a year to bring 'to the people the gospel philosophy'.[46] Preaching was central to the philosophy of St John's College and a northern member of Fisher's circle, John Fothede, Master of Michaelhouse, was the university preacher in 1509. In the sermons of these northern clergy the crisis of the challenge of lay piety and the consequent falling prestige of clergy was a prominent theme. William Melton outlined in his exhortative sermon to those seeking promotion to Holy Orders his ideals for candidates to the priesthood – a strong sense of the elevated nature of sacerdotal life; a firm belief in the Real Presence; and just and upright behaviour in priests, all of which was not possible without a grounding in good letters. He complained about the ignorance of the dissipated rural clergy and recommended the reading and contemplation of holy works as a remedy against sloth.[47] John Alcock wrote a pastoral letter on 6 March 1486 on clerical attire and non residence in which he complained the clergy were so dissolute and haughty that there was no difference between them and lay people. He commanded all clergy and curates to reside in their cures and if they had dispensation for plurality they were to reside in each of their benefices in turn. If they had been licensed for non-residence the ordinary had to see that suitable curates were provided for these parishes.[48] In a sermon to the synod of clergy in the diocese of Ely at Barnwell in 1498 he castigated the worldliness of his clergy and upheld the importance of the parish as the focus of regeneration in the diocese where people were held in good rule, serving God, preserving faith and where they could hear the truth proclaimed.[49]

However, it was the religious orders who were most threatened by the increasingly secular outlook in the late fifteenth century. Classical ideas on dedicated service to the state were by implication not very compatible with the monastic ideal. The Benedictine Chapter, during Wolsey's visitation of religious houses in 1532, realized that the monastic ideal was in trouble when it admitted that few monks were today prepared to follow the rule of St Benedict in all its forms, and it is significant that it was the Pastons (a literate family who were reading these translated works of antiquity) who took their chance in the sixteenth century to seize monastic lands forfeit to the crown. The clergy of the north did attempt some reform of monastic houses towards the end of the fifteenth century. John Alcock suppressed the Benedictine nunnery of St Radegund when he found it in bad order and replaced it with Jesus College.[50] Fisher wrote the foundation charter in 1496 and used it as an exemplar when suppressing the Hospital of St John in 1507.[51] Many sermons in this period were either addressed to, or concerned with, the regular clergy whose commitment to the spiritual life naturally came under closer scrutiny as mere laymen followed a daily routine of liturgical observance and private prayer. Alcock endorsed, in his exhortative sermon to religious sisters at the time of their consecration, the spiritual significance of the institution of marriage, depicting the nun's commitment to Christ as a marriage to an aristocratic lord and comparing the monastic virtues of service and obedience to those shown by a wife in marriage: 'to do all other thynge that perteyneth to a good wyf'.[52] This sermon appeals to the class-conscious daughters of gentry and aristocratic families and depicts their marriages to Christ as weddings that they could not achieve in lay society.

A far more serious challenge to the authority of the church was the increasingly secular outlook that stemmed from the growing interest in antiquity. Most of these northern clergy were themselves students of the new learning – Richard III's uncle, George Neville, the Chancellor of Oxford University and Archbishop of York, was a classical scholar. In a letter to Bishop Termi on the Battle of Towton he moralized on the dangers of civil war quoting from Lucan. In a letter written on his behalf to the University of Oxford on the question of the university securing the books bequeathed it by his brother-in-law, John Tiptoft, the writer stated that in his youth Neville 'acquired many books as possible, caused others to be copied for his use and valued nothing so much as they contained the voice of antiquity, morality, and religion' (in that order).[53] Melton owned a copy of Terence's plays and taught Euclid to Fisher and John Shirwood, Bishop of Durham, was commended by Richard III in a letter to Pope Innocent VIII for his knowledge of Greek. However, these churchmen were able to see how the new rational interest in history and society could erode church traditions. When Lefèvre of Etaples in his book on Mary Magdalene drew on the Greek orthodox traditions to distinguish the three different Marys in the New Testament, Fisher took an anti-critical and anti-humanist stance to maintain that they were all one and the same person.[54] The study of antiquity allowed crown officials to demonstrate that the church's power had not always been as great as it was in the fifteenth century and that concepts such as authority, society and moral order need not have a specifically religious basis. The author of *The Crowland Chronicle Continuations*, probably Dr Henry Sharp a chancery official, was a graduate of an Italian university and a professional administrator and politician trained in the new political ideas of the civil law school of the Renaissance Italy.[55] He saw the events of Edward IV's reign from a secular perspective and claimed he no longer believed the hand of God was the prime mover behind the swift and bloody changes he was narrating, while accepting that many 'simple-minded folk still did'.[56] Similarly Philippe Commynes, describing the death of Richard III at Bosworth and the crowning of Henry Richmond with his crown, asked whether fortune or God's judgement was behind the outcome; interestingly he added that he was not sure.[57] Sharp saw causes of events in personal rivalries for power and influence intertwined with major political grievances. He brought a new rationalism and Machiavellian amorality to historical events, describing with approval how

Edward IV demonstrated his political ability by waging war on the holiest day of the year. Returning from exile in 1471, Edward marched on London as Easter was approaching, hoping to capture Henry VI in the city while the pious king was spending his time in prayer. 'This foresighted (prudens) prince, . . . believing rather in response to immediate necessity than foolish propriety, set out for the city with his army on Holy Saturday of Easter . . . and set up camp at Barnet on the very same night as the Lord's Resurrection, thus ignoring the foolish convention the Peace of God'.[58] This chronicle upholds the creed of the prince and the state, relegating the role played by religion and the church. This was achieved in the reign of Henry VIII, when the king became head of the church, and it was anticipated by his predecessor, Henry VII's professional, bureaucratic approach to government.

The growth of the power of the state under the Tudors was the culmination of the changing relationship between high ecclesiastics and the crown. The leaders of the fourteenth-century church, Stratford, Thoresby, Islip and Arundel, were prominent state officials. However, in the late fifteenth century, while the Italian popes were aspiring towards the wealth and status of Roman emperors, the clergy of northern England, though still occupying positions in government, were mere servants of the state, instruments of, and witnesses to, the growth of state power. John Alcock's career and writings illustrate the way some high clergy responded to these pressures. Like his Cambridge-educated, fourteenth-century forbears, he was a holder of high office in church and state as Bishop of Ely, 1486–1500, keeper of the rolls of chancery, 1471–3, tutor to Edward, Prince of Wales and president of his council in 1473. However, he was never in a position to be able stand up to kings as Thoresby, Islip, Stratford and Arundel had done. He sought the crown's good will by requesting prayers frequently for Henry VII on public processions, and his Jesus College was founded to train chantry priests to say mass for the departed souls of the king and his relatives. There are many portraits of Alcock in stained glass with the royal family.[59] In his English sermon on the text *Qui habet aures audiendi audiat* (Luc viii), which he delivered to a mixed audience of layfolk, clergy and high ranking ecclesiastics and magnates,[60] Alcock reflected on the history of conflicting jurisdiction of church and state, one that he saw was inherent in the history of Christianity. Christ was born in Bethlehem because every man was commanded to make a profession to the emperor with a tribute and Joseph went to Bethlehem to make profession where he was born. During his ministry Christ was involved in conflict with the Pharisees over the issue of jurisdiction. For Alcock the subsequent history of the church was dominated by its attempts to maintain and defend hard-won and binding privileges from emperors, kings and councils. Alcock refers to *Magna Carta*, by which kings guaranteed the liberties of the church, recognizing that they could not be divided in any way and that no temporal judge should have jurisdiction over a spiritual person and temporal men should not deal with any spiritual person but let them have their liberty intact. For Alcock the focus of the liberties of the church and its influence over the people was (as it was for the York clergy of the fourteenth century) the parish church. Alcock traced its origins to Christ's birth at Bethlehem, which symbolizes the parish church where a man is born, baptized, shriven and buried. However, Christ was born at Bethlehem because Joseph was required to go to the place of his birth and make a profession of loyalty to the emperor, and the shadow of royal or imperial power looms large in this sermon. Even when Alcock discusses the necessity of parishioners knowing the sacraments and the laws of the church and obeying them he finds an analogy in a citizen's obligation to know the secular laws, proclaimed by the king's high command and under his seal in diverse places so no man can use the excuse of ignorance. The parish church is compared to the king's chancery (where many bishops served). The parish, Christ's court, was where people were informed about matters concerning the faith; in the same way as chancery, the most important of the king's courts, was where the king's proclamations were issued with his seal. In chancery the king is served by the lord chancellor and his lawyers and clerks, while Christ, the head of the church, is served in the parish by his ministers, pastors, saints, doctors and preachers. The most significant aspect of Alcock's use of the metaphor of chancery (which he seems to have taken from Walter Hilton's *Scale of Perfection*) is the way he uses it to reveal the tensions felt by himself and other leading clergy in their dual position as heads of the church and as state officials. Hilton used the metaphor of chancery to discuss different tensions – those experienced by ecclesiastics who were committed to fulfilling the public functions of the church and yet who were intent on pursuing a more private contemplative form of religious life. He explained the mystic's ambiguous relationship with his parish community with a metaphor concerning an outlaw who obtained a pardon from chancery to enable him to live in society. The pardon resembled the mystic's conformity to the sacraments of the parish church including compulsory annual confession.[61] In other words for Hilton it was the shadow of the church, represented by the parish community, that impinged on the consciousness of the pious man. For Alcock it was the shadow of the state.

The erosion of self-confidence of churchmen had been considerable since the late fourteenth and early fifteenth centuries when the medieval church was more powerful and exerted greater influence over people's lives than at any other period in its history. Thoresby, Islip and Arundel were godfathers; as great patrons with considerable financial and political power they had stood up to kings (Arundel had even helped to depose Richard II). Alcock's response to growing state power was to take refuge in the old consolations of the early church – the idea of an avenging God and the power of martyrdom. He reflected that Pharaoh, who despised the preaching of Moses and persecuted Israel, was drowned in the Red Sea. With more immediate relevance he preached that the chancery of the crown was transient, unlike the church of Christ: 'and this chancery with all the ministers thereof shall endure to the end of the world. And all the tyrants that ever was could never destroy it nor never shall . . . Christ ordained the angels, prophets, apostles, martyrs, confessors, virgins and all other for this church.'[62] The most potent and recent example for Alcock of the power of martyrdom was Thomas à Becket, England's most popular saint, who died 'for all the liberties of the church' and to whom Christ said: 'the same glory I gave to my apostles I give to you'. Alcock sensed the contemporary relevance of Becket's martyrdom: 'it is to presume brethren that Saint Thomas of Canterbury were now living they which directly now do against the liberties of the church would put him to death again', and he encouraged his audience with the words of David: 'touch not my priests nor malign my prophets. They that malign against priests be of the condition that Herod was'.[63]

Alcock's concern with what he perceived to be the growing secular outlook of society at large and even the increasingly secular view within the church itself, led him to cultivate the role of prophet and martyr. Alcock, however, focused on the spiritually indifferent among his own parish clergy. In his sermons to the clergy of the diocese he characterized himself as the preacher/prophet, a Christ-like man of sorrows undergoing rejection by his audience; he spoke of the persecution preachers must endure as they expose themselves to danger and ridicule. A woodcut, probably done to Alcock's instructions, that illustrates him delivering his first sermon, the *Gallicantus johannis alcock*, or 'Cock-crow of John Alcock', at Barnwell priory in Ely diocese in 1499, shows him as the preaching bishop in distress, faced by smiling priests who turn their backs on him. Alcock, punning on his name, associated himself with the crowing cock that appears on his buildings calling on men to repent, signifying the betrayal of Christ. The woodcut of Alcock shows him being humiliated by those he is trying to instruct. Alcock, faced with the worldly indifference of his clergy, closely resembles St Gregory the Great as he experienced his vision of the man of sorrows while celebrating mass. In this way he was identifying himself with a line of rejected prophets going back to Christ. The message expressed is that through humiliation comes power and institutional authority – those who reject the prophet's rejection are doomed. Alcock, with images of the crowing cock on either side, identifies with the preacher Ezekiel, who predicts the destruction of Jerusalem and its priests, thereby warning his own priests of their sins and predicting their ruin if they fail to repent.[64] Here too there is a contrast with late fourteenth-century, northern writers views on the devout cleric's relationship with his society. For Walter Hilton and Nicholas Love martyrdom was not a source of institutional power that could reinforce the church's authority, but a solitary stance that could reinforce isolation from the community of the church. Hilton and a circle of Cambridge lawyers saw themselves as a devout minority struggling to maintain their mystical outlook in a secular society that had little sympathy with religious introspection. The mystics identified with the spurned and rejected Christ, welcoming humiliation and rejection by men because it reinforced their isolation from society and their conviction that they were especially beloved by God.[65]

Alcock's fellow northerner, John Fisher, the last representative of the distinguished line of Cambridge-educated northerners, similarly saw himself as a prophet destined to martyrdom. In his sermons Fisher depicted a church under threat from the infidel outside and a decadent clergy within who ceased to proclaim the church's call to repentance to a sinful humanity. He too was preoccupied with the figure of Herod, the great emperor, and he identified with another martyr, John the Baptist (he had before him a St John's head when he celebrated mass to re-enact the sacrifice of Christ and martyrs in the face of earthly tyrants like Herod and Henry VIII).[66] Fisher, like Thomas More, died defending the inviability of the individual conscience against the secular state. This too was a considerable change from the late fourteenth century when the biggest threat to the individual conscience of the devout man was the church itself, which required conformity to the enquiries of the parish confessor and the penitential discipline of the parish community. Devout higher clergy of the diocese of York in this period voiced their concerns about these communal pressures, and by the mid-fifteenth century the relative decline in the administration of confession[67] and increasing participation in the devotional life by clergy and laity with secular responsibilities, encouraged in books of hours, gave them a brief period of relative freedom of conscience and worship. It was short-lived, for the state replaced the church as the agent of repressive conformity which inquired into people's lives and beliefs, and devout higher clergy like Fisher now found themselves in a less-ambiguous position defending the liberty of individual conscience and the church itself against the march of imperial monarchy.

If in relation to changes in the code of chivalry brought about by the impact of classical ideas Richard III can be considered a somewhat old-fashioned and individualistic figure, the same applies to his religion to which there is a very private dimension which contributed to his withdrawal into himself and the sense of alienation and betrayal he felt, especially towards his subjects in the south. In the second half of the fifteenth century important intellectual developments in the area of private ethics and notions of public duty and authority were occurring. They had a primarily secular context and made little reference to traditional pastoral teaching, the devotional traditions of the north-east or the privileges and liberties of the church. Richard III's role in these developments will now be examined. His adherence to the northern devotional teachings on the mixed life will be examined later, when we consider his private religion where we will see a very different sort of outlook from the secular detachment advocated by Seneca and Cicero, with which equally ruthless men like Tiptoft and victims of Richard III such as Anthony Woodville ordered their lives. Thanks to Shakespeare's portrayal it would appear that superficially Richard III was a ruthless political manipulator and wielder of tyrannical power. He certainly shared the ruthless attitude to practical politics of his brother, Edward IV, and John Tiptoft, but the secular teachings of antiquity left little impact on Richard beyond the common weal rhetoric already discussed. Richard's complex and contradictory character can be explained by the two very different influences – the chivalric traditions and innovations within his father's circle and the court in the south-east; and the religious influences from the female branch of his family, especially his mother, and his northern friends and neighbours and it is to these which we will now turn. We shall see in Richard III a strength of mind and self-belief fortified not by classical stoicism, but a fanatical brand of Christianity in which he believed himself to be first and foremost a servant of God and then the common good. However, first we shall consider ways in which Richard differed from his brother, Edward, and proved himself to be a loyal supporter of the church and a friend and patron to the northern, Cambridge-educated clergy, who were intent on defending and maintaining the traditions established by their predecessors.

RICHARD III, THE DEFENDER OF THE CHURCH

An equally formidable, though less-fashionable, intellectual legacy was available to Richard through his mother, Cicely Neville, her Yorkshire family and their neighbours. Richard's maternal grandparents were Ralph Neville the Earl of Westmoreland and Joan Beaufort, who were buried at Staindrop Church in County Durham. Richard was brought up as a Neville when he became a ward of Richard Neville, Earl of Warwick. The Nevilles of Middleham, though a junior line of the family, eclipsed the Neville Earls of Westmoreland and the Percys to control a large part of northern England around the estates of Middleham and Sheriff Hutton. Richard Neville also acquired the Earldom of Warwick through his countess, the heiress of Beauchamp. Between spring 1465 and the beginning of 1469, between the ages of twelve and sixteen, Richard was brought up in the household of Richard, Earl of Warwick, spending his adolescence at Middleham and Sheriff Hutton. He was present at the enthronement of George Neville as Archbishop of York in September 1465, with his future bride, Anne Neville, aged ten, and in 1468 he was received by the city of York with his guardian. Gloucester's reward for his loyalty to Edward IV during Warwick's rebellion in 1470–1 was that he became the political heir of Warwick in the north, and this was ratified in parliament in spring 1472 when Richard married Warwick's younger daughter, Anne, and he was granted the lordships of Middleham, Penrith and Sheriff Hutton.[68] By 1473 he was also in occupation of former Warwick Lordships of Richmond and Barnard Castle.

During this period Richard, Duke of Gloucester built up a northern affinity composed of old servants of the House of York, such as Sir Richard FitzWilliam of Spotborough and Warworth near Doncaster, Sir John Pilkington of Sowerby and Sir John Saville of Thornhill. It also included old Neville retainers such as Sir John Conyers and the Metcalfs, the lesser peerage of Yorkshire including the Lords FitzHugh, Scrope of Bolton and Scrope of Masham, and lesser gentry, such as Robert Brackenbury and Richard Ratcliffe of Cumberland, who settled in Selby, north Yorkshire after his marriage to Agnes Scrope, sister of John, Lord Scrope of Bolton.[69] All of the above became his counsellors. His patronage of these families is illustrated in the case of the wardship of Thomas Scrope of Masham, son of the fifth Lord of Masham, who in January 1476 was retained by Gloucester and was with his servants and tenants 'wholly at his rule and guiding'. The duke promised to be 'a good and loving lord' to all of them.[70] Thomas entered his father's lands and subsequently became a devoted follower of Richard. Much of Richard's time was spent in the north, and after the murder of his brother George in 1478 he dressed in mourning clothes and was rarely at the court; according to Mancini, Richard mistrusted the Woodvilles, whom he blamed for Clarence's death.[71] While Edward IV spent his time in manors in the Thames Valley, Richard's favourite residence was Middleham on the edge of the moors. He became a warlord of the north-west, the ruler of an independent palatinate of Cumberland. He also had a close relationship with the city of York and was very interested in its economy and the administration of local justice. The duke's council in the north acted as a court of poor requests, arbitrating in many disputes and enabling northerners' problems to be taken care of in York instead of London.[72] His power in the north defused aristocratic feuding and he gave a sense of regional identity to this region by presenting himself as an enemy of the common foe, the Scots.

The north also served as a platform for his bid for the throne. In 1483 Earl Rivers, Richard, Lord Grey and Thomas Vaughan were all sent north for safe custody at the beginning of May – Rivers was held in Sheriff Hutton and Grey at Middleham. Military help was summoned from the north-east. Richard, suspecting Hastings of conspiring against him, or perhaps anticipating that this former friend of Edward IV would oppose any bid to disinherit the princes and secure the throne, dispatched letters to York on 10 June claiming there was a plot of the queen and her family to 'murder and utterly distroy us' and to bring about the 'finall distruccion and disheryson of the north parties'.[73] An army, described as 4,000-strong, arrived in London in July in time to police the coronation. Several north-easterners attended the coronation, including the Earl of Northumberland, Scrope of Bolton and Masham and Gloucester's retainers Sir John Conyers, Sir Richard Huddleston, Lady FitzHugh and Lady Scrope of Masham. After the rebellion of autumn 1483 three dozen northerners were given forfeited estates in the counties of Cornwall, Devon, Somerset, Dorset and Wiltshire, including Scrope of Bolton, Richard FitzHugh of Tanfield, who was appointed Constable of Middleham Castle by Richard, Ralph Neville the third Earl of Westmoreland and Sir Richard Radcliffe.[74] They also filled offices in the south, sitting on commissions. Eight of his fifteen counsellors were from the north and six of the seven vacancies in the Order of the Garter during his reign were filled by northerners. Richard's dependence on York was such that he probably intended it to eventually be the focus of his dynasty. The highlight of his tour of the kingdom in 1483 was his entry into York. On 1 August, before his arrival he sent his Secretary, John Kendale, asking the mayor and aldermen to keep in mind the king's 'entire affection' that he bore towards the city and that he intended 'so to do unto you that all the kings that ever reigned upon you did never so much'. The sense of insecurity that Richard felt in the south is highlighted in the request in this same letter that the citizens of York receive him and his queen with pageants and good speeches and hangings of cloths of arras in the streets to impress the southern lords who will 'mark greatly how you receive their graces'.[75] In the last year of his reign Richard placed increasing reliance on northerners. The city of York, which consistently backed Gloucester, gave official minutes of the morrow of Bosworth, recording how Richard 'was piteously slane and murdred, to the grete hevynesse of this citie', and in 1487 the Earl of Northumberland was murdered by his tenants for deserting Richard at Bosworth.[76] Richard's commitment to his household and to his servants of all degrees was strong – his personal motto was 'loyalty binds me', and he remembered several associates of his youth. When he endowed four fellowships at Queens' College, he asked the new priests and fellows to pray for the souls of Thomas Par, John Milewater, Christopher Wursley, Thomas Huddlesham and John Harper, and all other gentlemen and yeoman servants and lovers of the Duke of Gloucester who were slain at the battles of Barnet, Tewkesbury and other fields and journeys. These men, all from northern families, were part of his personal following, slain around him in the thick of battle, some tracing their service to Richard, Duke of York and others to the earliest years in Richard's household at Middleham; and six years after their deaths they were still being remembered with affection.[77]

Many of these northern families with whom Richard had such firm connections were closely associated with the contemplative movement of the fourteenth century. One of Richard Neville's ancestors, William Neville, the Archdeacon of Durham, was Richard Rolle, the hermit of Hampole's original patron at Oxford. Margery Neville, née Thweng, a relative of John Thweng (or St John of Bridlington as he became known, another authority in the contemplative arts) was one of Rolle's aristocratic lay patrons.[78] Later in the fourteenth century the Nevilles became patrons of St John of Bridlington's priory, the Augustinian house at Bridlington, and supporters of his canonization in 1401. John of Bridlington's disciple, William Sleightholme, was a family confessor to John Neville the Lord of Raby and possibly to his son, Ralph Neville the Earl of Westmoreland and Joan Beaufort, Richard III's maternal grandparents.[79] The Scropes of Masham, who were loyal supporters of Richard, were among the original patrons of Margaret Kirkby, Richard Rolle's disciple, and they were also among the earliest lay owners of Rolle's writings. Richard Scrope, the Archbishop of York executed in 1405, was closely associated with Thomas Arundel, John Newton and Walter Hilton and the circle of Cambridge-educated, northern clergy who were adopting and moderating Rolle's teachings to apply them to teaching on the mixed life, a mode of living in which Richard III's mother, Cicely Neville, and his sister, Margaret of York, were notable exponents. Henry, the first Lord Scrope of Masham and Henry, Lord FitzHugh

The Neville family at prayer in a French fifteenth-century illustration. (Bibliothéque Nationale MS. Latin 1158 fo. 27v)

of Tanfield, an ancestor of another family prominent in Richard's northern retinues, helped to popularize contemplative teachings in the diocese of York and in the courts of Henry V and Henry VI. When we, therefore, come to examine Richard III's piety, it shall become clear that it was this spiritual heritage of the north-east, mediated through Richard's mother and her family and his northern neighbours and friends and servants, which was to prove more important in the development of his moral outlook than the courtiers and writers associated with his father's and brother's courts.

Richard's mother, Cicely, became famous for her piety, and each day at her principal residences of Beckhamstead and Baynard's Castle, London (which were decorated with tapestries of St John the Baptist and St Mary Magdalene and furnished with relics including one of the true cross) she followed the precepts of the mixed life by combing private devotion with public duty. A set of household ordinances, probably drawn up between 1485 and her death in 1495, gives a glimpse of how she spent the years of her widowhood and retirement. She rose at 7 a.m. and recited with her confessor the matins of the day; this was followed by matins of Our Lady and a low mass in her chamber. Dinner was accompanied by readings from Hilton's *Letter on the Mixed Life*, Nicholas Love's *Mirror of the Life of Christ*, the Bl. Matilda of Hackeborn, St Bridget or Catherine of Siena.[80] After dinner she gave audience to her suitors (during the reigns of her son Edward IV petitioners besought Cicely for a favourable word) and after the day's business she recited evensong with her chaplain; at supper she would relate to those around her the spiritual readings of dinner.[81] She maintained close links with monastic communities – among her books was *The Abbey of the Holy Ghost*, an account of monastic ideals for those living in the world, and she was a benefactor of Syon Abbey, where she was remembered in the Martilogue. She was granted confraternity of the Benedictines in 1480 and withdrew from public life into religious seclusion.[82] Two of her granddaughters became nuns – Anne de la Pole became Prioress of Syon and received from Cicely Nicholas Love's *Mirror of the Life of Christ* and Hilton's *Mixed Life*. Cicely also left to Elizabeth, a nun and sister of John Fisher, *The Revelations of Matilda*.[83] Her devotion to St Bridget is shown in her naming a grandchild Bridget in 1480; this grandchild entered the Dominican nunnery of Dartford.[84] As the last of three children to survive in infancy, Richard of

Gloucester would have naturally been close to his mother, especially after the death of his father, who died when he was eight, and after what was, in his eyes, the moral decline of his brother Edward. In one letter he addressed her in the following manner: 'Beseeching you in my most humble and effectuouse wise of youre daly blissing to my synguler comfort and defense in my nede. And madam I hertely beseech you that I may often hear from you to my comfort . . . and I pray God send you the accomplishment of your noble desires. Your most humble son'.[85]

Other devout women played an important part in Richard's life, especially Margaret, his elder sister. She was as famous as her mother for her piety. She was devoted to St Colette and in numerous miniatures she was shown either at prayer or performing deeds of charity. On her visit to England in 1480 she persuaded her brother, Edward IV, to introduce the reformed order of Observant Friars into the country. Margaret was a serious follower of the *devotio moderna*, a movement which originated in the Low Countries, and which had as its leading spokesmen Gerard Groote of Flanders, Jan van Ruysbroek, a brother of the Abbey of Groendael near Brussels, and St Thomas Kempis. Lay practitioners of the *devotio moderna* lived lives of worship, prayer, study and contemplation like followers of the mixed life in England. Their interest in private study and self-improvement led them towards involvement in religious reform, concentrating on restoring the purity of religious life within convents and monasteries (similar reforms were being undertaken in England through the initiative of clergy such as Alcock and Fisher). Among Margaret's friends in the reforming clergy were Denis van Rijkel, a Carthusian scholar and theologian.[86] There were twenty-five books in her possession, mostly of a religious nature including sermons, the contemplations of Augustine, and a book of hours with thirty-four miniatures.[87] The influence of Burgundian piety can be seen in illuminations in her books of hours showing her living a mixed life of prayer and performing the deeds of mercy;[88] Hans Memlinc's triptych, commissioned by Hastings while he was Captain of Calais, is a serene painting that shows Margaret as St Barbara affirming burgher values of charity and family life.[89] Richard seems to have been close to his elder sister and was brought up with her in early childhood;[90] when she married Charles, Duke of Burgundy in 1468 she set out from London accompanied by George and

Richard to make a pilgrimage to the shrine of Thomas Becket.[91] Richard met his sister again in the new year of 1470/71 when he fled to Burgundy with his brothers and Lord Hastings. Gloucester stayed in the Lowlands for five months and visited Margaret in February, staying two nights.[92] In 1474, during discussions of an invasion of France in support of Burgundy, Margaret met her three brothers in Calais on 7 June and Gloucester returned alone to visit her in St Omer. On 14 June all three brothers were entertained by Margaret and the Duke of Burgundy.[93] In June 1480 Margaret headed an embassy to England to draw the English into a Burgundian alliance. Margaret stayed at her mother's home at Baynard's Castle and Gloucester, who was already opposing the Scots, made time to come and see his sister.[94] Richard's mother-in-law and relative, Anne Beauchamp, may have been another influence. She was was probably present at his birth for she was described by John Rous as 'euer a full devout lady in Goddis seruys . . . to lov to be at and with women that traueld of chyld, full comfortable and plenteus then of all thyng that shuld be help to hem. And in hyr tribulacons she was eur to the gret plesure of God full pacient, to the grete meryte of her own soel and ensample of all odre that were vexid with eny aduersyte'.[95]

The other influences on Richard were the northerners who entered his service, the descendants of the Richmondshire families who had been patrons of Rolle and his followers and with whom Richard as a Neville had close links. The FitzHughs' base at Ravensworth was a few miles from Middleham Castle and Anne daughter of Richard's uncle, Richard Neville, Earl of Salisbury, married Richard, Lord FitzHugh, a member of Richard, Duke of Gloucester's council. The Scropes of Bolton and Masham were involved in the suppression of Buckingham's rebellion. John Scrope, the fifth Lord of Bolton, based at Teesdale, was another neighbour of Gloucester's and a member of his council in 1475; his widow, Anne, a member of the confraternity of Syon, left a white rose to her son, Henry.[96] Gloucester's links with the Scropes of Masham were even closer – on the death of the fifth Lord of Masham his widow, Elizabeth, arranged for the Duke of Gloucester to retain her sixteen-year-old son, Thomas, 'to guide him and be a good and loving lord to Thomas and his servants'.[97] Thomas became a devoted follower of Richard III and he and John, the fifth Lord of Bolton, were involved in the Lambert Simnel rebellion.

Younger members of these families found positions waiting at the duke and duchess's table. Among Gloucester's servants killed at Bosworth were the descendants of other gentry families prominent in the devotional movement of the fourteenth and early fifteenth centuries such as Sir Marmaduke Constable and Sir Brian Stapleton.

Richard was a man of clerical temperament and outlook. As he was the youngest son it is possible that his mother, or his uncle, George Neville the Archbishop of York, originally intended him for the church; he was after all present at the enthronement of his uncle as Archbishop of York in 1465 with his betrothed, the ten-year-old Anne Neville.[98] This would explain his knowledge of Latin, which is implied in the large proportion of Latin books in his possession, including those readily available in English such as *De regimine principum*, and the high quality of his handwriting.[99] The reservations of some historians notwithstanding, there is little doubt that Shakespeare was right about Richard's high intelligence (which he shared with the rest of his family); too many contemporaries comment on it for it to be mere sycophancy. *Hardyng's Chronicle*, while commenting on Henry VI's lack of intelligence, mentions the great intelligence of Richard, Duke of York and his knowledge of Latin, and Edward IV's phenomenal memory. Commynes noted Edward's ability to hold in his head the details of the administration of his kingdom. The Crowland Chronicler expressed his admiration for the legal knowledge Richard displayed in his dispute with his brother George over the Warwick inheritance: 'So much disputation arose between the brothers and so many keen arguments were put forward on either side with the greatest acuteness . . . that all who stood around, even those learned in law, marvelled at the profusion of their arguments'.[100] The Crowland Chronicler added that Richard was swift and alert with an 'overweening mind'. Polydore Vergil described Richard as a man to be feared for circumspection and celerity,[101] and in 1484 a Scots embassy at Nottingham to negotiate a three-year truce delivered a Latin oration before Richard by their leader, Archibald Whitelaw of Lotham, the archbishop of St Andrews and quoted and applied to Richard what was said by a poet of a prince of Thebans 'that nature never enclosed within a smaller frame so great a mind or such remarkable powers'.[102] That there was a recognition that intelligence was a family characteristic was shown in Richard III's description of his illegitimate son, John of Gloucester 'whose quickness of mind, agility of body and inclination to all good customs gives us great hope of his good service for the future'.[103] Most suggestive of the possibility of early clerical training is his lodging at Magdalen College to hear learned dissertations on theology and moral philosophy and his decision to purchase a second-hand book of hours which was originally put together for a clergyman (the *confiteor* includes the admission of having administered the holy office with an impure heart).[104]

Richard's clerical sympathies were clearly evident in his acts as the Duke of Gloucester and as king, and he did not share many of the Yorkist courtiers' enthusiasm for the concept of a more secular state. Throughout his life he was a firm supporter of the clergy. Richard established himself as a defender of the church, reversing some of the secular trends established by his brother Edward IV. Edward had appropriated 24 acres of land belonging to Pontefract Priory and Richard, as king, granted it back to the priory calling to remembrance 'the dreadful sentence of the church given against all these persons which wilfully attempt to usurp unto themselves, against good conscience, possessions and all other things of right belonging to God and his said church and the great peril of soul which may ensue by the same'.[105] Mancini observed in 1483 the good reputation of Richard's private life and public activities which powerfully attracted the esteem of strangers.[106] Thomas Langton, Bishop of St David's, said of Richard III in August 1483 to the prior of Christ Church, Canterbury: 'he contents the people where he goes best that ever did prince . . . I never liked the condition of any prince so well as his; God hath sent him to us for the weal of us all'.[107] Pietro Carmeliano, who came to England in 1480 and found employment as a chancery clerk in 1484,[108] dedicated a copy of his *Life of St Catherine* to Sir Robert Brackenbury, keeper of the Tower (St Catherine's symbol) and praised Brackenbury's master: 'If we look first for religious devotion which of our princes shows a more genuine piety? If we look for truth of souls, wisdom, for loftiness of mind united with modesty, who stands before our King Richard? What emperor or proud man can be compared with him in good works or munificence?'[109] John Rous, chronicler of the Earls of Warwick, also wrote glowingly of Richard before the king's death in 1485: 'the most mighty prince Richard . . . ruled his subjects in his realm commendably, punishing offenders of his laws . . . cherishing those that were virtuous; by the which discreet guiding he got great thank of God and some of his subjects rich and poor'.[110] During his public procession through his realm Richard was entertained for two days at Magdalen College, Oxford by its founder Bishop Waynflete and listened to scholarly disputations. After his visit Waynflete wrote in the college register: *Vivat Rex in Aeternum.* His patronage of learning won for him the acclamation of the clergy assembled in Canterbury Convocation of 1484 for: 'His most noble and blessed disposition' and Cambridge University remembered in their prayers 'the most serene Queen Anne' and 'the most pious king'.[111] Richard surrounded himself with northern graduates from Cambridge, many of whom were interested in the new humanist learning of Italy. Dr Thomas Langton from Appleby in Westmoreland, a student of Pembroke Hall, Cambridge, was chosen by Richard when he was protector for the bishopric of St David's.[112] He provided to the bishopric of Durham, John Shirwood, son of the town clerk of York; Shirwood was a protégé of George Neville, Archbishop of York and he owned one of the largest collections of classical literature in England.[113] Richard recommended Shirwood to the Pope in 1484 as one 'whose integrity of life, exceptional gentle manners, together with the unparalleled virtue with which he is endowed draw and attract our love to him'.[114] Other northerners in Richard's clerical circle were – his confessor, John Roby, who was licensed to hear confessions in the diocese of York;[115] William Beverley, Rector of Middleham, Dean of St George's College, Windsor in 1483;[116] John Gunthorpe, Dean of Wells and Keeper of the Privy Seal in 1484, a noted Cambridge Greek scholar who left a large collection of classical literature to Jesus College;[117] Dr Thomas Barowe of King's Hall, the holder of several benefices in the diocese of York in the 1470s from George Neville's patronage, appointed Keeper of the Privy Seal in August 1483 by Duke Richard;[118] and Richard's private chaplain, John Doket, a scholar of King's Hall who had studied in Padua and was the author of a commentary on Plato's *Phaedo*.[119] John Alcock's relationship with Richard was more ambiguous. The Duke of Gloucester removed him from the post as tutor to Edward IV's son, the Prince of Wales,[120] but he was a commissioner of Richard III with the Scots in 1484; he ordained Richard's nephew, Humphrey in 1491. The only Oxford graduates in Richard's circle were his chancellor, John Russell, Bishop of Lincoln, who was described by More as 'one of the best learned men undoubtedly that England had in this time',[121] and Robert Stillington, Bishop of Bath and Wells and Bishop of Ely in 1479.[122] It is significant that these clergy, and others noted for piety and learning, made no objection to Richard's assumption of the throne. John Alcock made no recorded protest, and he must have been in a position to know about Richard's intention to invalidate his nephew's claim to the throne – he was Edward, Prince of Wales' principal tutor at Ludlow and a pupil of Stillington's. According to the Crowland chronicler, Stillington did nothing without consulting him.[123] Likewise John Shirwood did nothing and he knew the princes' physician, John Argentine, who gave a grave report of their fate in the tower.[124] It was natural that Richard's patronage was weighted towards Cambridge University. In 1477 he made provision for the education of four priests and fellows at Queen's College, Cambridge; and the foundation statutes of Richard's college at Middleham a year later required that if no suitable dean could be found among the six priests in the foundation then he should be selected from one of the Queen's men.[125] Richard and his wife Anne gave £329 3s 8d to the college.[126] Richard also gave King's Hall £300 for its building programme.[127] Richard and Anne visited the university from the 9–11 of March 1484, where he was described as 'the most pious king'.[128]

Richard's support for the notion of a universal church and perhaps by implication his lack of enthusiasm for the development of notions of a secular, independent nation state can be seen in his enthusiasm for a crusade. Unlike the clergy who chose to identify with the suffering Christ, Richard would have regarded Christ as the one who, though apparently defeated, destroys his enemies at the Last Judgement. His patron saints were martial figures – commemorated at his foundation of Middleham College were St George and St Michael. A prayer to St Michael in his book of hours begins: 'O St Michael the archangel of God, defend me in battle that I perish not in the terrible judgment'.[129] The chivalric exemplar most prominent in Richard's imagination, however, must have been King David, depicted in his metrical *Old Testament* as a feudal warrior and guerrilla leader engaged in civil war with the allegiance of twenty barons against the house of Saul. In this poem Richard had the opportunity to see the Wars of the Roses and the struggles of his own house mirrored in the *Old Testament*. Richard's enthusiasm for the crusading ideal can be seen in his response to a papal letter to the princes of Europe warning of the

Turkish threat to the western church and culture and asking for speedy assistance. An important advocate of the crusading ideal for the new king was John Estney, Abbot of Westminster, who, on behalf of the abbey, made a large financial contribution to the papacy for the war against the Turks in return for being allowed to choose his own confessor. Estney organized much of Richard's coronation and advised the king before the coronation service.[130] Richard, in a letter to Dr Leonard de Prato, commissary of the knights of John of Jerusalem in Rhodes granting him access to visit houses in England, expressed his 'affection, zeal and devotion due to so great an order'.[131] In May 1484, while he was entertaining the ambassador from Emperor Frederick III, Nicholas Von Poppelau, at Middleham, Richard expressed a wish that his kingdom lay upon the confines of Turkey so that 'I would certainly and with my own people alone and without the help of other princes, easily drive away not only the Turks, but all my enemies'.[132] There is an echo of this in words attributed to Richard in the *Ballad of Bosworth Field*: 'King Richard smiled small,/ and swore by Jesu full of might,/ when they are assembled with their power all/ I wold I had the great turke against me to fight,/ Or Prester John in his armour bright'.[133] Richard's personal dedication to the crusading ideal is further suggested by a litany added especially for him to his book of hours: 'Let us pray almighty ever loving God, in whose hand are all the rights of kingdoms, come to the help of the Christians and let the peoples of the heathen who trust in their fierceness be destroyed by the power of your right hand'.[134] The supplicant then begs God to preserve him from 'langour', perhaps the slackness of princes of the Christian west in answering the call of Innocent VIII for a new crusade. Such devotion to the crusading ideal appeared decidedly old fashioned by 1483 and in this Richard has something in common with the unfashionable crusading knight of Chaucer's *Knight's Tale*, which was owned by Richard.

Given what we have seen about the new outlook of the intelligentsia in Yorkist circles, their interest in this world and posterity rather than the next world, Richard's excessive preoccupation with chantry masses and the fate of his soul appears rather startling. He had strong faith in the intercessory power of prayer and in his *Old Testament* poem it is claimed: 'even if we are too sinful ourselves for God to listen to our prayers, he will listen to holy men praying that we may by God's grace rise from our sins'.[135] He was responsible for ten chantry or collegiate foundations (apart from his patronage of Queen's College, Cambridge) and he distributed a stream of largesse to religious houses, parish churches, houses of friars, chapels and chantries. Many of his gifts were of a small scale and north-country establishments were conspicuous recipients of his charity. Most of his foundations were connected with the north of England. On 21 February 1478 he procured a royal licence to establish two colleges at Barnard Castle in Durham for twelve priests at 400 marks per annum and Middleham in Yorkshire at 200 marks per annum.[136] In the event only Middleham came into being. The statutes prescribed stalls in the collegiate church to be occupied by the dean and six chaplains who, along with five clerks and six choristers, were to form the collegiate establishment offering prayers for the souls of the king and queen and their children, for himself, his wife and son, his mother and sisters and for their good estate when alive and their souls when dead. Masses were also offered for the souls of his father and dead brothers and sisters, including George, Duke of Clarence (who was murdered three days before Gloucester procured the licence), Richard, his duchess and his family. It is possibly significant that one of the altars at Middleham was dedicated to St George.[137] In 1483 he set in motion as king a scheme for a college of 100 priests in York Minster which was intended to be his mausoleum and a focus for his dynasty, as St George's, Windsor had been for Edward IV, and as Westminster Abbey would become for Henry VIII. The proposed foundation at York would have made it the most impressive prayer house for a dynasty in the fifteenth century, one to rival Henry V's foundations of Sheen and Syon, Louis XI's funeral collegiate chapel of Clery and the mausoleum of Ferdinand V of Aragon and Isabel of Castile, St Juan de los Reyes at Toledo.[138] It is tempting to link these excessive measures with a guilty conscience and we shall return to this later, but there was undoubtedly a degree of social and moral purpose behind some of these schemes. Middleham and Barnard Castle were intended to contribute to the better education of clergy and the improvement of services in their localities. Richard gave the patronage of Cottingham to support the vicars choral of York Minster and paid a stipend for a chaplain at Hawes, an isolated village in Wensleydale, for a year while he was king. He donated £40 for the repair of the church of Coverham Abbey in the years of 1472, 1473 and 1483 and purchased and donated the advowson of Seaham in Durham worth £15 a year in 1476.[139] In Richard's short reign all this public patronage of religion stands in marked contrast to that of his brother Edward, whose patronage of religion was rather sparse and connected with his favourite Thames Valley residences of Sheen, Windsor and Greenwich.

THE MESSIANIC KING

Richard reversed the trends towards secular pragmatism shown by Edward IV and established a messianic tone to his reign. To some extent he was drawing on precedents set by his father when he made his bid for the throne. The *Letter to Stilicho*, which had legitimized the power of the peers to act as *vox populi* to choose a king, encouraged the Duke of York to interpret their will as *vox dei*[140] – he asked Henry VI to deliver to him his opponents for 'God who in heaven knows our intent is rightful and true'. When Henry VI refused, the duke promised to fight to save England from the peril it was in: 'preyng to that lord that ys kyng of glorye, that regneth in the kingdom celestyallll, to kepe us and save us this day in our right and throgh the help of his holy grace we pray be made strong . . . therefore we pray to our Lord to be our confidant and defender seiyng Lord be our defender shield.' However, his son brought a far greater religious dimension to his attempt on the throne, and one that had more disruptive social and political implications. His fanatical conviction that he was God's chosen instrument enabled him to apply to his usurpation of the throne and his brief rule as king a greater religious dimension than was present in the Duke of York's attempt on the throne. Richard's sense of moral superiority made him a more dangerous and ruthless man than his father. His first intimations of the awesome religious significance of monarchy would have occurred when, as an eight-year-old boy, he witnessed the coronation ceremony of his brother. His mother, Cicely, encouraged the theocratic conception of Yorkist monarchy. Her views on kingship as a priestly office are recorded by Thomas More. When she found out that Edward intended to marry Elizabeth Grey she objected to her widowhood 'sith it is an unsitting thing and a very blemish and high disagreement to the sacred majesty of a prince, that ought as nigh to approach priesthood in cleanness as he doth in dignity, to be defouled with bigamy in his first marriage'.[141] She arranged for the reburial of Edward and Richard's father, Richard, Duke of York, in Fotheringay in 1476; the duke's bones were taken from Wakefield to Fotheringay in a chariot bearing an angel clad in white wearing a crown of gold to signify his right to be king. Above the funeral image of the duke stretched a black cloth of majesty with a figure of Christ seated on a rainbow displaying the wounds of the Passion (a familiar image in primers).[142] The use of sacred emblems by the house of York can also be seen in the striking of the Angel, its distinctive coinage, with the sign of the cross and an invocation 'through your cross save us'. This and the king's touch for scrofula, maintained by Edward IV and Richard III (who was known to have touched for the king's evil) shows the Yorkist preoccupation with the sacred character of kingship.[143] At Richard's coronation he was anointed with oil, at which point he was informed he would experience a profound change in his spirit and be taken up into a special relationship with God. The ceremony was supposed to cleanse him of sins, and from this point he would achieve a quasi-sacerdotal status as God's anointed; if he had had ambitions to be a priest when he was younger he may have derived satisfaction from this ceremony. The anointing and subsequent investiture with a tunic, shaped like a dalmatic, the coif and gloves, to protect anointed places, recalled the consecration of a bishop.[144] The coronation itself, with the candlelit procession conveying the oil of St Thomas Becket to Westminster Abbey on the night of the vigil, was a religious service. Among the prayers said during the service itself was one entitled 'God in whose hand are the hands of kings'.[145] The investiture of Richard's son, Edward, as Prince of Wales shows that the new king retained the Yorkist symbolism of the sun and projected to his people an exalted ideal of his kingship as a divine vocation:

The charity and clarity of the sun's light is so great that when it is poured on other heavenly bodies the sun shines with no less light and splendour, nor does it suffer any diminution of its strength but is pleased to be seen, to shine as a king in the midst of us nobles and to adorn greater and lesser stars in the court of heaven with his outstanding light, which without doubt we should take as an example, seeing the vocation to which we are called by the favour of the almighty to govern and be set at the head of all mortals of this realm.[146]

Richard retained this conviction until his death wearing over his head armour at Bosworth the crown worth 120,000 crowns and saying, according to a ballad emanating from the Stanley household: 'Give me my batell axe in hand/ and sett my crowne on my head so hye,/ for by him that made both sunn and moone/ King of England this day I will dye'.[147]

Another indication of Richard's almost messianic conception of his kingship can be seen in his attitude to York, which he visited for the investiture of his son, Edward, as Prince of Wales on 29 August 1483, the feast of the decollation of John the Baptist (which was regarded as a second Corpus Christi feast). Although it was too late in the year to witness the performance of the mystery play, Richard (who was lodging in the archbishop's palace) called on the Guild of Corpus Christi, of which he and his wife Anne and his friend Sir Richard Ratcliffe had been members since 1477,[148] to perform the Creed cycle (a shorter version of the mysteries) before the king and the dean and chapter of the Minster at the Minster gates on the eve of the investiture ceremony. The royal entry of Richard and his wife into the city followed the same procession route as the plays.[149] So, whereas the citizens of York annually witnessed the drama which transformed them into citizens of Jerusalem and their city into a type of the heavenly and earthly Jerusalem, they could now observe their king, Christ's representative, the incarnate and temporal representative of divine order in which the citizens played an important role, tread the same path. The climax to the royal procession through the *via crucis* of York was a short ceremony in the Minster. Richard halted at a prie dieu placed specially by the font and before a congregation that included five bishops and all the cathedral clergy excepting the archbishop, and recited the *Pater Noster* in what was perhaps the first occasion that a king of England led the clergy and laity in spoken prayer. The *Pater Noster* was taken up by the clergy and followed by an anthem for the Trinity and a series of prayers including Dean Robert Booth's invocation to deliver the king from temptation.[150] This particular monarch chose York Minster as the site of the most ambitious chantry ever contemplated by an English king. Richard's special identification with York can be seen in the pun on Ebor/boar, his sign, and the link with York, the house into which he was born.

Behind this theocratic conception of kingship there lay a unique component of moral fervour and fanaticism that helps to explain the circumstances of the usurpation of the crown. Richard, Duke of Gloucester was puritanical in his attitudes to sexual morality (one of his patron saints was the ascetic St Anthony, the hermit in whose honour there was a guild in York). His disillusionment with Edward, the brother he idolized, probably set in with the king's secret marriage to Elizabeth Woodville, a middle-aged woman with children. According to Mancini, Richard and George were both displeased, but Richard was better at concealing his displeasure.[151] Mancini also thought Edward IV's licentiousness was encouraged by the relatives of the queen, especially her sons, Thomas Marquis of Dorset and Lord Richard Grey, and her brother Sir Edward Woodville, who were hated by the populace on account of their morals.[152] There is plenty of evidence of sexual immorality at Edward IV's court. Commynes testified to Edward's debauchery before he lost his throne: 'he began to give himself up wholly to pleasures and took no delight in anything but ladies', and after regaining it he lived 'a luxurious life and he grew very fat, and his excess making him to diseases in the very flower of his age he died suddenly'.[153] Hastings procured mistresses for Edward IV, and according to Thomas More, Edward seduced women at court and then passed them on to his other courtiers; he also had three regular mistresses including the one he loved most, Elizabeth (Jane) Shaw. Even Richard's sister, Margaret, had a reputation for promiscuity before her marriage, and before she arrived in the Low Countries for her marriage the Burgundians sang songs about her whoring. She may have identified with the Magdalene, the reformed sinner, for marguerites are prominent in her portraits. Richard seems to have disapproved of the Woodvilles and their Babylonian court and may have regarded the murder of his brother, George, as final proof of his brother's degeneracy. When he arrested Anthony Woodville, governor to the Prince of Wales, Richard told Edward V that the Woodvilles had ruined the health of his father by involving him in their debaucheries. He gave further hints in his correspondence about his alienation from his brother's court and close identification with his deceased father, Richard, Duke of York.[154]

Richard's puritanism and obsession with sexual morality was a personal conviction and cannot always be explained in terms of character assassination.[155] It was a passion he shared with his sister, who founded a house for reformed prostitutes at Mons which was known as the daughters of Magdalene. In his statutes for Middleham he issued instructions that his chaplains were not to haunt taverns or brothels. As protector in May 1483 he tried to drive prostitutes from London and a proclamation was issued by the mayor: 'for to eschew the stynkynge and horrible synne of lechery in all such strumpettes and misguyded and idill women . . . departe and withdrawe theym self and in no wise be so hardy to come ayen Resorte or abide within the said citee or liberte'.[156] Prostitutes had been banned from the city itself since the late thirteenth century, but the inclusion in his inhibition of the Bankside brothel quarter in the liberty of the Bishops of Winchester at Southwark is an indication of the protector's serious intentions. Like many puritans Richard had a repressed sexuality that became stronger as he got older and like some of the messianic self-appointed gurus discussed in the opening chapter he tended to project those aspects of his personality that disturbed him on to those who opposed him. Dr Thomas Langton observed the sensual streak in Richard and after praising him while accompanying him on his Yorkshire tour he broke into a Latin sentence which reads: 'I do not take exception to the fact that his sensuality seems to be increasing'. He had two illegitimate children whom he openly acknowledged – John of Gloucester he made Captain of Calais after the death of his one legitimate son, and he referred to him as 'our dear son our bastard John of Gloucester', and his illegitimate daughter, Katherine, married the Earl of Huntingdon. His closest friends seem to have shared his preoccupation with sexual morality. William Catesby Esq., a counsellor of the king who was executed after Bosworth, described his wife (Margaret, the stepdaughter of Lord Scrope of Bolton) in his will as his 'dear and beloved wife to whom I have ever be trew of my body'. Agnes, the wife of Sir Richard Ratcliffe of Sudbury, Yorkshire, the Duke of Gloucester's counsellor, took a vow of celibacy after she was widowed at Bosworth; she also left the nunnery of Marrick a copy of *The Dream of the Pilgrimage of the Soul*.[157] When Bishop Stillington revealed to Richard the news of Edward IV's pre-marriage contract to Eleanor Butler it was undoubtedly convenient for Richard, but it reinforced Richard's increasing preoccupation with sexual licence. He may genuinely have believed the consequent bastardizing of the princes was the final proof of the moral corruption of his brother and that it morally impelled him to seize the throne. His brother, George, was probably murdered because he had found out about the pre-contract, for at the time of George's execution in 1478 Stillington was also imprisoned in the tower. In his correspondence after Edward IV's death Richard, when referring to his eldest brother, always used the phrase 'whom God pardone'.[158] Richard's line was to be consistent – his nephews were illegitimate and the fruit of a degenerate stock. It is even possible to see the killing of the princes as the product of religious delusion. Richard had convinced himself they were the bastard fruit of his brother's degeneracy and the whole stock of the house of York, from Edward and Clarence, was sickened with sin and he was the only legitimate and sinless representative in the male line. Steeped as he was in *Old Testament* stories of sexual deceit and the relapsing of a line through immorality, Richard had little difficulty in rationalizing his proclamation of the illegitimacy of his nephews and in this he had not only canon law on his side but conventional moral opinion. Peter Idley, in his *Instructions to his Son*, denied that sexual union constituted marriage for this made sin the cause of union. He maintained that one was obliged to marry the first one loved not the second: 'If you give your trouthe to woman in secret and she pure and you give your trouth to second woman if your wits turned and take her for your wife your living in adultery to the first is thy will doubtless'.[159] On 22 June 1483 Friar Ralph Shaw, brother of the Mayor of London, expounded a Biblical text 'bastards shall not take root' and reminded his hearers of the duke's worthy character.[160] Richard may have had the tacit support of his mother Cicely. She had been opposed to Edward's marriage to Elizabeth Woodville and was, according to Mancini, prepared to assert her son's illegitimacy to prevent the marriage;[161] she did not attend the wedding and Richard was staying in her house at Baynard's Castle when he made his bid for the throne. Admittedly she did not attend Richard's coronation, though by this time she was living in contemplative retirement at Berkhamstead where Richard visited her in May, 1485.[162] His sister, Margaret, also gave her tacit support to his rule, refusing to believe he had had the princes murdered, and her Yorkist affiliations were commemorated in a Flemish Deposition portrait of about 1500, which shows Margaret as the Magdalen in a dress decorated with a white rose.[163]

On 26 June 1483 the throne was offered to the Duke of Gloucester on the basis of Edward's degeneracy and the illegitimacy of his offspring, and Richard was to be set up in his place as a divinely chosen, inspired king. In the bill offering Richard the throne the subjects of the realm are asked:

> to considre how that heretofore in tyme passed this lande many years stode in great prosperite, honoure and tranquillite, which was caused, forsmoch as the kings than reignyng, used and followed the advice and counseill of certaine lords spritulex and Temporelex, and othre personnes of approved sadnesse, prudence, policie and experience, dreding God, and havyng tendre zele and affection to indifferent ministration of Justice, and to the common and politique wele of the land; than oure Lord God was dred, lufffed and honoured; than within the land was peas and tranquillite, and among Neghbours concord and charite . . . But afterward, whan that such as had the rule and governaunce of this Land, delityng in adulation and flattery, and lede by sensuality and concupiscence, followed the counsaill of persones insolent, vicious and of inordinate avarice . . . ; the prosperite of this land daily decreased, soo that felicite was turned into miserie, and prosperite into adversite, and the ordre of polecye, and of the lawe of God and Man, confounded; whereby it is likely this Reame to falle into extreme miserie and desolation, which God defende, without due provision of couvenable remedie bee had in this behalf in all goodly hast.[164]

The marriage of Edward and Elizabeth on Walpurgis night is described as a perversion of the law of God and nature and so 'no Man was sure of his wif, Doughter ne servaunt, every good Maiden and woman, standing in drede to be ravished and defouled'. It is depicted as a match brought about through the sorcery and witchcraft of Elizabeth and her mother, Jacquetta the Duchess of Bedford, and claimed that it took place secretly in a private chamber, 'a prophane place' and not openly in face of the church, aftre the lawes of Godds churche'; and in any case it was invalidated by the previous marriage: 'the said King Edward duryng his lif, and the said Elizabeth lived together sinfully and dampnably in adultery, against the Lawe of God and of his church; and therefore noo marvaile that the soverain Lord and the head of this Land, being of such ungodly disposicion, and provokyng the ire and indignacion of oure Lord God'.[165] The full text of this bill was incorporated into an act of Richard's only parliament on 23 June 1484 confirming his title.

Richard continued to see the Woodville faction as representatives of moral corruption. His proclamation against the leaders of the rebellion of the southern counties headed by the Duke of Buckingham on October 23 1483, which he issued from Leicester, was headed: 'Proclamation for the reform of Morals'. In it he granted a general pardon to his immoral and adulterous subjects in August 1483 trusting all: 'oppressours and extortioners of his subjectes, orible adultres and bawdes, provokyng the high indignation and displeasure of God, shuld be reconsiled and reduced to the wey of trouth and with the abiding in good disposition. This yet notwithstanding, Thomas Dorset, late Marques of Dorset, which not feryng God, nor the perille of his soule, hath many and sundry maydes, widowes, and wifes dampnably and without shame devoured, defloured and defouled, holding the unshampful and myschevous woman called Shore's wife in adultry'.[166] He named other conspirators of Buckingham who intended 'not oonly the destruccion of the riall person oure seid soveraign Lord and other his true subjectes, the brech of his peace, tranquillite, and common wele of this his reame, but also in virtue and the letting of virtue and dampnable maintenaunce of vices and syn as they have done in tymes passed to the greate displeasur of God and evyll exemple of all cristen people'. The king then calls on his subjects to resist and punish 'the grete and dampnable vices of the seid traytours, adultrers and bawdes so that by true and feithfull assistens virtue mey be lyfte up and praysed in the reame to the honour and pleasure of God, and vice utterly rebuked and dampned'.[167] The rhetoric, strongly reminiscent of the sense of self-righteousness and persecution in the prayers in Richard's book of hours, suggests he identified with Old Testament kings witnessing the destruction of Sodom and Gomorrah. The same obsession with sexual impurity surfaces again when he was faced with the escape to Brittany of the Woodville faction led by the Marquis of Dorset. In his proclamation to the sheriffs of the counties of the realm on 7 December 1484 he claimed that these men 'be knowen for open murdrers avoutrers and extorcioners contrary to trouthe, honor and nature'.[168] Furthermore he claimed that in finding the support of Henry Richmond they had found a like-minded spirit and that all true Englishmen should defend themselves and their wives. This proclamation was renewed on 22 June 1485 and issued from Nottingham to every shire against these same supporters of Tudor claiming that they were adulterers 'contrary to the pleasire of god'.[169] This obsession with adultery explains his misfired attempt to make a scapegoat of Elizabeth (Jane) Shaw, the former mistress of Edward IV, the Marquis of Dorset and Lord Hastings, who was said to have encouraged Edward into 'vicious living and inordinate abuse of his body with her'.[170] She was charged with witchcraft and conspiracy after allegedly helping the Marquis of Dorset to escape from England and was required to do public penance as a harlot through the streets of London, clad only in her kirtle and carrying a lighted taper. Richard's intolerance contrasts with the sympathy shown by Thomas More, who knew Shaw as an old woman and praised her compassion. A hint of Richard's dour puritanism can be seen in Sir William Stanley's replying to a friend who invites him to go hunting that he is pressed by his duties and has no hope of getting leave from 'Old Dick'.[171]

Richard's moral austerity helped him to believe that his own virtue placed him above the law and that it was God's will that he take the throne. His childhood experiences of civil war and exile must have increased his conviction he was being chosen by God – like David he always remained loyal to the king anointed by God and waited to take the opportunity presented by the Lord. That Richard saw himself as one who could deliver the nation from sin can be seen as early as 1478 when he instructed a preacher at Middleham to say a *de Profundis* for him and concluded with the line 'He alone will set Israel free from all their sins'. This psalm would have had profound significance for Gloucester at the time of Clarence's murder and when the Woodville power was growing. It is significant that Gloucester, who blamed the Woodvilles for Clarence's murder in a letter, was now exclusively based in the north (wearing black mourning clothes[172] and hinting in a letter to the Earl of Desmond at his alienation from his brother's court) was arranging a public profession of his relationship with God and a recitation of this psalm in his collegiate chapel. John Russell, Bishop of Lincoln, in his draft sermons for the abortive parliaments of 1483 planned to tell the peers 'God speed with the prince, which is like our God on earth.'[173] At the opening of Richard's first parliament as king, Chancellor Russell gave a speech expressing the idea that Richard was monarch through God's inscrutable decree which should not be questioned. Men must now strive to heal the divisions in the realm and not question God's ways: 'Is it not a dark way for a man to take on himself the most privileged and secret office of his maker God'. Richard himself, in a letter to the Duke of Milan, Gian Maria Sforza, said 'since we have attained this royal dignity by divine favour we have thought nothing more laudable and more worthy of our princely dignity than to benefit our subjects'.[174] John Norton, the Prior of Evesham, in a letter to Richard described the prayers of royal foundations as 'contributing to the glory of him through whom princes rule'.[175] The Crowland Chronicler wrote of the evil befalling Edward and his progeny and hinted at the providential destruction of his two sons because of his own sins.[176] Even John Alcock, in an English sermon delivered after Richard's death, tried to make sense out of the disinheritance of the princes by reflecting on the goodness and charity of the Lord's secure succession of lands and titles among the Israelites to Jacob, Joseph and David, all usurpers who succeeded on their own merits.[177] Such a sermon obliquely alludes to the sins of Edward IV and the eventual succession of Henry Tudor. Richard's self-appointed role as an Old Testament king and deliverer of a nation from sin was expressed in the open letter to the bishops on 10 March 1484 at Westminster urging them to repress and punish immorality: 'Our principalle entent and fervent desire is to see virtue and clennesse of lyving to be avaunced encresed and multiplied and vices and alle othre thinges repugnant to vertue, provoking the highe indignacion and ferefulle displeasure of god to be repressed and adnulled. And this perfitely folowed and put in execucion by persones of highe estate . . . enducethe persones of lower degree to take thereof example, . . . but also thereby the great and infinite goodnesse of god is made placable and graciously enclyned to thexaudicion of our peticions and prayers'.[178] In other words by upright rule a king who delivers his people out of vices and brings about the multiplication of virtue appeases a sincere and vengeful God. The success of a people's prayers depends on the conduct and rule of the king. Richard further exhorted the bishops to be vigilant in punishing clergy and laity who wandered off the path of true living and promised his full support. 'We therefore wol and desire you that acccording to the charge of youre professione you wol see within thauctorite of your Jurisdiction and on goddes behalf inwardly exhort and Require you that alle such persones. as set aparte virtue and promote the dampnable execucion of synne and vices to be reformed repressed and punysshed condignely after theire demeryts not sparing for any love, favor drede or affeccion'. In this he concludes you will 'do unto God righte acceptable pleasure'.[179]

Richard's proclamations represent an attempt to distance himself from his brother and to be identified more closely with the saintly Henry VI (Richard staged the removal of Henry VI's body from Chertsey Abbey for reburial in St George's Chapel, Windsor alongside Edward IV). After the translation there were forty-nine pilgrimages to the tomb between 22 August 1484 and 2 November 1484.[180] It is also possible that John Blacman, the Carthusian of Witham Charterhouse in Somerset, wrote his 'Compilation of the Meekness and Good Life of Henry VI' to coincide with this move.[181] In this biography Blacman vividly recalls the low opinion Henry VI expressed about Edward IV's disinterest in spiritual matters. Henry, while he was a prisoner in the Tower in 1471, reflected that he had always, since he was a child, tried for the kingdom of heaven and told his chaplain 'of the earth I do not care. Our kinsman of March thrusts himself into it as is his pleasure.'[182] Unlike his elder brother, Richard observed holy days, even delaying his move to Bosworth field from Nottingham because he refused to leave on 15 August, the Feast of the Assumption.[183] However, his puritanical convictions and a messianic sense of his destiny to rule and deliver his nation from sin, combined with his patriotism, his desire to lead and reform the clergy and to found prayer houses for his dynasty and his chivalric ambitions and crusading zeal made Richard a monarch very much in the mode of Henry V. However, despite his undoubted piety and intelligence, Richard did not have as much success as Henry V in harnessing the forces of communal religion in support of his monarchy or in establishing the trust of his subjects. A consideration of the reasons for this failure will take us into the more private and idiosyncratic areas of Richard's religion.

4

THE PRIVATE RELIGIOUS LIFE OF RICHARD III

THE MIXED LIFE AND PRAYER IN THE NORTH OF ENGLAND IN THE FIFTEENTH CENTURY

In the fourteenth and fifteenth centuries there was a general recognition of the importance of solitude in enabling people to achieve integration with their inner selves. For this reason recluses and the eremitic orders such as the Carthusians and the Brigettines were patronized by courtiers and the nobility and devotional texts were written, translated and copied and (towards the end of the fifteenth century) printed. The most convenient way of achieving this state of solitude and meditation, especially for those living the mixed life, was prayer. Although prayers said at funerals, in chantry chapels, and in response to orders from bishops for prayers for the successful prosecution of the crown's military campaigns had an important public dimension, corporate worship undertaken as a means of achieving social integration and harmony has been emphasized (see chapter 1) at the expense of the more private function of prayer, which was to put the worshipper into the presence of God and in touch with his or her deepest feelings and needs. The prayer book, especially one as frequently used and adapted to the needs of its owner and bearing the impact of his personality as Richard III's book of hours (in the calendar there is an entry for October in which Richard in his large, untidy hand has added 'on this day was born Richard III king of England at Fotheringay in the year of our Lord 1452)[1] can be used to indicate the workings of the imagination of the worshipper. A book of hours was something people could turn to in trouble for comfort as it provided prayers for those in exile, in prison, facing danger, illness, death and betrayal. Richard's prayer book contains the Hours of the Virgin, which are the psalms of David (then believed to have been composed by a beleaguered and penitent king) arranged according to the liturgical hours of the day, and a number of separate devotions, some common such as the fifteen Oes or invocations to Jesus which originated in the Brigittine order. It also includes long prayers to Jesus and the Virgin, meditations on the Passion of Jesus and Mary, and more unusual prayers, including a prayer for the beginning of Lauds commencing 'O Lord come to my aid, O Lord make haste to help me' which is preceded by an eight line initial D^2 and a prayer to the Cross and a prayer to St Veronica. Some of the prayers including two to the Virgin, a prayer to the Trinity and a prayer to a good angel appear to be unique to this manuscript.[3] Others are both unusual and, as we shall see, have direct relevance to the king. These include prayers to St Michael, St Joseph and St Julian the Hospiteller. Added to the book at the king's request were a litany composed for him and a personal prayer asking Jesus for protection and deliverence from his enemies which contains the king's name. No man was probably more surrounded by people and more alone than a late medieval English king, especially one as mistrusted as Richard III. I hope to demonstrate how Richard used this prayer book to enable him to live a mixed life like his mother and sister, and that by doing so in prayer he would have used the psalms and his chosen private prayers in an individualistic way to reinforce a self-image. This was derived from identification with Old Testament rulers, especially King David, who were persecuted, misunderstood and penitential leaders chosen by God. This takes us into a private, religious world which was as individualistic as anything Rolle could have imagined and one that had profound consequences for English history.

An indication of Richard's austerely religious devotion to the mixed life, which was formulated through the influences of the Cambridge clergy who were at the forefront of reform of the church, and above all northern, and family influences, especially that of his mother Cicely Neville, can be seen at Middleham. His devotion to daily mass at his chapel at Middleham would have pleased Cicely. He was a strict enforcer of daily worship in his own chapel – an ordinance made by the king for those in his household in the north stipulated that 'the hour of goddes service, diet and rising be at a resonable time and convenient hours'. Anyone breaking this ordinance was to be punished.[4] Music played an important part in the daily celebration of hours in his chapel – in 1484 he gave a licence 'to his well beloved servant, John Melyonek, one gentleman of our chapel, knowing his expertise in the science of music to licence him and give him authority in all chantries, chapels, religious houses, and colleges to take and seize for us in our name all singing men and children who are experienced in the science of music'.[5] The elaboration of Richard's daily mass at Middleham in May 1484 and the beauty of the music was admired by Nicolas von Poppelau, the Silesian diplomat.[6] This was more than mere show – Richard showed a knowledge of and interest in the liturgy that was unusual for a layman. In his foundation statutes for Middleham, after long deliberation with his ecclesiastical counsellors including the first dean, William Beverley, he stipulated that the use of Sarum was to be sung exclusively, and he spelt out in detail the daily round of divine service, instructing the anthem of St Ninian, confessor, to be daily sung after matins. These statutes indicate the importance of the Divine Office in Richard's life. He requests a daily mass of Our Lady, a mass of Jesus on Fridays and on every Wednesday a Requiem mass.[7]

There was also a literary dimension to Richard's religion. His reading tastes were different to those of the Yorkist court. Instead of showing an interest in the classical literature read by Worcester, Woodville and others, he was interested in the more old-fashioned mystical and religious literature of the north of England, tastes he shared with his mother and sister Margaret. From early childhood Richard was surrounded by religious books. One of his earliest was a metrical paraphrase of the Old Testament, which was written between 1400 and 1410 in the north-east of England and influenced by the York Corpus Christi plays.[8] Richard's interest in the stories of the Old Testament and in the cycle plays that dramatized them is attested by his membership of the York Corpus Christi Guild and his attendance at performances of the Creed Play in York on 7 September 1483; and performances of the Corpus Christi plays in York on 17 June 1484[9] and in Coventry on 2 June 1485.[10] He was also, apart from Henry VI, the only English king to have owned an English New Testament.[11] The influence of his mother, Cicely, can be seen in the joint ownership by Richard and his wife, Anne, of *The Booke of Gostlye Grace* by Mechtild of Hackeborn.[12] Richard's in-laws shared this interest in female visionaries: Anne Neville's mother, the Countess of Warwick, commissioned the Pageants of Richard Beauchamp, fifty-three drawings celebrating the life of the Earl of Warwick, including one commemorating the prophecies of the York anchoress Emma

Rawghton.[13] This work gives useful precepts for the living of the mixed life and especially significant is a meditation on the different fingers of the hand – the last finger signified doing service for others as Christ had done; whenever the reader was tempted by pride he was advised to put his finger to that finger and think of the subjection and meekness of God.[14] Such a meditation would have been appropriate for Richard who, like his sister, Margaret, had strong notions of public duty.[15]

Richard's taste in books, with his preference for religious literature and works in Latin and English, suggests he was introspectively pious in a way that is in marked contrast to some of his predecessors as kings of England such as Edward III, whose religion was ceremonial, dynastically orientated and unaffected by the trends for private devotion based on books of hours,[16] or Richard II who was more interested in French romances.[17] While this accords with the tastes of fellow northerners from the families of FitzHugh or Scrope, it contrasts with the more secular, classical tastes of the literary circles of the south-east, such as the circle of Sir John Fastolf where there is a marked preference for classical literature in French translations, or even in the court of Edward IV. Sir John Howard, a servant of Edward IV who was granted the dukedom of Norfolk by Richard, had a library composed entirely of historical tales and light romances, mainly in French.[18] The most important book in Richard's collection, however, and one that gives closest insight into his piety, was his book of hours modestly illuminated and decorated, which like many of his books, he acquired second hand and therefore presumably owned for private reading rather than display. This manuscript was probably produced in London in the 1420s. It shares decorative features in common with the book of hours of John the Duke of Bedford and another book of hours, which were both illuminated by an artist influenced by Herman Scheere who was working in London in the 1420s.[19] Originally produced in about 1420 for a cleric (a model confession contains admission of negligence and inattention while celebrating mass) it probably came into his possession while he was king, for the calendar entry giving his date of birth describes him as *Ricardus Rex*. This book of hours takes us into the private world of prayer, the most important manifestation of lay religion and one little studied or appreciated.

The key to Richard's self-image is prayer, the way he communicated with himself and God, and it was his fanatical conviction that he was God's chosen instrument that gave his usurpation and brief reign a religious dimension lacking in the Duke of York's unsuccessful attempt on the throne. Richard's sense of moral superiority made him a far more dangerous man than his father. The most important manifestation of lay piety in the second half of the fifteenth century was the growth of private prayer. Many were sceptical about the value of the teachings of antiquity in achieving peace and detachment. Jean Battista Alberti wrote: 'how can we live the indifference to ill fortune of which the philosophers speak when the goods of the world are all we live for. It is necessary to purge the soul with a reason and method stealing from ancient ruins does not bring us this possibility'.[20] Prayer was seen as an alternative means to achieving this peace and emptying the mind. Sophisticated concepts concerning self-knowledge and discipline through prayer that were once the preserve of monks now, with the decline of monastic ideal, were circulated among the laity at large with the help of the printing presses. The Brethren of the Common Life and the Observant Friars (whose order was established in England by Richard III's sister, Margaret) and writers such as Richard Whytford, William Bonde and the author of *The Mirror of Our Lady*, who were associated with the Brigittine house of Syon (where Richard's niece was professed) demonstrated how the purpose of prayer was to focus and empty the mind, compared by Gerard Zerbolt to a mad mill forever grinding.[21] They asserted the sanctification of marriage and daily work which was seen as a means of anchoring and emptying the mind and showed that laymen could in their daily lives attain the sort of self-discipline and concentration once attained only by monks.

The importance of prayer in the lives of many members of the Yorkshire nobility is shown in the way they projected an image of themselves as people who devoted an important part of their lives to solitary, devout communion with God. Funeral monuments usually depicted the departed with hands clasped in prayer, one such monument is that of Richard's maternal grandparents, Ralph Neville the Earl of Westmoreland and Joan Beaufort in Staindrop church and the monuments of his retainers in Harewood church. Owners of books of hours frequently had illuminations of themselves on bent knees praying to a patron saint or God. Richard of Gloucester's sister, Margaret of York, was frequently

The private chapel of the Scropes of Bolton Castle with reclusarium. (A.D. Worsnop)

A brass rubbing of William Catesby at
prayer. (BL MS. Add. 32940)

depicted in miniatures at prayer either by herself or accompanied by her ladies in waiting.[22] Private prayer was facilitated among the nobility in this period by family chapels, of which there are examples in Middleham Castle and the manor houses of Leconfield, Wressle (Percy) and in the gentry manors of Thorp Perrow (Danby) and Sedbury (Boynton).[23] Even more personalized were the oratories which could be reserved for masses in times of sickness and mourning (a concession allowed Joan Boynton in 1455 when she was mourning her first husband) but which were almost exclusively associated with private prayer. The licence of Joan (the mother-in-law of Richard III's servant and friend Sir Richard Ratcliffe) was extended in 1474 when she was granted the privilege to have service in an oratory wherever she chose. Licences for the use of oratories

Funeral effigy of Richard III's maternal grandparents, Ralph Neville, Earl of Westmoreland and his wife, Joan Beaufort, at prayer in Staindrop church, County Durham. (Geoffrey Wheeler)

were issued between 1480 and 1481 to Edward and Elizabeth Saltmarsh, Henry Percy the Earl of Northumberland, his wife Maud and Robert Haldyngby Esq. and his wife Elizabeth in the parish of Howden. These oratories were also increasingly associated with books of hours – in the household book printed by Wynkin de Worde, the chamberlain of Lady Margaret Beaufort's oratory at Christ's College is instructed to lay carpets and cushions and her book of prayers in the morning and then to draw curtains which opened on to the interior of the chapel.

However, it is the increasing ownership of the primers themselves that indicates the growing significance of private prayer in the lives of laymen and women in the north of England and the rest of the kingdom. The book of hours was a layman's abbreviated version of the Psalter consisting of the gradual psalms, Marian antiphons, lessons and collects celebrating the beauty and mercy of the Virgin, the penitential psalms, litany of the saints, the Office of the

Alabaster funeral effigies of William Gascoigne and Margaret Percy, 1487, at Harewood church near Leeds. Gascoigne accompanied Richard, Duke of Gloucester on his Scottish expedition and was knighted by him on this campaign. He fought for Richard at Bosworth. (Geoffrey Wheeler)

Alabaster funeral effigies of Sir Edward Redman and his wife, Elizabeth Huddleston, 1510, at Harewood church. Edward Redman fought for Richard III at Bosworth. He was possibly an esquire to the body of Richard III. (Geoffrey Wheeler)

dead, and psalms of Commendation and the psalms of the Passion, which offered laymen the opportunity to share in the monastic round of prayer over the seven monastic hours of the day.[24] These books of hours, or primers as they were known, were produced in increasing numbers in the Low Countries and England in the early fifteenth century and were owned by most members of the Yorkshire nobility who handed them down to their children. Richard III himself, his son and his servants and friends all owned their personal books of hours. Elizabeth, Lady FitzHugh of Ravensworth, widow of Henry, Lord FitzHugh of Tanfield, patron of the Brigittines and owner of an autograph of Rolle's writings, left primers to her son, Robert, her daughter Margaret and Malde Eure, and her god-daughter, Elizabeth FitzHugh. One book, written in about 1410, and illuminated by Herman Scheere and containing an office of Richard Scrope, may have been specially written for this family.[25] Thomas Cumberworth, who owned Hilton's *Letter on the Mixed Life*, bequeathed his red

Alabaster funeral effigy of Nicholas Fitzherbert of Norbury, the head of a
Derbyshire family. (Geoffrey Wheeler)

primer and a roll of prayers,[26] and Thomas Dautre, clerk of York, left primers to his son, John, also a clerk of York, and his daughter Margaret.[27] William Catesby, one of Richard III's inner circle, owned a 'great and a little primer'[28] and Sir Brian Roucliffe, one of Richard, Duke of Gloucester's servants, left a primer once owned by his wife to his son John,[29] and Lady Elizabeth FitzWilliam, wife of Sir Richard FitzWilliam, a servant of Richard, Duke of Gloucester, left her best primer to her daughter Katherine Skipton.[30] These prayer books were often described as precious, personal items to be used daily and often to be continually carried around. Sir Brian's kinsman, Peter Ardene, Baron of the Exchequer, left his 'daily' primer to his wife in 1467; Robert Constable Esq. of Barnby by Bossard, bequeathed to his son, Robert, 'my Portative which I say to myself', and to his friend and executor, Thomas Witham, who lived at Cornburgh a mile from Gloucester's castle at Sheriff Hutton (where he founded a church to keep divine services) he bequeathed his diurnal (a shortened form of the breviary written for the convenience of laymen) which 'I bear in my sleeve daily'.[31] Primers suitable for such daily use were produced and naturally do not survive in such numbers as the de luxe editions displaying wealth and position. One that is extant and of northern origin is small enough to fit into the palm of the hand and could be read while riding a horse. John of Lancaster, Duke of Bedford, besides owning a large illuminated Hours, had a small prayer book which he carried with him daily on campaigns.[32] One contemporary witness to the daily reading of the Psalter was John Rous, the antiquary of the Earls of Warwick, who claimed that Henry Beauchamp, Duke of Warwick (d. 1445) recited the entire Psalter daily: 'he wolde dayle sey the hole daved sawter with owt he had the gretter besiness he cowd hyt will owt the boke perfyzzle [perfectly]'.[33] This was probably an abridged version of the Psalter ascribed to St Jerome which consists of a few lines from each of the psalms that are found in most primers.[34] Psalters and primers constituted an important part of the education of the nobility – Sir Brian Roucliffe wrote to Sir William Plumpton to tell him that his daughter, Mary Plumpton, had just learned her psalter.[35]

The popularity of these books makes them important sources for the study of lay piety in the fifteenth century (possibly more so than the devotional literature emanating from the north east). It is, therefore, necessary to study the standardized contents of the books of hours, and Richard III's primer will be cited for this purpose. Later, when we consider how Richard conformed to and deviated from these patterns of religious behaviour, we shall look more closely at the king's personal additions to his prayer book and his own individualistic and idiosyncratic attitudes towards some of the prayers in the books of hours. While the works of Hilton and Nicholas Love circulated widely in the fifteenth century and gave general and practical advice to laymen who wished to live a mixed life, it was the book of hours, the most widely read religious text in this period, that enabled laymen to come closest to living a fully religious life.[36] Fifteenth-century prayer, we shall see, was an emotional, individualistic and amateur activity that allowed worshippers to apply the prayers in their primers to their own secular worlds of family, career, their individual personalities and situations, and above all their own self-images. This enabled them to live more fully a mixed life.

The arrangement of the psalms according to the monastic hours enabled owners to pray in ways appropriate to the changes in the day, stages in an individual's life and individual moods. In the early morning the psalms for matins and lauds praised God's creation and the birth of Christ the redeemer: 'I will praise thy name, O Lord; for it is good'. At none, in mid-afternoon, the psalms emphasize achievements culminating in the birth of the saviour. By compline the emphasis is on the longing and disquiet of the soul: 'Hail Mary, we sigh groaning in this valley of tears, turn to us your merciful eye . . . out of the depths have I cried to thee O Lord. My soul watcheth for the Lord more than they that watch for the morning'. Apart from expressing different moods, these psalms and other prayers could help reconcile laymen and women to the crises and sufferings of life and these could be applied to people with vastly different horizons. A meditation on the seven blood-lettings of Christ, known as the Revelation of the hundred Pater Nosters, was owned by a monk of Mount Grace and copied by a Yorkshire parish priest for a local husbandman who 'used hit dayly as devoutly as he coude' and turned to the prayer in desperation to revive his oxen which one of his farm labourers had beaten senseless.[37] A moving instance of turning to the psalms to come to terms with the suffering caused by violence occurs in the funeral of Sir Henry Vavasour in 1499. Vavasour, when making his will, had to deal with a tragedy of biblical proportions, a case of fratricide within his own family (in 1488 his son, William, had killed his brother, Richard). Sir Henry, identifying with Jacob faced with his quarrelling sons, asked his two surviving sons, Henry and William, to stand with chantry priests around their brother's grave singing the psalm about the departure of Israel from Egypt (Psalm 114): 'when Israel went out of Egypt, Judah was his sanctuary . . . tremble thou earth, at the presence of the Lord at the presence of the God of Jacob'.[38] Archbishop Rotherham, who had handed over Richard Vavasour to the rural dean for purging, also quoted from the Book of Job in his will, asserting his belief that he would see the face of his redeemer.[39]

The penitential psalms enabled supplicants to face their own sins: 'I acknowledged my sin unto thee, and mine incapacity have I not hid . . . the sacrifices of God are a broken spirit a broken and contrite heart'. The Office of the Dead, with readings from the Book of Job, emphasizes God's support and power, and provides comfort and guidance for those in trouble and prayers for those in exile or facing death or betrayal. It is intended to relieve the worshipper from feelings of guilt, self-loathing, hatred of the world and even of the Lord and enables him to praise God's creation. The Office of the Dead also encouraged in a worshipper an acceptance of the inevitability of the deaths of members of the family, friends and the self: 'Man that is born of woman is of few days, and full of trouble. He cometh forth like a flower, and is cut down; he fleeth also as a shadow, and continueth not'.[40] The resignation and pathos of the Office of the Dead made its mark on the wills and funeral monuments of the north. William Fitzwilliam Esq. of Spotborough prefaced his will in 1474 by a long Latin preamble in which he considered the 'lacrimose and ever-mutable human condition . . . in this vale of tears where nothing is stable or permanent and all mankind is bound to the preordained end in darkness and invisibility' and quoted from Psalm 144 'man is like to vanity: his days are as a shadow that passeth away'.[41] A key figure in Richard III's northern affinity, Sir Marmaduke Constable of Flamborough, a knight of the body who was at Bosworth,[42] willed in 1518 that his body be buried quickly as soon as God called him out of this transitory life.[43] He left a brass epitaph on his tomb (which contains the remains of an effigy of a skeleton) in the high altar of Flamborough church in which he reviewed his military past, including the French campaigns of Edward IV and the Scottish wars, and reflected on the transitoriness of life:

But now all thes tryumphs ar passed and set on syde,

ffor all worldly joyes they wull not long endure.

They are sonne passed, and away dothe glyde,

And who that puttith his trust in them I call hym most unsure;

ffor when deth strikith he sparith no creature,

Nor geuith no warnyng but takith them by one and one.

And now he abydyth Godis mercy, and hath no other socure

ffor, as ye se hym here, he lieth under this stone.[44]

Above all the epitaph expresses the sense that this old Yorkshire soldier and servant of the king depended not so much on the intercession of priests, but on the consolation of the prayers of those with whom he was most intimate: 'I pray you my kinsmen louers and frendis all to pray to oure lord Jhesu to have mercy on my sowl'.[45] The usual recipient of these world-weary prayers was Jesus. William FitzWilliam left his soul to Christ, who redeemed him from the Cross, with as much devotion as he could muster.[46] Thomas Witham Snr of Cornburgh, a friend of Richard, Duke of Gloucester whose house was in sight of Sheriff Hutton Castle, had a perpetual chantry in the church of Sheriff Hutton (where Edward of Middleham was rumoured to be buried) and a marble slab with the inscription 'Christ pity Thomas Wytham and his wife Agnes';[47] she prefaced her will in 1490 with a prayer 'knowing I am to pass from the prison of this world of nature, I give my soul to Christ and his blessed mother'.[48]

If the psalms helped owners of primers to emerge from crisis and face rites of passage, they were also important in affirming the ties and responsibilities of the household. Christ and the Virgin, guardian angels and patron saints offered the sort of protection available from leaders of families and households.[49] God and Christ were addressed as feudal lords and the Virgin was addressed as a patron. They provided power, patronage and protection that could be tapped through prayers that used the language employed throughout society by those seeking the patronage of the great: 'O glorious Lady Virgin Mary think me worthy my unworthy petition which I pour forth from the heart to your sweetest son'.[50] The patron saint and patrons were linked in paintings and illuminations. In the Donne altarpiece, executed in about 1480 by Hans Memlinc for Sir John

Donne, servant of Edward IV, and his wife Elizabeth Hastings, sister of the Duke of Gloucester's friend, William Hastings, saints and supplicants share the same courtly world – St Barbara bears a resemblance to Margaret of York (Richard III's sister) as she stands behind Elizabeth Hastings. Service was an important part of the social, economic and political lives of all the nobility. Service given to a lord in the return for protection, employment, financial rewards, and grants of local influence contributed to a person's self-esteem, and service to God was conceived in similar terms. There was, therefore, a close link between prayer and the language of household and service. God, like the lord of the manor, was a source of power to be tapped. Many prayers in primers begin with the phrase 'your servant N', and Richard, Duke of Gloucester, after years of dispensing and receiving patronage, expressed himself in his private prayers to God as a servant seeking the patronage and protection of a feudal lord. In the prayer added especially for him in his book of hours he describes himself to God as 'your servant',[51] a phrase that is echoed in his own warrants to his household servants as 'your well beloved squire'. The language of prayer was also used in appeals to Richard as king. Subjects appealed for his help to his grace, and if they had served him, to his lordship.

More important, however, was the way prayer helped affirm the duties and joys of family life. Many prayers were addressed to God the Father and the Virgin Mother as parents to be revered and loved, and guardian angels and patron saints offered similar protection. The psalms, the brief Hours of the Cross, the Hours of the Compassion of the Virgin, individual prayers to the Virgin and illuminations depicting the Annunciation, affirmed the need for wives and mothers to accept the fate of childbearing, and gave a religious dimension to feelings of well being and happiness experienced at pregnancy, and to anxiety and bereavement. The close identification of female owners of books of hours with the Virgin was emphasized in illustrations which show the Virgin at the moment of the Annunciation reading her book of hours which would be identified with the owner's.[52] Some of the most popular prayers to the Virgin celebrate the beauty and goodness of womanhood. In *Obsecro te domina* the supplicant appeals to Mary as the 'mother of orphans' to provide comfort by showing her face at the hour of death 'through that inestimable humility in which you responded to the archangel Gabriel'.[53] This contemplation, near

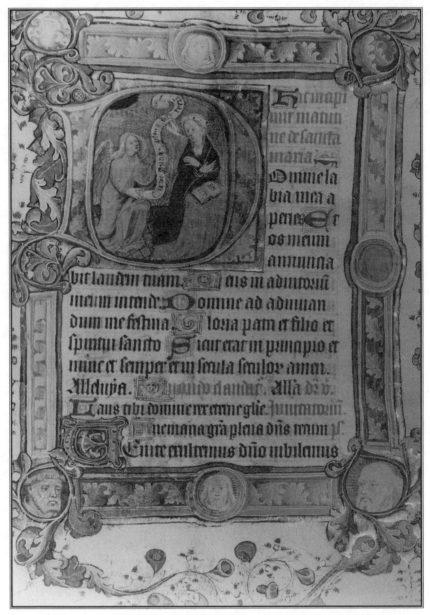

Richard III's Hours, Lambeth MS. 474 fo. 15. The Annunciation and the beginning of the Hours of the Virgin.

death, of the Virgin's fatalism during the Annunciation was presumably practised in 1488 by Joan Boynton of Yarm, the mother-in-law of Sir Richard Ratcliffe, who paid for an image of the Salutation of Our Lady and St Gabriel on her gravestone.[54] The prayer *Obsecro te homina* reaches a climax with a breathless appeal to a mother who is full of joy at the Annunciation, sorrow at the sufferings of her son, and pity for the supplicant. The prayer on the Five Joys of the Virgin evokes the happiness of the divine family 'Hail to you who gave milk to the son of God. Hail to you who cradled and swaddled the son of God';[55] the prayer on the Five Sorrows of the Virgin encouraged the supplicant to face painful emotions because Christ too had felt them.[56] Prayers on the joys and sorrows of the Virgin celebrated the human body and the warmth and sorrow of life in the same manner as the *Corpus Christi* plays. The most important emotion from the supplicant's point of view was the love of the mother Mary for Christ; this appreciation of an indulgent and unqualified love expressed in a prayer such as *O intemerata* gave worshippers confidence that the Virgin would intercede on their behalf and secure the forgiveness of her son. 'I believe he who wants to be yours will belong to God, for you can obtain whatever you ask from God without delay . . . I beseech you to offer your glorious prayers so that my heart would be made worthy of being captured, entered, and inhabited by the holy spirit'.[57] This assertion of the religious significance of emotions within the family, the serene affirmation of the values of family life, contrasts markedly with the indifference shown towards the family in confession manuals of the fourteenth century. These stress integration into the parish, and the hostility shown towards the same emotions in some of the penitential handbooks written in the north of England such as the *Prick of Conscience*, which anticipates a Last Judgement where saved mothers willingly separate from their children if they are sentenced to damnation.[58]

Affective prayers in books of hours encouraged worshippers to empathize closely with the sufferings of the Virgin and Christ. Illustrations in prayer books identified female owners (especially expectant mothers) with the Virgin Mary. Illustrations of the Annunciation usually showed the Virgin at the moment of Gabriel's appearance praying from the book of hours. In the Donne altarpiece Donne's wife, Elizabeth Hastings, prays holding an open book of hours before the Virgin who is also reading a book of hours. A prayer such as *Stabat Mater*

Dolorosa takes the worshipper into the sufferings of the mother of Christ: 'Can the human heart refrain from partaking in her pain . . . make my heart with thine accord. Make me feel as thou hast felt . . . let me share with thee this pain. Let me mingle tears with thee'.[59] The Fifteen Oes, a prayer ascribed to St Bridget, shows how sharing the pain of the Virgin and Christ was a way of convincing oneself of God's love: 'sweet Jesu, for your great pains that your innocence suffered Lord heartfully I require you to defend me from my foes both soul and body and grant me to find in high order your shield defence of hell and always to dwell with you in'.[60] The supplicant in this prayer is encouraged to confront his/her limitations, especially the inability to feel another's pain, and to try to escape the prison of the self and give and live for others by meditating on the mysterious and unfathomable well of mercy within the Virgin and Christ, and their selfless generosity and love; through intense prayer the supplicant can feel Christ's pain and follow his example and feel the pain of others. Such affective meditating had been advocated by two northern writers, Walter Hilton and Nicholas Love, but it was the teachings of St Bridget that made an impact on prayer books in the region, possibly because of her early popularity among such northerners as Henry, Lord FitzHugh of Tanfield. In a northern book of hours illuminated between 1405 and 1413 by Hermann Scheere, which was possibly owned by Henry, Lord FitzHugh or his son William, there are several lengthy readings from the *Revelations of St Bridget*.[61] A series of prayers to the saint occur in a book of hours of Flemish origin commissioned between 1420 and 1450, which bears the arms of de la Pole of Hull together with a miniature showing St Bridget dictating her revelations to a scribe.[62] William Scargill of Leeds gave two chaplains at his chantry chapel in the parish church of Whitkirk in 1448 a psalter and a *Life of St Bridget*.[63] The inclusion of extracts from devotional writers in prayer books is appropriate when the mystical potential of the psalms is appreciated. The rhythm of psalm and antiphon maintained when saying these hours aloud, especially if a friend provided the responses, would have recalled the alternation of voices in the monastic recitation of the Divine Office, and it was while listening to the chanting of the psalms in the Daltons' private chapel that Rolle first felt the fire of God's love. Walter Hilton said in *The Scale of Perfection* that the prayers people generally found most helpful were the Our Father and the psalms; the Our

Father for simple people and the psalms, hymns and other devotions of the church for the educated. Those engaged in active works, he observed, pray with a loud voice or normal tone, and their prayers are worthy and commendable even though, preoccupied as they are with with worldly matters, they often have one thing on their mind while the words of the psalms express another. The devout, touched by grace, will utter their prayers in a very low voice and with deep feeling because their minds are not troubled or distracted by outward things.[64] Fifteenth-century illuminations of books of hours, especially the Annunciation, convey the numinous atmosphere that could accompany private prayer. The portrait of Mary of Burgundy (the adopted daughter of Richard III's sister, Margaret of York) at prayer in her oratory in about 1490 opens on to a vision of the Virgin and child in the holy and peaceful atmosphere of a cathedral.[65]

However, the most socially significant parallel between books of hours and the contemplative literature written in the fourteenth century was in the challenge they posed to institutional, parish-orientated religion. Richard Rolle's first works were commentaries on the psalms and the Book of Job; he saw in them an affirmation of a close relationship with God expressed in terms of alienation from society, and he went on to expound to his followers a way of life that involved rejection of the world in pursuit of God. The pastoral reformers of the church of York in Arundel's circle, especially Walter Hilton and Nicholas Love, tried to moderate the extreme individuality of Rolle's message in their writings. They also tried to reconcile their own reservations about the communal pressures of the parish with their individualistic, introspective piety and their public pastoral duties which included strengthening the bonds within family and the parish.[66] However, by the late fifteenth century the widespread use of books of hours exposed these individualistic prayers to a far wider number of laymen than the devout minority who were reading the works of Rolle and Suso. While public prayers could strengthen such communities as families, institutions and even a realm in times of war, prayers in the primer reinforced individuality, emphasizing the close relationship that exists between the worshipper and God, who provides a source of strength against the hostility of neighbours, the frustrations of dealing with people: 'thou preparest a table before me in the midst of my enemies . . . though a host should encamp against me, my heart shall not fear: in time of trouble he shall hide me in his pavilion'.

In the psalms of the Passion, David's isolation and his dependence on prayer anticipates that of Christ and echoes the image of Christ the rejected, isolated man of sorrows that occurs in Nicholas Love's *Meditations*: 'Into thine hand I commit my spirit for you have redeemed me O Lord. Mine enemies daily swallow me up: for they be many that fight against me'. Furthermore the penitential psalms convey a highly individualistic, intuitive conviction that sin was a private matter between the individual worshipper and God, and that salvation could be achieved through intimate prayer: 'Against thee, thee only have I sinned and done this evil in thy sight'. This conviction of the efficacy of private prayer lies behind the many rubrics to individual prayers which promised the supplicant forgiveness of deadly sins and deliverance from Hell or Purgatory. A prayer found in the book of hours of the Bolton family, fifteenth-century merchants of York, is accompanied by the promise that 'He who says this prayer daily with bent knees will never die in mortal sin'.[67] One rubric in a northern primer to a prayer to Christ on the cross instructs the owner 'wane ye rise on morn of youre bed say this orisonys after' and concludes with the words 'Cross of Christ protect me, Cross of Christ defend me from all insinuations and temptations of the devil'.[68] Another prayer in the same manuscript requests release of the soul of a friend from Purgatory: 'I pray omnipotent and eternal God. I pray to you that you raise the soul of your servant'.[69] In a northern book of hours in York Minster library a rubric accompanying a prayer to Christ explains: 'To each saying this prayer it is considered that if he be in a state of eternal damnation God transfers punishment to punishment in purgatory. If he would be in purgatory for a maximum time, God changes this punishment of Purgatory and reduces or delivers you outside Purgatory to eternal bliss'.[70] In one northern prayer book the owner, Sir Brian Roucliffe, Baron of the Exchequer, who signed himself with the rebus of the chess rook, writes 'if ya be in dedely syn or in tribulaccon or in any deses goy to the kerke and falle on thy knes'.[71]

Because reconciliation between God and man was seen to be such a private matter, in the primer there was no acceptance of the social ideology propounded in confession manuals of the fourteenth century, which defined sin as a form of social hostility and stressed the need to reintegrate penitents into the community. Sin was seen instead as a private matter between the supplicant and God, and the penitential psalms became egocentric confessions of a worshipper who confesses to God a sense of isolation and being at odds with the world, persecuted by his enemies: 'They also that seek after my life lay snares for me and they that seek my heart speak mischievous things, and imagine deceits all day long. For I am ready to halt, and my sorrow is continually before me. I will declare mine iniquity; I will be sorry for my sin. But mine enemies are lively and they are strong and they that hate me wrongfully are multiplied'. This egocentric and abrasive expression of social hostility lacks the pathos and humility of the mystic's sense of rejection which had been communicated by Hilton and Nicholas Love, and as the psalms became more widely known and used in private prayer in the fifteenth century the possibility of others apart from Rolle reacting to them in an individualistic and unorthodox way was increased.

The Cambridge-educated clergy of Yorkshire enthusiastically endorsed the power of private prayer, seeing its individualistic potential. Their fourteenth-century forbears had found in contemplative literature an opportunity to escape the communal pressures of the parish. Now in the late fifteenth century such literature and the increasing availability of prayers in the primers offered the devout man a refuge from the secular pressures of the state. Like his mentor, Arundel, Alcock was interested in the contemplative life and took a close interest in the Carthusian order – he addressed his first sermon to the Carthusians of St Anne of Coventry. In his capacity as Bishop of Ely he repeatedly endorsed the power of private prayer, although it is significant that in the process of describing such a private activity he used imagery from the court, and compared those who frequently prayed to the most valued servants of the king, who would defend those whose names were on his check roll. He granted a perpetual indulgence to all those who said the Lord's prayer three times with an angelic salutation before the image of St Ethelred in Holy Trinity chapel of Snaith parish church, indulgences to all who visited in prayer the chapel of St Mary at the Cross in Great Orkyshe, Essex and indulgences to those who said the entire office of the Virgin. He also issued indulgences to all those who said an entire psalter of the BVM and a twenty-day indulgence to all who attended divine offices.[72] In his *Mons Perfeccionis*, (or 'the hyl of perfeccon'), a sermon delivered to the Carthusians of St Anne in Coventry in 1496, Alcock endorsed the power of prayer, 'A man never ceaseth to pray but when he ceaseth to have the name of a just man', neglecting to mention fasting and only discussing prayer, obedience and chastity (of which only the two former would be applicable to laymen). By recounting the benefits of prayer in a resounding repetition of *ora, ora*, he emphasized its function of stabilizing the thoughts and emotions, bringing peace of mind, and he claimed that the Holy Ghost would be served with no other thing but psalms and prayers. Alcock's concept of mystical intuitions was the regular routine of prayer in a monastery (away from the noise of children and servants), where from the first knell of the bell the monks prayed from the heart with singing of psalms and hymns and other devout prayers with a harmony and melody that exceeded all manner of harmony of instruments and music.[73] The man who more than anyone initiated the contemplative movement in England, Richard Rolle, first had his experience of the fire of love when he was listening to the chanting of the psalms and responses in the Daltons family chapel 160 years earlier.[74] By the time Alcock was writing many laymen were participating in the aesthetic and spiritual pleasures to be gained from chanting the psalms in private chapels. John Fisher also enthusiastically endorsed private prayer and wrote a treatise on the necessity of prayer, drawing on the traditions established by Hilton and the author of *The Cloud of Unknowing*, and he wrote an exposition on the penitential psalms for Margaret Beaufort which was printed by Wynkyn de Worde in 1504. These northern clergy evoked the mysticism of the Yorkshire contemplative writers and the psalms and prayers of the books of hours in a less ambivalent way than their fourteenth-century forebears. Thomas Rotherham declared in his will his belief 'that my redeemer lives and that in the flesh I shall see him after death' and stated his intention to found a college of the Name of Jesus (a devotion first popularized by Richard Rolle).[75] Alcock shared this devotion and bestowed the Name of Jesus on his Cambridge College. William Melton was similarly devoted to Christ crucified and possessed a cloth picture showing Christ crucified between two thieves.[76] Fisher's admiration for Rolle's emotive piety was, unlike Hilton's, unqualified and uncritical, and he brought the hermit's writing to reach a wider audience through the printing presses.[77] The extent to which personal mysticism had become a way of preserving the sanctity of an individual's inner life from the prying of the state by the late fifteenth and early sixteenth centuries is demonstrated by the way those clergy and laymen who were continuing the devotional traditions of the diocese of York, Fisher, Thomas More and the Carthusian monks, stood up to Henry VIII. The staunchest defenders of the old religion were religious houses such as Syon and Sheen, where the devotional influences of the north were strongest and where the religious, pastoral innovations occurred that helped forestall the reformation for 100 years. It was in these houses and in the north of England that Catholicism persisted and was manifested in such movements as the Pilgrimage of Grace.

RICHARD III AND PRAYER

So far we have considered the way books of hours and private prayers could facilitate the same sort of mystical individualism that was encouraged by such religious writers of the diocese as Richard Rolle and Nicholas Love. Now we examine how Richard III responded to them in a way that was as idiosyncratic as Rolle's, but which had more profound social and historical consequences than the withdrawal from society advocated by the hermit of Hampole and his followers. The significance of prayer was probably impressed on Richard when, as an eight-year-old boy, at his brother's coronation he was made a Knight of the Bath and conducted to the Chapel of St John in the Tower of London, where he remained in prayer with his fellow knights before a lighted taper until dawn. At daybreak he made a confession and attended mass.[78] As a layman Richard would have been expected to make his prayers vocally on bended knee, but given his piety it is probable that he acquired the habit of what Hilton defined as mixed mental and vocal prayer suitable for the devout layman. It is even possible, given the hints of early clerical training, that he prayed silently to himself, the type of prayer that Hilton labelled mental that required the total concentration pertaining more to a contemplative person.[418] In Shakespeare's *Richard III* Buckingham, when orchestrating the offer of the crown to Gloucester, says to the assembled citizens of London: 'O see, a book of prayer in his hand,–/ True ornaments to knowe a holy man.'[80] The persistence of the image which was so uncomfortable to the Tudors cannot be so easily explained away in terms of ostentatious hypocrisy, as Shakespeare does.

Richard's prayer book was not lavishly illustrated like the Duke of Bedford's. There are only three illustrations and it was a second-hand copy clearly chosen by the king or his confessor, John Roby. Incorporated into the book were a number of unusual prayers found nowhere else, a prayer and a litany, one copied and one composed for the king. The book was part of the booty of Richard's tent at Bosworth and went to Richmond's mother, Margaret Beaufort, who may have given it to Elizabeth, Lady Scrope of Upsall.[81] The most revealing indication of his private religion is the prayer copied for him and incorporating his name and title – Richard, King of England. The prayer dates from the mid-fourteenth century and is usually attributed to St Augustine. The king's sister, Anne, Duchess of Exeter, owned a prayer book containing the same prayer and John, Duke of Bedford owned a small prayer book that he carried on campaigns for daily use that contained a prayer of St Augustine to be said in times of trouble for thirty days.[82] The rubric to Richard's prayer is missing but was probably the same as the one accompanying the same prayer in the primer, copied in 1491, of Prince Alexander of Poland who became king in 1501 and who died in 1506: 'Whoever is in distress, anxiety or infirmity or has incurred the wrath of God, or is held in prison, or has experienced any kind of calamity, let him say this prayer on thirty successive days and he must be without mortal sin. It is certain that God will hear him completely, that his trouble turn to joy and comfort . . . And this is proven by many persons'.[83] The supplicant in the prayer appeals to Christ to deliver him from sin, captivity, consolation grief, temptation, illness and immediate danger. The editors of Richard's book of hours argue that this prayer was known and used by rulers throughout Europe and therefore cannot be used to indicate Richard's private beliefs. But when the content of this prayer, and indeed others in his book of hours, and their relevance to Richard's situation is considered, along with his undoubted intelligence and the fact that he must have read many of these prayers daily, then it is reasonable to assume that they had some personal meaning for him, as indeed prayers and psalms would have for merchants who thought of their competitors, or craftsmen of their creditors. The appeal of such a prayer to a king who was faced with the rebellion of his subjects in south-east England in 1483 and the subsequent deaths of his son and wife and the Tudor rebellion of 1485 is obvious. It is likely that Richard began to rely more on such prayers at this time of his life when the normal sequences were broken by bereavements and he was forced to stop and reflect.[84] Nearly all the rubrics to this prayer stress the need to say it over thirty days on bended knees, and biblical examples are used to point to the effectiveness of prayer. Although the prayer was copied into the manuscript after he became king, it is likely that Richard knew the prayer before he acquired the manuscript, for at one point it closely resembles part of his 1478 foundation charter for Middleham College. The prayer concludes: 'What am I Lord and what is my family that thou hast brought me thus far? O Lord god it was thy purpose to spread thy servants fame and so thou hast raised me to this I give and return thanks, and for all the gifts and goods granted to me because you made me from nothing and redeemed me out of your beauteous love and pity from eternal damnation by promising eternal life'.[85] The foundation charter for Middleham says: 'Know yet it pleased God creator and redeemer of his manifold graces to enhabile, exhaunce and exalte me his most simple creature, nakedly born into this wretched world, destitute of possessions and enhereatments, to the grete estate, honor and dignite that he hath called me now unto, to be named, knowed, reputed and called Richard Duc of Gloucestre . . . bot also to preserve, kep and deliver me of manyfold benyfets of His bounteouse grace and godnesse to me, without any desert or cause'.[86] In this document Richard expresses his consciousness of his personal circumstances as a younger son and testifies to his conviction that God has elevated him to a high position and has preserved him from many perils, and in the prayer he is asking God to continue to do so. The conviction that he is chosen by God takes the form in the prayer of a close identification with the heroes of the Old Testament who are delivered from peril by the power of prayer, and this is strengthened by the incorporation of the king's name in the prayer. Above all the prayer appeals for deliverance from, victory over, or reconciliation with, one's enemies in accordance with the militaristic spirit of many of the psalms:

Keep concord between me and my enemies . . . Deign to assuage, turn aside, destroy and bring to nothing the hatred they bear towards me, even as you extinguished the hatred and anger that Esau had towards his brother Jacob. Stretch out your arm to me and spread your grace over me, and deign to deliver me from all the perplexities and sorrows in which I find myself, even as you deliver Abraham from the hands of the Chaldees, Isaac from sacrifice by means of the ram, Jacob from the hands of his brother Esau, Joseph from the hands of his brothers, Lot from the city of the Sodomites . . . Moses and Aaron and the people of Israel from the land of Pharaoh and the bondage of Egypt and Saul of Mount Gilboa. King David from the power of Saul and from Goliath the giant. Even as you delivered Susannah from false witness and accusation, Judith from Holofernes, Daniel from the lion's den, three young men from the burning furnace, Jonah from the belly of the whale. Therefore Lord Jesus Christ, son of the living God, deign to free me, thy servant, King Richard, from every tribulation, sorrow and trouble in which I am placed and from all the plots of my enemies, and deign, lord Jesus Christ to bring to nothing the evil plans they are making or wish to make against me, even as you brought to nothing the counsel of Achitophel and Absolon against King David.[87]

The prayer ends with an invocation of Christ's triumph in the judgement to come and of all the benefits hitherto bestowed on the king. Victory over his enemies is hinted at in the petition for assistance of the archangel Michael against the imitators of Achitophel.

Such prayers were popular towards the end of the fifteenth century and their use among princes was encouraged in that standard manual for rulers, the *Secreta Secretorum*, with which Richard must have been familiar. In this work prayer is described as the remedy of all troubles – a prayer to God can turn harm to good. It suggests a prayer can deliver a man from shame and peril of death, the power of wicked princes, the malice of enemies and it can secure victory in battle.[88] The reader of this book is instructed that 'we should pray everywhere, for in every place there is danger and in every place we need help of God'.[89] In the *Secreta Secretorum* Richard would also have found endorsement of his exalted view of a king's relationship with God – the king, like the wind and the rain, is described as the origin of all good. He would also have found an endorsement here for his ruthless attitude towards his opponents for it is claimed that it is an aspect of justice never to spare your deadly enemy. The prayer, and others like it, was used throughout all sections of society. One of

Richard's clerical servants, John Alcock, when he was recounting to the Carthusians of St Anne the power of prayer to protect men from sin and to deliver them from danger, cited similar examples of deliverance or comfort including the stories of Moses, Joshua, Ezekiel, Jeremiah, Daniel, Job and the three children cast in the furnace; he recommended his audience to occupy their minds continually with the prayer 'Lord stretch out and help me Lord, hurry to my aid.'[90] Robert Thornton, who belonged to the lower ranks of the gentry and owned an estate in East Newton in the North Riding of Yorkshire, copied into his collection of devotional writings and romances between 1422 and 1453 a number of prayers including a prayer to the Trinity for patience, courage and 'victory over all my enemies, that they be not able to oppose me nor harm me, nor to speak against me'. In this prayer Thornton also begs Christ to deliver him as he freed Susannah from a false accusation, Daniel from the lion's den, Jacob from the hands of his brother Esau and Joseph from the hands of his brothers.[91] A similar prayer occurs in a commonplace book, a collection of devotional verse and carols owned by Richard Hill, a London grocer active in the 1520s.[92]

The editors of Richard's book of hours conclude that the popularity of this prayer throughout Europe precludes its being used to make deductions about Richard's, or anyone else's, piety.[93] Duffy, although acknowledging that Richard Hill in a similar prayer beseeching Jesus to keep his unworthy servant 'from the malicious foe and all who hate me' had earthly enemies in mind, is similarly cautious in discussing Richard III's and Robert Thornton's use of this prayer. Duffy suggests that the enemies they had in mind are primarily spiritual – the devil and his demons exorcized by the priest at the commendation of the departing soul, the original source of this prayer.[94] However, a reluctance to apply these related devotions to the individual's personal life can result in a failure to appreciate the vastly different mental horizons that worship could encompass.

For an ambitious judge like William Paston, who used his position to acquire land for himself and his clients, the social inferiors who obstructed his sharp practises became the focus of his prayers. In 1426 he wrote to three monks of Bromholm: 'I preythe the Holy Trinite, lord of yowr cherche and of alle the werld, delyvere me of my iii adversaries, of this cursed bysshop for Bromholm,

Aslak for Sprouston, and Julian Herberd for Thornham.'[95] Although Paston was primarily the aggressor, he expressed in his prayer to the Trinity the same sense of persecution (which included the bishop's excommunication) that is communicated in Richard III's prayer: 'I have nought trespassed a-geyn noon of these iii, God knowith, and yet I am foule and noysyngly vexed with hem to my gret unease, and al for my lordes and frendes matieres and nought for myn own'.[96] Daily use of psalms and prayers that referred to one's enemies clearly had special relevence in such a competitive society, and it is likely that merchants in using such prayers had in mind their competitors, creditors and craftsmen.

Robert Thornton's perspective as a small landowner of the gentry class was very different from Judge Paston's, and when he also prayed to the Trinity specifically asking for deliverance from enemies visible and invisible, including those who spoke against him, he was preoccupied with aggressive and acquisitive social superiors. A consideration of the contents of the manuscript Thornton compiled can provide some hints as to the origin of his enemies and the specific nature of his anxieties. The Thornton manuscript enabled the owner and his family to live a mixed life by providing theoretical advice on spiritual improvement from northern writers such as Hilton and practical help in prayers and meditations. Thornton, through his knowledge of the devotional literature of the diocese of York, a selection of which is in his manuscript, would have been familiar with Rolle's and Hilton's analysis of the sense of persecution that the devout felt when confronted with the hostility and resentment of less spiritually advanced parishioners who were resentful of their introspective detachment and their special relationship with God. However, Thornton's manuscript also gives more specific indication of these tensions and how they could be related to social and economic conflicts. The tail rhyme romances in the volume, such as the early fifteenth-century *Sir Degrevant* and *Sir Eglamour*, show how minor gentry could aspire to improve through honest endeavour and a moral approach to their duties in estate administration, marriage and the rearing of children and thereby sanctify their secular lives. In the course of doing so they aroused the jealousy of their less morally disciplined feudal superiors, the higher nobility, and the plots of the romances revolve around their struggles against neighbouring earls who raided their lands. It is significant that Sir Degrevant finally obtains victory over the earl with whom he is in a property dispute 'through his humble prayers for victory' after commending his soul to God.[97] Thornton was a member of the same class as the gentry heroes of these romances and it is possible that he had in mind when praying for victory over, or reconciliation with, his enemies, neighbours who resented his spiritual and social progress. His prayer was certainly couched in the language of feudal service and advancement. The preface promises 'say this orysone deuotly at that messe, and bere it wretyne appone the byfore kyng or prynce or any other lorde: and thou sall fyne grace, helpe and favore byfore thame'.[98] The prayer itself begins with a plea to the Trinity to 'give me your servant, Robert, victory over all my enemies'. The appeal of the prayer to the Trinity, symbol of unity, which for the fifteenth-century members of this family may have signified the unity of the family and its lands, would have poignant significance for later generations of this Catholic family, who were to feel, in the aftermath of the Reformation, an even greater sense of social and spiritual exclusiveness and persecution. Dorothy Thornton, who was charged with recusancy in July 1607, wrote her name alongside the following prayer: 'Omnipotent eternal God, who hast given it unto us thy servants to know the glory of the Trinity in the confession of the true eternal faith and to worship the unity of God in the power of thy majesty: we beseech thee that in the strength of that faith we may always be fortified against all our enemies, through Christ our Lord Amen'.[99]

The Thorntons clearly brought to the art of private worship a sophisticated self-awareness. It is my contention that Richard III identified with his version of this prayer, and the others in his primer, in an even more personal way and applied to the plea for deliverance from his enemies his perception of his situation as an embattled and misunderstood monarch. There can be no doubting the personal importance of this prayer for Richard III.

Since childhood Richard would have read in the 'Book of Kings' in his Old Testament poem about these heroic leaders who are delivered from peril through prayer, and he closely identified with them. Particularly relevant, in the light of Richard's attempt to prove his brother Edward was illegitimate, was the story of the rivalry between Jacob and Esau, who struggled in Rebecca's womb. Jacob, on the advice of his mother, Rebecca, covered himself in hair to trick his elder brother, Esau, out of his birthright.[100] Richard may have seen parallels in his own relationship with his eldest brother and father, and in the passive role played by his own mother, Cicely, in the usurpation. He would have found encouragement in the amoral use of cunning in his metrical Old Testament, where it is explained that the name Jacob signifies one who obtains by subtlety what he cannot obtain by right.[101] Also of potential relevance to Richard was the visionary nature of Jacob, the man of prayer who survives the plots laid against him by his elder brother because he is suspicious by nature. The potential for identification was even greater with the story of Joseph, the child of his mother's old age (Richard was Cicely's last of twelve children and her previous three children died in infancy). Joseph too was the youngest son who usurped the eldest brother's birthright. In Richard's prayer book there is a rare prayer to Joseph, son of Jacob, which was especially added for the original owner near the end of the book before the prayer to St Julian and the devotions added for Richard III. It begins: 'O God who gave wisdom to the blessed Joseph in the house of his Lord and in the presence of Pharaoh and freed him from envy and hatred of his brothers but also raised in honour I pray to you Lord God Omnipotent that similarly you deliver over your servant Richard from the plots of my enemies and to find grace and favour in the eyes of my adversaries and all Christians'.[102] Here again there is a strong suggestion that Richard was identifying with the younger brother, the man of prayer, who was raised by God to high honour. In Richard's Old Testament there is a further sanctioning of the usurpation of the younger brother when Jacob blesses Joseph's younger son, Ephraim saying 'his younger brother shall be greater than he and his descendants shall be a whole nation'. Interestingly it was Richard's elder brother, Edward IV, who introduced biblical references to family strife in his struggles with his relatives in the house of Lancaster. According to Whethamstede's register, before Edward's victory at Ferrybridge in 1471 he caused northerners to flee because 'like the other sons of Ephraim they were unwilling to keep the covenant of the Lord and walk in his law, which required that the elder son must always precede the younger'.[103] Here Edward was alluding to the precedence of the York line over Lancaster through Lionel, Duke of Clarence, the elder brother of John of Gaunt, the Duke of Lancaster. There are in Richard's prayers and in the Book of Kings in his Old Testament explorations of family conflict and relationships between father and sons, mothers and sons and fraternal rivalries which are strangely neglected in fifteenth-century explanations of human conduct. This may be because the educational institutions that provided the models for moral behaviour and relationships in this period were the aristocratic household and the parish. The penitential manuals were the most important sources of psychological analysis and because their authors had grown up almost exclusively in such communities as monasteries, cathedral chapters and colleges, they evaluated the individual and his tensions almost exclusively in terms of his relationship to his parish community. It was Shakespeare, with his knowledge of classical tragedy, who first showed a special insight into the importance of the family and family relationships in determining character and history and it is this understanding which underpins his great tragedies from *Richard III* to *King Lear* and *Hamlet*.

Richard's identification with Old Testament figures helped him to conceive his religion in aggressive terms. Many of the individual prayers in his book of hours are militaristic and call for God's help in defeating his enemies. One, a prayer to Christ by Berenger of Tours (d. 1088), which also appears in the *Ancren Riwle*, calls for his help and protection against spiritual enemies or opponents: 'By thy right hand, that shattered Acheron's infernal gate, Break mine enemies in pieces lest mine enemies uprising/ Fierce reproaches on me pile./ Let them be destroyed and perish,/ who desire my soul to slay;/ Make them, to their own confusion, Fall by snares themselves did lay. Be from henceforth my Protector,/ My defender and my shield:/ So will I against my slanderers, . . . / Thou my captain, take the field . . . under that triumphant banner [cross] on to victory make me ride'.[104] The most important Old Testament figure with whom Richard identified was King David, who figures prominently in Richard's prayer. From his youth he owned a manuscript, which was written in the north of England in about 1420, that contained a Middle English metrical paraphrase of the Old Testament and *The Knight's Tale*. From this work he would have learned about King David who was depicted as a feudal warrior and a guerrilla leader. Also in Richard's hours is a prayer to the cross (his mother Cecily owned a portion of the true cross) which is contemplated as a military standard belonging to the line of David: 'Behold the cross of our Lord: flee ye adversaries, overcomen by the lion of the tribe of Judah, root of David, the wand of Jesse, saviour of the world, save me, the which

by your cross and blood has redeemed me . . . Christ of cross defend me'.[105]
The youngest of seven sons of Jesse of Bethlehem, David was chosen by God's
prophet, Samuel, to be king of the Jews instead of his eldest brother, the tall and
beautiful Elijah, who was rejected by the Lord who judges the heart.[106] When
Richard read this in his Book of Kings he could not have helped drawing the
parallel with himself and his handsome brother, Edward, who was 6 ft 3 in tall.
The depiction in the Middle-English version of The Book of Kings of the civil
war among the Hebrews between Ishbosheth, son of Saul, and his Duke Abner,
and David and his Duke Joab during the royal minority occasioned by the death
of Saul, allowed Richard to see parallels with the power struggles of his own
time and his own rise to power. David's claim during this royal minority was not
lineal but based on divine inspiration. David was a man after Richard's own
heart, a ruthless guerrilla leader who refused to kill Saul when he was at his
mercy because he was God's anointed, but who was capable of cold duplicity in
sending Uriah to his death so he could possess Bathsheba. Richard, with his
strong identification with northerners, may well have taken to heart David's
psalm: 'I will lift up mine eyes unto the hills, from whence cometh my help'[107]
when he summoned his northern supporters to London in August 1483.

However he identified most strongly with David as a man of God betrayed by
those closest to him. David, described in the Old Testament as an angel of the
Lord who can decide between right and wrong, finds out through spies that
Absolom is, with the help of Achitophel, organizing a rebellion and obtaining
the allegiance of most of the men of Israel. He leaves Jerusalem and goes up the
slope of the Mount of Olives barefooted to pray 'frustrate O Lord the counsel of
Achitophel. With the help of his agents this is achieved and Absolom is defeated.
Richard while praying and using the psalms of David would have seen parallels
in his own situation, faced with the betrayal of Hastings and Buckingham and
the large scale rebellion in the south-east; and like David he reacted by using a
network of spies and informers. He expressed his sense of betrayal and
persecution in a number of letters. To the mayor of Windsor he wrote on 6
December 1484 stating that a number of false reports, invented by 'our ancient
enemies of France' were circulated by seditious persons, to provoke discord and
division between the king and his lords. To check this the mayor was
commanded that if any such reports or writings got abroad he was to examine

as to 'the first stories and utterers thereof whom when found, he was to commit to prison and sharply to punish as an example to others'.[108] In a letter to the Pope informing him of his assumption of rule he explained why he had not done so sooner: 'had not the unexpected perfidy and evil conspiracy of certain people hostile to us, to loyalty and their oath prevented us'.[109] Richard reacted to the news of Buckingham's betrayal with his characteristic personal oath 'Here, loved be God'. He also wrote in his own hand a postscript to a letter to the chancellor requesting him to send the Great Seal which he needed urgently in dealing with the rebellion that says: 'Her loved be God ys all well and trewly determyned and for to resyste the malysse of hym that hadde best cause to be trewe the duc of Bokyngham the most untrewe creature lyvyng whom with Godes grace we shall not be long tyll we wyll be in that partyes and subdewe hys malys. We assure you was never fals traytor better purvayde for as berrer Gloucestre, shall shewe you'.[110] This is strikingly similar to the outbursts of David to the treachery of Achitophel who counselled David's son, Absalom, to rebel. In Psalm 41, which is in the Office of the Dead in Richard's hours, David says 'Yea, mine own familiar friend, in whom I trusted, which did eat of my bread, hath lifted up his heel against me. But thou, O lord, be merciful unto me, and raise me up, that I may requite them. By this I know that thou favourest me, because I knowe mine enemy doth not triumph over me.' From Psalm 55 Richard would find a similar reaction to betrayal: 'for it was not an enemy that reproached me; then I would have borne it; neither was it he that hated me that did magnify himself against me; then I would have hid myself from him: but it was thou, a man mine equal my guide and mine acquaintance'.[111] Something of the extremity of Richard's reaction to Buckingham's rebellion and even the reported plot against him by Hastings can be seen in the same psalm: 'we took sweet counsel together, and walked unto the house of God in company. Let death seize upon them quick unto hell: for wickedness is in their dwelling; and among them. As for me I will call upon God; and the Lord shall save me'.

In his identification with David, Richard would have turned to the psalms because they reinforced his sense of isolation and persecution and strengthened his belief in his special relationship with God and the power of prayer. Many of David's psalms communicate a sense of the hostility of enemies and the need to defeat them through prayer. The devotional writers of the diocese of York, especially Richard Rolle, used the psalms to reinforce the mystic's conviction that introspective experiences could separate one from the rest of one's society. John Fisher, the confessor of Margaret Beaufort who was the subsequent owner of Richard's book of hours, was a late fifteenth-century representative of the Cambridge-educated northerners who followed the contemplative path first mapped by Rolle. In writing his commentary on the penitential psalms at Margaret Beaufort's request, he saw in the psalms the same sense of isolation from others that came from a close relationship with God: 'If ye were of the worlde, the worlde shoulde loue you. But bycause ye be not of the worlde, therefore it hateth you. They that take upon them the waye of penaunce dooth forsake worldly conuersacyon and in no wyse be conformed to it, for the whiche they be forsaken of the worlde. What shall we do the deayl may dyneth greueth us, the world pursueth and foloweth us, what remedy may be goten amonges so many aduersaryes'.[112] The remedy, Fisher urges, is to be found by turning to the psalms. However, Fisher, presumably with Margaret's many tribulations in mind, her periods of exile and her long struggles on behalf of her son, intimated that there was potential in the psalms for a more direct identification with David, with his sins and misfortunes and sense of grief and weakness and his feeling that he was opposed and misunderstood by others:

Davyd remembrynge it calleth to mynde all his offences and trespasses, whereby he may shewe his wretchedness to be grete and ouer heped, he spake before of the inwarde partes of mysery, now he remembreth nombrynge the outwarde partes of it. This prophete sayth thus, my wretchednes standeth not onely in the trouble of myn herte which is very grete, not in the feblenes of my strength depressed and put downe by the tyranny of my soule, but it is otherwyse encreased, and by that wherof my chefe comforte and consolacyon ought to be had whiche is a very unhappe kynde of wretchednes veryly they that be my frendes and nygh aboute me be myne aduereryes and moost ayenst me. Perauenture it sholde seme that we haue sayd a thynge ayenst reson to saye our frendes and they that be next us be rather our enemyes that our frendes. But and we wyll call to mynde and remembre how much they do lette us from getynge the helth of our soules it sholde to no man be a doubte.[113]

This sense of isolation and betrayal that Fisher extracts from the psalms has more than just devotional potential. The poet Wyatt translated the penitential psalms while he was in prison in 1535 and intended them to provide Henry VIII with a model of how a penitential king should behave. Surrey wrote that in Wyatt's psalms 'Rulers may see in a mirror clear/ the better fruit of false concupiscence'.[114] It is likely, given Richard's connections with northern laymen and clergy familiar with the devotional literature of the diocese, and his upbringing by a mother who daily read the works of Hilton and Nicholas Love, that he would have used the psalms as an aid to achieving a sense of closeness with God defined in terms of his isolation from others. But Richard III would not have used the psalms of David merely as devotional texts; the daily round of prayer would have had a far more directly political purpose, to strengthen his resolve to act ruthlessly against the enemies he regarded as traitors. Richard's book of hours gives insights into the function of prayer among high-ranking noblemen and the religious component that it provided for the Wars of the Roses. Richard would have found on almost any page of his prayer book an echo of his sense of persecution and an affirmation of the power of prayer to defeat one's enemies: 'strangers are risen up against me, and oppressors seek after my soul: they have not set God before them. He shall reward evil unto mine enemies: cut them off in thy truth. I will freely sacrifice unto thee I will praise thy name . . . for he hath delivered me out of all trouble; and mine eye hath seen his desire upon mine enemies'.[115] This is the sort of prayer Richard may have said before Bosworth. Even when things were at their worst and Richard felt his kingdom was most precariously in the balance, he had these psalms to turn to for reassurance: 'I called on the Lord in my distress and the Lord answered me . . . the Lord is on my side: I shall not fear in what can man do unto me? The Lord taketh my part with those that hate me. It is better to trust in the Lord than to put confidence in man or princes. All nations compassed me about: but in the name of the Lord I will destroy them'.[116]

There is a self-righteous sense of mission and of persecution in these psalms, 'But many are my enemies, all without cause, and many are those who hate me wrongfully, those who repay good with evil oppose me because my purpose is good'.[117] This suggests that Richard may have identified closely with the persecuted man of sorrows, David, who prefigured Christ in the psalms of the

Passion: 'they part my garments among them and cast lots upon my vesture. They pierced my hands and feet. When the wicked even mine enemies and my foes, came upon me to eat up my flesh they stumbled and fell.'[118] These prayers had the potential to assist Richard in identifying with fellow outcasts such as David and even Christ. For Alcock and Fisher such identification led to passivity and martyrdom; in Richard's case it would strengthen his ability to fight: 'Those that seeking my soul to destroy it shall go into the lower parts of the earth. They shall fall by the sword; they shall be a portion for foxes. *But the king shall rejoice in God*'.[119] Richard probably had a different concept of prayer to most people because he had the power to act against his opponents and bring many of his wishes about: 'Deliver me O Lord from mine enemies: I flee unto thee to hide me. Teach me to do thy will for thou art my God. And of thy mercy cut off mine enemies, and destroy all them that afflict my soul: for I am thy servant'.[120] This would convince him of the efficacy of his prayers: 'thou shalt stretch forth mine hand against the wrath of mine enemies and thy right hand shall save me'.[121] It was not only in the psalms of David that Richard would have found encouragement for his isolated and grandiose self-image. Many of the prayers in his book of hours, some unusual and even unique, have the same embattled and desperate outlook. A prayer to his good angel, found nowhere else says: 'Show me where to go and how to serve and how to act and how to please Christ. Shine through all Angel. Help me loving friend and true physician and my fellow citizen defend me against all my enemies visible and invisible'.[122] The more unpopular Richard became in 1484 and 1485 the more prayers, such as the commendation of souls, could reinforce delusions that he alone was right and understood by God: 'Surely I shall hate those who hate you Lord and I shall destroy your enemies. I shall hate with perfect hate those who do evil to me'. Besides his personal prayer, the prayer that may have done most to reinforce his conviction that he belonged to the line of Old Testament misunderstood, persecuted leaders chosen by God was a prayer to Christ and his favourite saint, Michael, against his enemies: 'O God be my helper and guardian all the days of my life. God of Abraham, God of Isaac and God of Jacob, have mercy on me and send in my help Michael the archangel who shall be my protector and defend me from all my enemies visible and invisible. O St Michael and all the holy angels get ye help to me that no enemy condemn or oppress, in house of without house, sleeping or waking. Behold the Cross of Our Lord: flee ye adversaries, overcome by the lion of the tribe of Judah, root of David'. In the manuscript this prayer is accompanied by a drawing of the cross to give the worshipper strength.[123] Richard's messianic view of himself led to a preoccupation with what he perceived to be betrayal of trust. It would not have escaped his attention that he had ordered the arrest of his former ally against the Woodvilles, Lord Hastings, on Friday the 13th.

Richard was not unique in his identification with biblical figures, only perhaps in the extreme nature of this association. It was common to see political events in the light of biblical history. At Edward III's last parliament Chancellor Houghton likened the people of England to the Old Testament Israelites, the chosen people, and referred to the king as a vessel wherein resided God's grace. Thomas Arundel, the Archbishop of Canterbury, opening the first parliament of Henry IV after the deposition of Richard II, described the new king as Saul chosen by God through the prophet Samuel to lead his people. The Crowland chronicler, referring to the murder of Henry VI, alluded to David's refusal to kill God's anointed. The Bible was used to justify anxieties arising during a royal minority. Walsingham, speaking in *Historia anglicana* of the effects of Henry V's death on his people, quoted the words of Solomon 'woe to the land whose child is king' (Eccles 10.16), and a man was condemned to death for applying the saying to Henry VI in 1444.[124] Such proverbial wisdom would not have escaped Richard, Duke of Gloucester. In the book of hours executed for the marriage of John the Duke of Bedford to Anne of Burgundy there are marginal roundels showing King David (about whom it is said 'by God's will was a good and devout king and conquered the peace of Israel') speaking parables to his servants with illustrations from his life. One, showing Joab killing David's son Abner, alludes to the betrayal of fathers by sons and the sacrifice of sons by fathers, and refers to the assassination of John the Fearless by the Dauphin and his sentence to exile by his father, Charles VI.[125] Even that ruthless pragmatist, Sir John Fastolf, during the lingering illness of his old age when he made arrangements for prayers for his soul, identified himself with the suffering Job. In his will he said: 'my soul, vexed in peynefull angwysh, with holy Job, be not compelled to say with great lamentacion and mornyng, have mercy on me, namely yee that my freendes shuld be, for the hand of Goddes punysshynge hathe grevously touchyd me', and he too had his moments of self-pity when he felt himself to be misunderstood. In a note to a memorandum to a debt owed him by Sir William Chambelyn, Sir John added in his own handwriting: 'for my good wille, my fortune is to have trouble'.[126] A member of the Fastolf circle, Friar John Brackley, used scripture to reinforce religious convictions that like Richard's were combative and self-righteous. Preaching a Whit Sunday sermon on complacency about wealth, he exclaimed 'rejoice that your name is written in heaven' and in his letters to John Paston he used the Bible to dismiss his enemies. Referring to Tuddenham and Heydon in October 1459 he said 'fret not thyself because of evil doers . . . for they shall soon be cut down like the grass and wither as the green herbs'. Casting himself in the role of a Jeremiah (the Book of Daniel being his favourite text), he commented on the Earl of Warwick's opposition to Henry VI in October 1460, 'Whoever will not do the law of God then let judgment be executed speedily upon him' and he publicly preached at St Paul's from the text 'Never trust your enemy'.[127] An illuminated roll executed before 1465 juxtaposes scenes from the life of Edward IV with biblical stories. For the marriage of Richard's sister, Margaret of York, to Charles, Duke of Burgundy, pageants at Damme enacted the marriage of Esther to King Ahaseurus, anticipating that Margaret would have the same sort of influence over her husband and save his people from destruction.

It has been suggested that Richard, either innocent of some of the crimes attributed to him or incapable of acknowledging his guilt, used his private prayer to identify with Susannah when she was tried by the elders. Such identification is not without precedent. Master John Stacy of Merton College, an astronomer and sorcerer, was arrested for forming a plot with Thomas Burdet, a Cheapside merchant and one of Clarence's household, to make leaden images to procure the death of Edward IV and the Prince of Wales. Burdet spoke at length on his way to the gallows at Tyburn and in his last words exclaimed with Susannah, 'Behold I must die, whereas I never did such things as these'. Richard was probably unique in the extreme way he saw his social, political world in religious terms, though it was a trait he shared with his elder sister Margaret, and no doubt his mother, Cicely Neville. Margaret a lonely, childless woman neglected by her husband, devoted herself to charitable causes,

Margaret of York and the resurrected Christ, illustrating the *Dialogue de la Duchesse de Bourgogne à Jesus Christ*. (BL MS. Add 7970 fo. 1v)

including the education of orphans and the children of her step-daughter, Mary of Burgundy. Her patron saints included St Colette to whom she prayed for pregnancy; St Barbara, patron of pregnant women and infants; and St Catherine, protector of young girls and unmarried women. In *The Vision of Tondal*, which was completed for her by 1475 at the time when her husband Charles was engaged at the siege of Neuss, the duchess meditated, wistfully no doubt, on the vision of a worldly knight who was taught to focus on the welfare of his soul by making peace with the enemy and devoting himself to charity and faithful marriage.[128] Like her younger brother, her close identification with patron saints and the Bible encouraged her to believe that as an important head of state her prayers would obtain divine inspiration. In her *Dialogue de la Duchesse de Bourgogne à Jesus Christ*, Margaret is shown kneeling on a pillow in her bedroom in the pose of Mary Magdalene in *Noli me tangere* images as she is given a beatific vision of the resurrected Christ who praises her piety and informs her that he is the lord of the Apocalypse.[129] In her illuminated Apocalypse, made for her in 1475, Christ, in the form of a spectral image, addresses her: 'I have sent my Angel to make these revelations to you'. At the end of the picture cycle, in a miniature accompanying the text 'I shall indeed be with you soon', she is given direct access to St John's vision (known only to the Trinity for which Margaret had a special devotion); the enthroned lord in his second coming descends on an earth whose horizon is already engulfed in smoke.[130]

The use of the book of hours to mirror the immediate political and emotional environment of the owner is compellingly demonstrated in the respective books of hours owned by Edward V and Richard III. William, Lord Hastings, friend and chamberlain of Edward IV, procured while he was Captain of Calais a book of hours illustrated in Bruges before 1483. It has been recently suggested that he commissioned it for the Prince of Wales, possibly with the assistance of Margaret of York, who visited England in 1480. The prince's ownership is suggested in the prominence given to the Welsh saint, St David. Furthermore a number of the illustrations allude, in a way that would be appealing to a child, to Prince Edward's world. The portrait of St Christopher bearing on his shoulders the Christ child, who is pulling the saint's hair as he crosses a high river, alludes to the joke of Edward IV's jester about the rivers being so high one can scarce escape through them. In this context it is possible to see Christ as Prince Edward and St

Christopher as his guardian and friend, Hastings or Anthony, Earl Rivers (it is ironic that Cicely Neville left a relic of St Christopher to Prince Edward's mother, Elizabeth Woodville). The other illustrations explain the proverbs contained in Christine de Pisan's book of proverbs translated by Anthony Woodville in 1477 and presented at the court of Edward IV. They include, besides more punning references to the Woodvilles, illustrations condemning extreme largesse, warnings about the wheels of fate, exhortations to greater self-control and advice on the rearing of children. All such proverbial advice contained in the pictures is intended to prepare the young prince for the conquest of France, which is symbolized by a royal barge rowed by flagellants blowing a challenge to France. If the book of hours was presented to Edward V during his last days before 13 June when Hastings was involved in a desperate attempt to rescue him then its owner would have prayed from it knowing his hour was up.[131] His identification with the child on the shoulders of the avuncular St Christopher would have taken on a poignant significance when the prince realized that his guardian, Rivers, was dead. Hoping vainly for rescue from Hastings, the only father-figure left him after the execution of Rivers, Edward must have felt the shadow of his uncle lengthening over him, and he could only have taken solace in identifying with the infant Christ, seeing Richard, as others were to do, in the role of Herod. His physician, John Argentine, reported to Mancini that the young Edward 'like a physician prepared for sacrifice, sought remission for his sins through daily confession and penance, because he believed death was facing him'.[132] A blue smudge on a page containing a painting of the Virgin Mary suggests that one of the owners of this book of hours, perhaps the Prince of Wales, had in his hour of need kissed the dress of the Virgin.[133] This book became for Shakespeare a symbol of the innocence of the princes 'Their lips were four red roses on a stalk,/ And in their summer beauty kiss'd each other./ A book of prayers on their pillow lay, which once, quoth Forrest, almost chang'd my mind'.[134] How different is the mindscape of Richard III's book of hours. A comparison between this prayer book and the Hastings Hours reveals the clashing of the destinies of nephew and uncle. Edward's book of hours reveals the elaborate support system that underpinned the prince's life, such as the moral advice that his tutors gave him to enable him to assume the duties of kingship, advice that reflected the secular interests of a Woodville-dominated court steeped, like Sir John Fastolf's circle, in the literature and secular ethics of Roman antiquity.[135] Richard's book of hours, on the other hand, reveals the isolation of the ambitious younger brother and uncle, the outsider who only has his God to turn to, whose imaginative world is not the New Testament or classical antiquity, but a more private, chivalric world, that of the Old Testament chronicles of war and exile which reflected so compellingly his childhood and youth.

If this is how Richard saw himself it raises the following question – why did he not attempt to project a public image of himself as a man of prayer who was patiently suffering the blows of fortune and the hostility and misunderstanding of others while he was intent on serving his people and his God? His mother, Cicely, preserved the record of her daily routine of prayer and meditation in a household ordinance to publicize her devout method of living as a precedent for other noble ladies. The most obvious way to spread one's reputation for piety was through visual images. Richard's sister, Margaret of York, became the first Burgundian duchess to develop a distinctive portrait image that shows the diverse aspects of her religious character, especially her devotion to daily prayer.[136] There are nine portraits in the thirty books she owned or patronized, including books of advice on how to approach prayer and contemplation. Sometimes she is shown providing a clear example to her court, as in the miniature accompanying a book of nine moral and religious texts, which shows her under a canopy, kneeling at a prayer bench before a book of hours and a painting of Christ, accompanied by her ladies in waiting and watched by a vain but curious young man.[137] At others she is shown in private prayer, for example in a compendium of moral treatises in Brussels she is depicted in a side chapel before an altar showing the Trinity.[138] In a miniature accompanying a text of the Seven Acts of Mercy, written for her by her almoner, she is shown at her devotions at a prayer bench in the robes of the Duchess of Burgundy to emphasize her spiritual duties as head of state and the public importance of her prayers. Most significant for our purpose is the possibility that she and the illuminators in her household, especially the Master of Mary of Burgundy, influenced the way Richard III had himself painted as a man of prayer. Richard spent two nights with his sister in February 1470/1 during his five-month exile in Burgundy with his brother, Edward and William Hasting. In June 1474, during the discussions about an English invasion of France in support of

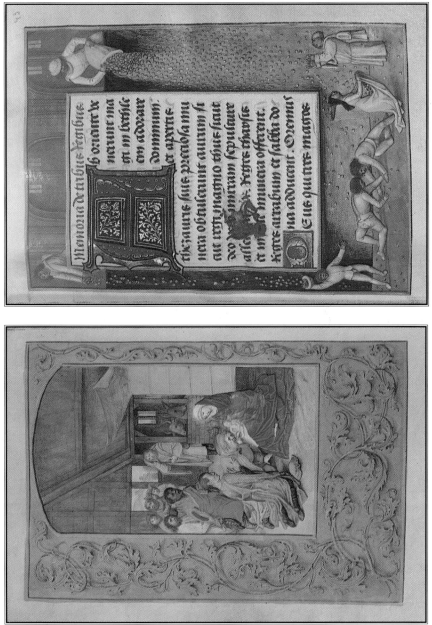

The Hastings Hours showing where the Virgin's blue gown has been kissed, possibly by Edward V in the Tower? (BL MS. Add. 54782 fos 42b, 43)

Richard III, Royal Collection, Windsor. This is a copy, created between 1518 and 1523, of an original probably dating from the last year of Richard's reign; alterations include narrowing of the lips and the raising of one shoulder. This portrait is the source of all surviving copies.

Richard III, Society of Antiquaries. This was faithfully copied between 1516 and 1522 from an original made during Richard's reign.

'The Vigil of the Dead' – Richard's Hours. (MS. 474 fo. 72)

St Catherine of Alexandria (patron saint of Margaret of York) pledging herself to a life of chastity and prayer. Jewels in the background and on the hat and collar of Engelbert II are similar to those in the Windsor portrait of Richard III. (Bodley MS. Douce 219 fo. 40)

Burgundy, he visited the duchess alone and was subsequently entertained, along with his brothers, by Margaret and the duke.[139]

Two almost contemporary panel portraits of Richard III survive in the Netherlandish style (see colour plate section). One, the source of all the later copies, is in the royal collection, Windsor, with the subject facing to the viewer's right. It was copied between 1518 and 1523 from an original dating from probably the last year of Richard's reign. Copies were made at the same time of contemporary portraits of Henry V and Henry VI which adorned Henry VIII's new palace at Bridewell. They were all given a red brocade background (which was probably only original to the portrait of Richard) and they comprise a natural trio of three pious kings. The original portrait of Richard III was probably intended to have a close relationship with that of Henry VI. Both kings wear similar heraldic collars – Henry VI the Lancastrian SS and Richard the white and red roses. In 1484, at about the time of the painting of this portrait, Richard translated the remains of Henry VI from Chertsey Abbey to St George's Chapel, Windsor, and he may have wished to be associated with a king with a posthumous reputation for sanctity. This portrait is also related to the royal collection portrait of Edward IV, copied between 1534 and 1550 for another of Henry VIII's palaces from an original made shortly after Edward's death at the same time as Richard's portrait. The other portrait of Richard is arch topped and shows Richard facing to the left (the heraldic right) and was faithfully copied between 1516 and 1522 from an original made during Richard's reign. Originally it would have faced an arch-topped painting of Edward IV in one of Richard's palaces and demonstrates the continuity of his rule with Edward.[140] However, both portraits emphasize the difference in personality between the two brothers. Edward's features show a smug, complacent, sensual though clever man. Both the royal collection portrait of Richard, despite the Tudor copyist's alteration of the setting of his eyes, and the Antiquaries' portrait's faithful likeness, show a serious, determined man with anxious, careworn and hounded features that are entirely in accord with the tone of his private prayers and devotions. In the *Dialogue de la Duchesse de Bourgogne à Jesus Christ* (written for Margaret of York in 1470 by Nicolas Finet) Christ, to whom Margaret is shown praying, urges the duchess to devote herself to spiritual concerns as befits the sister of the King of England. Edward must have disappointed Margaret in this

Margaret of York at prayer watched by a curious, vain young man. (Bodley MS. Douce 365 fo. 115)

regard, but the portraits of the two brothers, both of which have Burgundian influences, assert that her younger brother lived up to these expectations.

This was given more specific expression, and in a more subtle way than a simple gesture of hands clasped in prayer would allow, in the rich symbolic details of flowers, jewellery, colour and clothing.[141] The key to the significance of these details lies in the *Liber Specialis Gratie* of Bl. Mechtild of Hackeborn, an English translation of which, known as *The Booke of Gostlye Grace*, was owned by Cicely Neville, her son, Richard, Duke of Gloucester and his wife Anne Neville.[142] The visions of St Mechtild coincide with the liturgical hours of the day and are full of details of court life; it is a work that is close to Richard's world. *The Revelations* are also rich in symbolism, the significance of which is explained to St Mechtild by Christ and the Virgin; and these explanations can be applied to the portraits of Richard III. The most striking aspect of both portraits is the prominence of red roses which occur in the Windsor portrait in the brocade red background – in the diamond-shaped lozenges, which contain in their corners fleurs-de-lys to represent the purity of the Virgin, that are interspersed with further pairs of roses in the king's collar; and in the centre of his hat badge. In the Society of Antiquaries' portrait they occur around the gold collar with garnets in the centre; the hat badge forms a prominent red rose, and gold roses, representing the sun and Christ, with five petals occur on the king's overcoat. Roses traditionally represented the Virgin and Christ – the red of the rose, alluding to Christ and the Virgin's suffering, and the five petals to the five wounds. The Virgin was known as the Lady of the Rose and prayers to her had been known since the twelfth century as roses. The primer, or the little office of the blessed Virgin Mary, was known as a rose garden. By the fifteenth century there was a tight knot of associations of prayer and roses. It was recognized that the prayers one said formed a chaplet of roses which were worn by the Virgin and that they corresponded to the rosary beads.[143] Therefore, when Richard chose to be depicted in a gold collar of roses it would have had specific associations of prayer and the rosary. At the time this portrait was executed there was a cult of the rosary throughout northern Europe – a confraternity of the rosary was founded in Cologne in 1475 in which a Yorkshire knight, Sir Robert Plumpton, was enrolled.[144] Richard's mother, Cicely, owned a large rosary of six sets of gold beads divided by square enamel stones from which hung a gold cross.[145] The significance of the roses in Richard's portrait is revealed in a series of St Mechtild's visions. While praying to Our Lord to teach her how she should worship him she is granted a vision of Jesus, and from his heart springs a beautiful rose with five petals (echoed on Richard's coat) which represents the five senses through which Christ should be worshipped. The Virgin appears to Mechtild clothed in saffron embroidered with red roses and which, the Virgin explains, represents the stability of patience that allows her to suffer all things;[146] and in another vision Jesus explains to Mechtild that 'y am that am a rose ande borne without a thorne ande, prykkynge y am with many thornys'. Roses were used in their religious as well as heraldic sense by the Burgundian painters employed in the household of Margaret of York and her stepdaughter, Mary of Burgundy. In a votive portrait of Margaret in the Louvre, executed in about 1468, showing her at prayer, she wears a collar of alternating red and white roses or marguerites to signify her descent from John of Gaunt and Richard, Duke of York and her identification with the sorrows and joys of the Virgin. These motifs occur in illustrations of Margaret at prayer – in the border of the image of her praying before Christ revealing his wounds to her there are five petalled roses.[147]

The predominant colours in Richard's portrait are red, which is so prominent in the jewelled roses and the background of the Windsor portrait; purple, the colour of Richard's doublet in the Antiquaries' portrait; and gold, the overcoat of the Antiquaries' portrait is a plain cloth of gold with stylized acanthus leaves that incidentally occur in the borders of Netherlandish books of hours of the 1480s illustrated by the Master of Burgundy; gold also features in the jewellery, collars and hat badges and the doublet of the Windsor portrait. In a series of visions Mechtild is instructed by Jesus on the colours she should wear and their significance – purple represents Christ's meekness; red the patience that allows him to take on all things hard and grievous that Christ showed when he took on himself man's humanity; these clothes, Jesus informs her, should be surrounded by gold, representing the charity and love that Christ showed to all people on earth and which the worshipper should emulate.[148] In another vision Christ appears in glory to St Mechtild wearing a gold collar and a shield, under which there is a beautiful rose to represent his great patience.[149] Gold is further emphasized in the doublet in the Windsor portrait, which is possibly a piece of armour,[150] and is without parallel in its display of gold circles that represent

Christ. When Richard, therefore, chose to wear for his portraits purple, red, gold and a gold collar with roses he was identifying himself with a patient Christ who suffered and was misunderstood and rejected by others.

The jewellery in the portraits conveys the same message – the most prominent items are the hat badges, which appear in the form of a rose in the Society of Antiquaries' portrait, and a crucifix in the form of a gold Greek cross with a rose centre and pearls dividing the arms that occurs in the Windsor portrait. The significance of the cruciform hat badge is explained in Mechtild's vision of a gold cross. She is told that each person must bear their cross and follow Christ – the right arm of the cross represents love of neighbour, the left patience in adversity, emphasized by the rose in the centre of Richard's cross and in the other hat badge.[151] The hat badges themselves are explained in Mechtild's vision of a gold hat brooch, which signifies the way people's sins are transformed through prayer.[152] Margaret of York's illuminator, the Master of Burgundy, was aware of the symbolic significance of this cruciform jewellery for it occurs in a book of hours illustrated in 1485 for Engelbert II of Nassau, Margaret's Lieutenant of the Realm, and Philip the Fair, the son of her stepdaughter, Mary of Burgundy, on a page containing a prayer to St Catherine of Alexandria (one of Margaret's patron saints). The illustrator shows Catherine pledging herself to a life of chastity and prayer in a symbolic marriage to Christ and the cruciform jewels relate symbolically to this picture.[153] Interestingly the hat Richard is wearing closely relates to the hat of Engelbert II in a panel portrait of about 1480. The importance of prayer is also emphasized by the pearls hanging down from both hat badges and in the gold collar of the Windsor portrait. This is explained when Mechtild, listening to Psalm 148, 'praise him heavens, and your waters above the heavens', is granted a vision of pearls underneath water which betoken the virtues of the saints which are attained through prayer.[154] The Master of Burgundy frequently associated pearls with prayer, and in a book of hours owned by Charles the Bold and Margaret of York there is an illustration showing a pearl rosary on a prayer cushion near a book of hours before a window that overlooks Christ crucified. In the border of the miniature showing St Catherine of Alexandria being instructed to marry Christ there is, besides the cruciform cross that occurs in Richard's portrait, a pearl rosary.[155]

The hands, prominent in these portraits may also have symbolic significance. By the late fifteenth century lay followers of the new devotion, Observant Friars and Brigittines, were accustomed when praying to use the hand, and even diagrams of the hand, as artificial memory techniques, associating an intention or virtue with a part of the hand which was stroked while praying the psalms to strengthen and deepen attention.[156] Similar methods of association may explain the placing of finger rings in these portraits. The other jewels in the portraits are the finger rings. The most prominent of these is the ring Richard places on the fourth finger of his left hand (the wedding finger) in the Society of Antiquaries' portrait. In the Windsor portrait of Edward IV, the original of which may have faced a portrait of Elizabeth Woodville, Edward is shown insouciantly playing with a ring that could be a wedding ring or a coronation ring, the symbol of his authority. The significance of Richard's more serious, determined treatment of his ring can be explained in one of Mechtild's visions of the Virgin. Mary gives her a gold ring and Mechtild offers it to Christ, who places it on his finger. Mechtild then desires him to return the ring to her as a symbol of her dispensation from sin and her marriage to Christ; she even asks him to give her a perpetual pain in this finger to remind her of this dispensation. Christ gives her a ring of seven stones to represent the seven articles of his godhead, including his sacrificing himself for man and wearing the purple and red clothes of his Passion.[157] Given that this portrait probably dates from 1485, after the death of Anne Neville during an eclipse of the sun, it is hard to escape the conclusion that Richard was not nervously playing with this ring, as Vergil implies, but consciously intending to quell rumours that he intended to marry Elizabeth of York. He was stating his intention to put on the coronation ring, the wedding ring of England, and to pledge himself to Christ in suffering and prayer. A letter of exhortation by Mechtild to a nun on the meaning of the five fingers she joined to Christ's in prayer gives clues to the significance of the rings on Richard's right hand in the Windsor portrait. The little finger, on to which he is placing a ring, betokens Christ's meekness in coming to earth to serve others, and could, therefore, emphasize Richard's profession of his devotion to his kingdom and the common weal. The fourth finger, which also has a ring, represents the soul's devotion to God. The thumb, which on Richard's hand bears a ring with a death's head, represents God's power and protection, and the soul's manly exercise of virtue and its refusal to despair of the mercy of God, who nevertheless allows the soul to be troubled and withdraws from it relieving comfort and grace.[158]

Taking all these things together, both portraits can be read as complex, symbolic representations of the self-image Richard wished to convey to his people. This was the image of a suffering, tormented man who, despite his bereavements, refused to despair of God's grace and who believed his sins would be forgiven through diligent prayer and Christ's intercession. It was the image of a man who had sacrificed hopes of worldly felicity to enter a symbolic marriage to Christ, with whom he identified in his suffering, and who he followed in dedicating his life to the subjects who did not appreciate or understand his sacrifice. In this identification with Christ he was remarkably similar to Bishop John Alcock and, therefore, reveals that his piety had something in common with the leading reforming clergy of the north. The image confronting us in these portraits is that of a man of prayer, a David whose strength of will and determination is in strong contrast to the soft, ineffectual piety that is stamped on the features of portraits of Henry VI.

5

CONCLUSIONS: 'THE CONSCIENCE
OF THE KING'

O Lord' when thou shalt come to judge the earth, where shall I hide
me from the face of thy wrath? For I have sinned full much in my
life'.[1]

If these portraits allude to a king's sins and the forgiveness that assiduous
prayer merits, they raise the controversial issue of Richard's alleged crimes. We
have seen how, to some extent, he was driven by a private religiosity that gave
him the confidence and conviction to act ruthlessly. There is independent
evidence that Richard's code of morality was unusual and that he was at odds
with the rest of his society, which explains why between July and August of 1483
it was relatively easy for him to step outside the bounds of what most people felt
was right and wrong. Some of Richard's individuality stems from his position as
the youngest child in a large family. He had no hereditary expectations – apart
from his wife's Yorkshire inheritance everything he held was granted to him in
person. Unlike his contemporaries, who felt obliged to keep intact for their heirs
what they inherited, he was free to alienate land he acquired and he was in a
position to buy, sell and reshape his estates in an unparalleled way. A recent
examination of Richard, Duke of Gloucester's register of grants of land and
offices suggests that for Richard possession of land and the consequent
obligations of providing a secure inheritance for the future did not act as a
moral imperative the way it did for most aristocrats who were compelled to
think of their families and unable to alienate land to the church freely.[2] Richard
had none of these restraints and, therefore, demonstrated both a selfish egotism
and the sort of attitudes expected of a monk or priest who had no stake in the
future of his family dynasty. He was free to alienate land to the church in a way
that was unparalleled among his fellow aristocrats and he showed no sense of
familial obligation towards his heirs, neglecting to obtain a dispensation for his
marriage to Anne Neville, to whom he was closely related, which meant that if
he died his wife's estate would terminate with him. Richard's priorities were his

own political ends and the salvation of his soul. As a rootless and, by fifteenth-century society's standards, amoral younger son he anticipates Shakespeare's charismatic villains, especially Edmund, Duke of Gloucester, the illegitimate son in *King Lear* and the younger brother of Edgar who had only his ambition, talent and his title and who was free from the old feudal restraints that come with the ownership of land. Richard too had little sentimental attachment to his family, betraying the memory of his elder brother and even his mother. The emotional force of prayer, as we have seen, was usually derived from images of kinfolk and patrons. The violent destruction of this network of relationships within the York affinity was to some degree Richard's responsibility, and it is not surprising that in his prayers he could appeal only directly to God. His recourse to the psalms probably justified his sense of isolation: 'Thy commandments hast made me wiser than mine enemies: for they are ever with me'.[3] He was driven by a sense that he was an instrument of God: 'I have done judgment and justice, leave me not to mine enemies'.[4] The meditation in his copy of *The Revelations of St Mechtild* on the fingers of the hand as an instrument of providence and prayer would have been significant for him. The great finger represented the ordinance of God's providence who gives man prosperity and adversity. When readers put their fingers to Christ's in prayer they were accepting that all things come from God. This is how Cicely or Anne Neville would have understood the meditation, as an invocation to accept providence. Richard, however, would have identified his hand with the hand that dispensed mercy and justice, vengeance and misery.

However, there are indications that Richard had a disturbed conscience and experienced moments of doubt as early as 1478. After publicly proclaiming in the opening preamble to the foundation statutes to his college of Middleham about the sinful state of his soul and how he had nevertheless been favoured and elevated by God, Richard instructed the dean of his college to say the *De Profundis* and asked the local people to pray for his soul and to say a *De Profundis*, either secretly to themselves or with companions when it pleased them. The significance of this psalm of David's, which occurred among the penitential psalms in his book of hours, would have increased after July 1483: 'Out of the depths have I called to thee, O Lord; Lord, hear my cry./ If thou Lord shouldst keep account of sins/ who, O Lord could hold up his head/ But in thee is forgiveness'. His doubts and anxieties would have increased after July 1483 when rumours concerning the disappearance of the princes spread and his unpopularity increased, despite his displays of piety. In the expression of religious sentiments in this period there was considerable affection for young children, and in Richard's own copy of the *Revelations of St Mechtild* there are many visions of the Christ child appearing as a twelve-year-old boy. What must have taken Richard by surprise, however, was the widespread, instinctive reaction of horror to what was presumed to be the murder of two innocent children. Mancini told his readers he had seen many men burst into tears and lamentations when mention was made of Edward V after he had been removed from men's sights. According to the Crowland Chronicler the spreading of rumours of their deaths was the reason for the rebellion in the south-east. Richard seems to have turned to prayer and expressed his anxieties in his investiture of his only legitimate son, Edward of Middleham, as Prince of Wales: 'We have turned the gaze of our inward eye to the greatness of this noble state and of its members, having great care that, in the great anxieties that press upon us, those who are necessary to support us should not now seem to be lacking'.[5] An indication that the image of an embattled anxious monarch was Richard's public persona can be seen in Caxton's dedication of Lull's *Order of Chivalry* to the king: 'I pray almighty God for his long life and prosperous welfare and that he may have victory of all his enemies and after this short transitory life to have everlasting life in heaven where as in joy and bliss without end'.[6] Richard's addiction to the regular performance of divine hours at his collegiate chapel at Middleham and his own private chapel at Middleham Castle reflects his need for a regular reassuring routine. He would have turned to the psalms knowing that David too was a king, who despite the fact that he had sinned, was chosen by God. There was a widespread belief at this time that David composed the penitential psalms in remorse for his unlawful passion for Bathsheba, and the murder of Uriah, her husband. John Fisher, in his *Commentary on the Penitential Psalms*, says they were written by David, 'a man syngulerly chosen by almyghty God . . . afterwarde he synned full greuously agaynst God and his lawe, and for the occasyon of a grete offence, he made this holy psalme, and thereby gate forgyuenesse of his synnes'.[7] Richard's dependence on the penitential psalms and his identification with David would have increased after the death of his son, Edward of

Middleham in April 1484. Even before Edward of Middleham's death Richard, given Anne's relative infertility, regarded children as a sign of God's grace. In his Middleham College statutes he asked for daily divine service for his only legitimate son 'and such other issue as shall please God to send me whilst I live'. He read in his Old Testament that David was punished with the death of his son for his adultery with Bathsheba and for arranging the murder of Uriah, and that Nathan prophesized that David would henceforth never be free from fighting by the sword. He must then have reflected on his own complicity in the murder of Henry VI and his son, Edward, whose widow he had married, and the death of the child of this union and seen it as divine retribution. Richard may even have been able to see some parallels in incidents in the life of David and the notorious disappearance of the princes. A number of David's opponents were killed in suspicious circumstances including Absalom, Abner and Ishbeth. David mourned Absalom's death, because of which the people said he should not be king, but after the death of Abner, Saul's commander, David walked behind his bier in sackcloth and the people believed in his innocence. Richard III may have persuaded himself, as well as others, that he did not have full control over the disappearance of the princes and identified with the partially innocent and penitent King David. According to the Middle English Old Testament version of the story owned by Richard, David's reaction to these tribulations was to pray all the harder and he composed *misere mei Deus* in response to the death of his son 'to god that gouerans all/ forgyfnes forto gete,/ yf we in care be cast'.[8] This penitential psalm must have had a poignant significance for the bereaved King Richard: 'My iniquities are gone over mine head; as a heavy burden they are too heavy for me. My wounds stink and are corrupt because of my falseness I am troubled; I am bowed down greatly'.

The second half of the litany written and included for Richard is a plea for deliverance from misfortune, illness and death, the sort of sufferings alluded to in the penitential psalms and which were afflicting Richard in 1484 and 1485. Used as an introit to the mass 'to avert death', it was especially connected with pestilence and sudden death and gives the impression that Richard was asking for protection for himself and his companions and dependents: 'look down Lord, upon this your people for whom Our Lord Jesus Christ did not hesitate to deliver himself to those that would harm him and to suffer the agony of the cross. Remember, Lord your covenant and say to the destroying Angels Now stay your hand! And let not the earth be made desolute and do not destroy every living soul'. To which there is a verse response 'May your anger, Lord, now be lifted from your public'.[9]

A reading of the psalms could also have encouraged Richard to think, like the penitent king and reputed author of these prayers, that he was only answerable to God: 'Against thee, thee only have I sinned and done this evil in thy sight,' and that merely by following in David's footsteps and using his prayers he would obtain forgiveness. Fisher, recounting the story of the sins of the proud king who received great benefits from God writes: 'Beholde the accumulacyon and hepynge of synne upon synne'. He reveals that David:

> made this psalm with grete contrycyon and sorowe in his soule, whereby agayne he obteyned forgyveness. Now ye understande who made this psalme, what occasyon caused hym to wryte it, and what proufyte he gate by the same. . . . Syth we now therefore haue herde tell for a trouth how gretely seke and dyseased this prophete Dauyd was, not with sekenes of his body, but of his soule, and also whith what medycyne he ws cured and made hole. Let us take hede and use the same when we be seke in lyke maner . . . he dyd halysome penaunce makynge this holy psalme whereby he gate forgyueness and was restored to his soules helth. We in lyke wyse by ofte sayenge and tredynge this psalme with a contrite herte as he dyd, askynge mercy shall withoute purchase and gete of our mercyful lorde god forgyuenesse of our synnes.[10]

Fisher gives an indication of the way King David provided a model of repentance through prayer and living a religious life, and it is likely that Richard was following such precepts in his private devotional routines and public acts of charity, for which he was criticized as a hypocrite: 'For euery man knoweth this prophete Dauyd was a wretched and greuous synner, neuertheless afterwarde he lyued holyly, and by the merytes of his lyfe was lyffte up unto heuen . . . with grete dylygence made these holy psalmes which he dayly offred up unto almyghty god with grete deuocion as lettres of supplycacyon, by the whiche he moued gretely his goodness for to forgyue hym'.[11]

In Richard's prayer book, as in all primers, there is a *confiteor* which catered for all manner of sins;[12] but there are also a number of devotions specifically concerned with a sense of guilt, and it is likely that the king would have turned to these after the events of July to August 1483. It is significant that his personal prayer is preceded by a suffrage to St Julian the Hospitaller who accidentally killed both his parents and then did penance by ferrying travellers across the marshes until he atoned for his sin.[13] This tale appears in a version of the Golden Legend that Caxton printed towards the end of 1483. Although it is unlikely that Richard added this devotion, it is an unusual prayer and the fact that it occurs near the end of the book preceding his own prayer, which also pleads for Christ's forgiveness for his sins: 'I ask you most sweet Jesus Christ, to keep me, your servant King Richard, and defend me from all evil, from the devil and from all evil present, past and to come and deliver me from all tribulations, sorrows and troubles which I am placed and deign to console me',[14] means he may have regarded the saint as the one most able to help him to atone for his crimes against his family. Unfortunately only the rubric survives and the text of the prayer is missing but all of these prayers at the end of the volume were meant to be used by a particular person in a particular situation. The unique litany added for Richard III at the end of his book of hours is a plea for forgiveness of his sins on the basis of his great suffering: 'Keep us from weakness, Jesus, for the sake of your name, cleanse us of offence and all crime' which is followed by a verse response which asks 'Do not remember our former sins' and a response 'Have mercy on us because we have been brought very low'.[15] One basis of the appeal for forgiveness in this litany, apart from his Job-like tribulations, is his status as king: he appeals for protection for the house of York. The other basis of his appeal for forgiveness is his devotion to the Holy Name, in which it is possible to see echoes of the individualistic concept of sin and forgiveness to be found in the teachings of Richard Rolle:

Response: And for the glory of your name rescue us and forgive our sins for the sake of your name.

Verse: Lord, save the king. Let us pray. Hear us, Lord Jesus, almighty, ever-living God, and deign to send your saints from the heavens to keep, support, protect, visit and defend all who are here in the house through Christ Our Lord.

Richard could also find in fifteenth-century devotional literature an avocation of an individualistic view of sin and penance, including a rejection of the morality of the community which demanded restitution to the community and penances that integrated a sinner into his society in favour of the special relationship with God who could alone judge the heart. Of special relevance to Richard's situation as king and the unfeasibility of his making any conventional penance and atonement for his sins is a passage in the well known *Revelations of St Bridget* (first popularized by Henry Lord FitzHugh of Tanfield, an ancestor of the family who were supporters of Richard III) in which St Bridget witnesses a debate taking place in the soul of a king just before his death. A conflict occurs between two types of conscience. A worldly one desires security and comfort and instructs the dying king to obtain forgiveness by restoring his ill-gotten goods, making peace with his neighbours and rectifying the injustices of his rule; a conventional confession that serves the purpose of social reconciliation. The other type of conscience regrets only that the soul has been deprived of God's company. All it desires is union with the Lord. Such contrition not only obtains forgiveness for all social crimes, but is the only form of conscience that will secure eternal life.[16]

A number of the rarer prayers that are included in Richard's book of hours are also special pleas for forgiveness of sins. A prayer to the owner's guardian angel begins: 'O Angel approach and teach me and incline my will to God and in all hours to console me at night and day remain and show me the way that I shall please through prayer.'[17] An appeal to Christ begins 'My most merciful judge. Do not judge me according to my sins. Pity me Jesus, consider my distress you sweet delectable name the comfort of sinners. Truly what is Jesus but salvation. Pity me while there is time.'[18] Most moving are the appeals to Mary. One prayer, of which there is no copy, cries: 'Pity all who are tormented. My God sting me with worthy contrition.'[19] The prayer ascribed to Theophilus, a cleric who repudiated the Virgin and became penitent, would have especially appealed to Richard: 'of which of my sins shall I suppose I most miserable sinner shall first get remission? What shall I do? To whom shall I go? What shall I answer on the day of Judgment when all shall be revealed naked? Who shall pity me? Who will come to my assistance? Or who will protect me? . . . I adore, I embrace and this my prayer offer myself, to you holy and immaculate Virgin

mother of God . . . do not reject and despise my prayer. Release me blessed
Virgin, from the cries that lay hold of me; and from the turbulent storms that
possess me, because I am exposed and full of sins'.[20]

There is some external evidence to suggest that these prayers can be used to
indicate Richard's state of mind and the workings of his conscience. Polydore
Virgil said of him 'the whyle he was thinking of any matter he dyd contynually
byte his nether lyppe, as thowgh that crewel nature of his did so rage agaynst yt
self in that lyttle carkase. Also he was wont to be ever with his right hand
pulling out of the sheath to the myddest, and putting in agane, the dagger
which he also alway were'.[21] The death of his son must have shattered his
confidence in God's favour, and like David he prepared to face a troubled reign
full of plots and betrayal. His chosen prayer and his portraits show the strain he
was under. In a letter dated March 1485 he wrote 'evil disposed persons . . .
enforce themselves daily to sow seed of noise and dislander against our person
to our great heaviness and pity'. The Crowland Chronicler commented on his
reaction to the death of Edward: 'You might have seen the father and mother
almost out of their mind for a long time when faced with sudden grief'. They
remained in mourning in Nottingham for over a month. A tradition developed
that Richard referred to this castle when he first learned the news as his 'castle
of care', a phrase taken from Langland's *Piers Ploughman*. The earliest surviving
portrait of him shows him with the lined features of a man of care.[22] The
Crowland Chronicler also gave an account of Richard's nightmares on the eve
of the Battle of Bosworth at his camp at Sutton Cheney: 'that morning the king
declared he had seen dreadful visions and imagined himself surrounded by a
multitude of demons and he presented a countenance which, always attenuated,
was on this occasion more lurid and ghostly than usual'.[23] Polydore Vergil gave
the most complete account of Richard's doubts and fears on this night:

'yt ys reportyd that king Rycherd had that night a terryble dreame; for he
thowght in his slepe that he saw horryble ymages as yt wer of evell spyrytes
haunting evydently about him, as yt wer before his eyes, and that they wold
not so muche stryke into his brest a suddane feare, as replenyshe the same
with heavy cares: for furthwith after, being troublyd in mynd, his hart gave
him theruppon their thevent of the battale folowing wold be grevous'. He

reported this dream to many in the morning and Vergil commented '(I beleve) yt was no dreame, but a conscyence guiltie of haynous offeces, a conscyence (I say) so muche the more grevous as thoffences wer more great, which, thowght at none other time, yeat in the last day of our lyf ys woont to represent to us the memory of our sinnes commyttyd, and withal to shew unto us the paynes immynent for the same, that, being upon good cause penytent at that instant for our evell led llyfe, we may be commettyd to go hence in heavyness of hart'.[24]

Robert Fabyan, the author of *The London Chronicle*, said King Richard led his life in great agony and doubt, trusting few about him.[25] There is a tradition in the Wyatt family that Richard cross-examined Henry Wyatt (sent by Henry Tudor into Scotland) and lamented that his own servants showed no such fidelity.[26] Thomas More, who was brought up in the household of Bishop Morton and was in a position to call on eyewitnesses, claims to have heard from the king's attendants that almost every night of his reign he was troubled by 'fearsome dreams'. In the light of all this it is possible that there was a penitential motive behind Richard's excessive proposals for a chantry at York of 100 priests, which would mean incessant celebration of mass for the dead without a break. The motive may have been the same as that stated in the foundation charter of his collegiate church at Middleham 'in part of satisfaction of such things as at the dreadful day of judgment I shall answer for'.

This insecurity, which is such an important background to Richard's religion, and which stares out from his earliest portraits, and according to graphologists from his handwriting, may have been a chronic condition relating to anxieties created by civil war during his unstable childhood. In 1460 his father and second eldest brother were killed at Wakefield and he went into exile in Burgundy with his mother. A few months later his eldest brother captured the throne and he was, at the age of eight, made a duke; but in his teens all this was undermined when his brother was deposed and they had to return to Burgundy in exile. After the recapture of the throne at Tewkesbury and Barnet he did enjoy twelve years of security, but all this was jeopardized when Edward died unexpectedly in 1483 in the same year as the heir of the Earl of Warwick, leaving Richard dependent on the good will of the Woodvilles for continuing lordship of his Neville lands in the north. It is possible that Richard feared for his own life at the hands of the Woodvilles, given the fates of his predecessors as Duke of Gloucester – Humphrey, Duke of Gloucester (whose reputation was rehabilitated by Richard III's father) possibly murdered on the orders of his nephew, Henry VI; and Thomas Woodstock (the great-grandfather of Richard III's ally and confidant, the Duke of Buckingham) who was murdered on the orders of his nephew, Richard II. Such feelings of insecurity among the great were an inevitable consequence of the Wars of the Roses and they were expressed in Caxton's translation of the *Curiale*, which gave clear warnings of the dangers of court life. Men study, he says, to entrap you and you need to use bribes if you are not to be replaced by another. In such an environment paranoia becomes the norm and there were different ways of responding to such stress. Anthony Woodville, to whom the *Curiale* was originally addressed, cultivated an ideal of Ciceronian retirement; the works of antiquity gave him a mirror image of himself as a public man of high office whose real love was study and who longed for release into solitude and a detached contemplation of the vagaries of a world governed by the vagaries of fortune. Woodville probably had an impersonal, classical notion of the deity, but Richard's God was an Old Testament God intervening in the affairs of the kingdom in response to heartfelt prayer; Richard's reaction to the court he mistrusted so much was different. He was nearer to the top and he, like Shakespeare's Mark Antony, must have felt that there was nowhere for him to flee, no *otium*. His inspiration was the Bible and the psalms and they encouraged in him a suspicious watchfulness and a readiness to take the initiative and respond to divine intervention from God. Instead of seeing himself, like Woodville, as a philosophical victim of fortune he saw himself as an Old Testament king, an instrument of heaven. His insecurity was probably further rooted in childhood than Woodville's, a chronic condition relating to the traumas of the loss of his father, the deposition of his brother and his own exile. It is something he shared in common with his equally ruthless and suspicious political opponent, Margaret Beaufort, who had experienced similar cruel twists of fate. Her confessor, John Fisher, noted the tears of foreboding she shed in times of triumph;[27] but Richard's insecurity manifested itself in an egocentric identification with King David, a preoccupation with his own political survival. The piety of the two most powerful women of the age was in contrast dictated by their maternal interests in their sons – Cicely was depicted with her son Edward IV before an image of the trinity and was described as the true heiress of the crown of England.[28] Margaret was devoted to the political interests of her son, Henry Tudor, from whom she was separated for many years, and in her religious practices she devoted herself to Christ, the Son, and the Virgin Mother of God and her students at St John's College, Cambridge, for whom she was a mother.[29] Her book of hours, like Richard's, can be seen as a mirror of a political destiny (in her case her son's) and recounts the outcomes of the battles of Bosworth, Stoke and Blackheath.[30]

Only the king's confessor, John Roby, could have revealed how Richard saw his chances in the next world. He may have believed, until the Battle of Bosworth, that if he prayed hard enough he would obtain God's forgiveness and approval. The prayers in the primer of his father, Richard, Duke of York are preceded by indulgences ranging from 7 years to 2,000 years, and in Richard's prayer book there is a levation prayer to Christ that has a rubric promising whoever says this prayer between the elevation of the host and the third *Agnus Dei* 2,000 years indulgences to be granted by Pope Boniface VI.[31] In Richard's book of hours many prayers were accompanied by indulgences (including probably the missing indulgence to the king's prayer) that promised release from the punishment of Hell for mortal sins. Another penitent king who, though treated more sympathetically by Shakespeare, was probably more pessimistic about his chances of salvation, was Henry IV. According to his confessor, John Tille, Henry was able, through his encouragement, to show repentance for the killing of Richard II and Archbishop Richard Scrope, for which he gained papal absolution. However, he could not make restitution for his third sin, the occupation of the 'wrong title of the crown' without disinheriting his own children. Richard was in a position to make full expiation for his sins: both the princes were dead and after the death of his son he was free to distribute the crown to the rightful surviving heirs. He accordingly named first his nephew, Edward, Earl of Warwick, son of George, Duke of Clarence, as his heir, and then his other nephew, John de la Pole, Earl of Lincoln, the eldest son of the Duke of Suffolk and Richard's sister, Elizabeth. Richard was able to read in his Middle-English Old Testament that the only sin for which he could not be forgiven was Judas' sin of despair: 'What syn so we have done,/ yf we to trowth wyll tent,/ God wyll forgyf als sone/ as we wyll rygt repent'.[32] He would also have read in this book that, even if he could not pray effectively because he thought his sins were of such an unforgivable nature, he could be reassured by the chantries he had founded and was in the process of founding: 'All yf our self so synfull be/ par god wyll not our prayers here,/ of holy men pen here wyll he pat for us profers par prayer'.[33] What is certain is that his fellow northerners were profoundly affected by the apparent fall from grace of such a great and pious prince and patron of the church who was afflicted by attacks of conscience. John Dalton, a merchant and Mayor of Hull 1487–95, who was married to a niece of John Alcock's, began his will with a long prayer in which, after meditating on the transience of life and the inevitability of death and God's omniscience, reflected: 'I seyng daily dye prynces and grete estates, and men of all ages ther daies; at deth giffes no respect certayn to levyng creature but takis thayn sodaynly'. Perhaps thinking of the dead king's alleged crimes, he further prays that when he (Dalton) dies he will die a true son of the church, fully confessed, contrite and repentant for all the sins that he has done since 'the first houre I was born of my moder into this synful world onto the houre of my deth' and beseeches the intercession of the Blessed Virgin and her blessed son 'who suffered pain and passion for me and for all sinful creatures'.[34]

Richard's crimes, coupled with his religious convictions and his hopes of salvation, would have contributed to his double-mindedness, his inscrutability and complexity, and this must have baffled and disturbed some of his contemporaries. It is a quality he shared with another high-minded and ruthless operator, John Tiptoft, the Earl of Worcester, and with another religious fanatic, Gilles de Rais, canon of St Hilaire de Poitiers, the founder of the Chapel of Holy Innocents at Marchecoul, the companion as Marshal of France of Jeanne d'Arc and a sexual abuser and murderer of children. Rais' faith was that with patience and hope in God he would achieve Paradise.[35]

The image of Richard III that still dominates is Shakespeare's and the Tudor tradition he drew from. The historical figure of Richard undoubtedly contributed to the composition of Shakespeare's villains – he is in Macbeth, the good man undone by ambition, a tradition started by the Crowland chronicler who noted with regret the destructive rivalry between the three Yorkist brothers and their outstanding talent,[36] and handed on by Robert Fabyan who sadly noted that if Richard had allowed the children to have prospered he would have triumphed over all.[37] He can be seen in the incestuous and ambitious Claudius; the scheming and talented Iago; and above all in the disinherited younger brother, Edmund, Duke of Gloucester. What Shakespeare distorts is the image of Richard at prayer, which he and subsequent historians have seen as a cloak of hypocrisy to give moral credibility to a ruthless usurpation of power. This tradition was started by Polydore Vergil, who arrived in England in 1502 and who in *Anglicana historia*, completed in 1513, reported that Richard determined to abolish the infamy with which his honour had been stained and repented of his evil deeds and began to take 'a certain new form of life and to give the countenance and show of a good man'.[38] However, Richard III was in reality far removed from Shakespeare's modern Machiavelli, a rational man motivated by the amoral quest for power. He was a more old-fashioned figure, out of touch with the intellectual developments of the late fifteenth century, the rational, secular interests shown in the circles of Anthony Woodville and William Worcester in the south-east.[39] Stephen Scrope's and Anthony Woodville's versions of *The Dicts and Sayings of the Philosophers* and William Worcester's *On Friendship and on Old Age* all emphasize the importance of self-knowledge and the prudence and detachment that it can bring: 'konnyng is lif and ignorance is dethe; therefore he that knowith is lif for he undrestandithe the whate he dothe and he that knowith not is dethe, for he undrestandithe no thin that he dothe'. That could sum up the difference between Woodville and his foe, Richard III.

While one cannot talk exclusively about a regional division of religious sensibility in this period, the devotional movement was a northern phenomenon and Richard was an important representative of this tradition. It was Henry VIII, the would-be emperor, who was prepared to harness the increasingly secular outlook of the educated circles in the south to create a powerful state, who embodied Machiavellian amorality. Richard's outlook was superstitious, subjective and irrational. His most important political decisions were dictated by fear of witchcraft – at the council meeting on Friday 13 when Hastings was arrested, Richard, according to More, accused Elizabeth Woodville and Elizabeth (Jane) Shaw of witchcraft and giving him a withered arm (his brother George, Duke of Clarence had previously claimed that his dead wife had been bewitched by Elizabeth Woodville, a charge of which Richard took note). He was very aware that his two predecessors as Duke of Gloucester, Thomas Woodstock and Humphrey, both protectors during royal minorities, died in prison and this probably influenced his pre-emptive strike against his nephew. Furthermore it was distorted by a fanatical religiosity, and absorption in the psalms which fortified his sense of persecution and his conviction that he had a God-given right to trample over others. While most leading lay intellectuals of the period were looking outwards to the active life and relationships in society, Richard's piety took him inwards to an individualistic isolation. His private religious impulses remained primarily destructive. Under his kingship the church could not so easily perform its task of social integration. In this he contrasts with Henry V, the monarch he most closely resembles as a thinking layman. Henry V defined firmly the political, social role of the church and provided the inspiration for the ideal of contemporary kingship that was worthy to be compared with the rulers of antiquity. According to the author of the *Gesta Henrici Quinti* (possibly John Stevens, a clerk of Exeter), once Henry began his private prayers no one could interrupt him; but Henry successfully incorporated his private religious impulses into a public religion of liturgical music, saints' cults and processions that became the foundation of an ordered state. His religious propaganda, employed in the invasion of France, his adoption of the role of the true elect of God as a monarch ordained to rule was entirely successful, and he integrated his spiritual energies and his people's spiritual energies in public religion that served the interests of the state. The architects of this religion were Henry V's clergy, especially Thomas Arundel, and the events of July to August 1483 show that Arundel's reservations about the growth of lay piety and the reading of the Bible in English were more well founded than he could have known. He and the clergy associated with him, Walter Hilton, Nicholas Love and John Newton, and Henry V himself, were preoccupied with the growth of heresy and anti-social forms of religious enthusiasm. They could not have anticipated the phenomenon of Richard III, a man driven by a sense of religious mission and his belief in the power of prayer which reinforced a self-image at variance with the one entertained by his subjects in the south. This misunderstanding, thanks to the private, idiosyncratic nature of Richard's religion, has been perpetuated by historians. Richard's failure, whatever his crimes, was a failure in communication; whereas men like Anthony Woodville, true to the teachings of antiquity, were mindful of posterity and their posthumous reputations and developed the appropriate social skills, Richard, confident in his special relationship with God, left little behind for posterity. The appropriate epitaph for Richard III should be delivered by his most intellectually distinguished victim, Anthony Woodville: 'There abideth not bot good name and loue, the which passethe the good dedes of aunsient peple abiden in the hertis of thaire successors; strengthe you ther to gete a good name, the whiche failethe no tyme; and bi this good name thi noblesse shalle endure'.[40]

Shakespeare's vision still dominates popular perception of Richard III and indeed the concept of the English nation in the fifteenth century. By creating this national epic Shakespeare was consciously emulating Virgil and claiming for England a destiny to rank with that of Rome. It is fitting that this grammar school-educated boy should also apply his knowledge of popularized views of the classics to create a series of characters who shared the outlook of men like Cicero and Seneca, stoics who contemplated the aloneness of the self and the possibility of there being no afterlife. Shakespeare differs from other creators of national epics, like Virgil and Dante, in that he expresses through his characters no real recognition of God, of a divinely ordered universe. This is not to say that no relationship existed between the contemplative movement of the late fourteenth century and the interest in antiquity in the fifteenth century. Both ultimately became important manifestations of popular culture. By the second decade of the fifteenth century the contemplative literature of the north-east was no longer read merely in Yorkshire and court circles but among gentry families throughout the south-east and among merchants, especially in London. This is the substratum upon which the growing interest in antiquity among courtiers, gentry families in East Anglia and the citizens of London (Caxton's audience) was built. In the first instance this was a court culture, represented by such cultivated noblemen as John Tiptoft the Earl of Worcester and Anthony Woodville the Earl Rivers. By the late fifteenth and early sixteenth centuries this too was becoming a popular culture spreading through the grammar schools of England.[41] Both types of literature constituted the basis of moral edification of a high-minded literate class and different people reacted in different ways to both types of literature. This can be seen in the York dynasty – Richard III, as has been shown, was influenced by both classical and devotional literature but he reacted more emphatically to the religious traditions of the north-east than his brothers Edward and George, in ways more akin to the spiritual traditions maintained by his mother and his sister, Margaret. In a sense Richard was rediscovering the intellectual bedrock of the culture of his class through his northern connections. Both traditions, as has been shown in the turbulent history of this family, were popular and vital throughout the fifteenth century and neither had anything directly to do with the more famous cultural movements of the sixteenth century. The fifteenth-century translations of the classics which provided a moral guide to people leading an active life did not lead to, or have any relationship with, the more elitist and scholarly Italian humanism studied by Weis. The religious texts composed, translated and copied for the laity at the beginning of the fifteenth century also had nothing directly to do with the development of Protestantism in the sixteenth century (which initially was also an ideology maintained by an elite minority). In both cases we are dealing with a genuinely popular culture, which in the case of the interest in antiquity lead to the creation of an intellectual environment in which the plays of Shakespeare were written and performed. Shakespeare's Richard III may reflect this environment, but the real Richard III, as we have seen, did not share this perspective.

However, Shakespeare's secular vision of the inner dimension of the lives of courtiers does apply to a section of the fifteenth-century lay aristocracy which included, as we have seen, members of the Yorkist court. Through their access to texts emerging from France from the libraries of Charles V, popularizers of the classics such as Anthony Woodville were expressing in their writings the same secular outlook as characters like Macbeth and Hamlet, who faced depression and death alone with only the self for support. Richard III was an educated layman who was an exception to this trend – clerical in outlook, he reacted to the depression he experienced as a king by creating a grandiose self-image, a delusion that was appropriate to the religious values of his day. Other educated courtiers faced despair and the question of self-image in a more analytical way by writing about their self-image and their relationships in poetry and letters which showed a sceptical attitude to chivalric and religious role-playing. In conclusion it would be instructive to compare what we have suggested is Richard III's view of his relationship with God to the attitudes expressed by near contemporary writers connected with the English court. These writers displayed an ironic, detached attitude towards themselves and the objects of their emotions that contrasts markedly with Richard III's egoistic and subjective religiosity.

Sir Richard Roos, a younger son to Sir William the 6th Lord Roos, was, like many of his generation, profoundly affected by war. His two eldest brothers fell at Bauge and a third was drowned at Paris in 1430. Sir Richard himself was a prisoner of the seneschal of Normandy from 1453 to 1463. With his brother, Sir Robert, he moved in Lancastrian court circles.[42] Sir Richard's wife, Margaret, was in Margaret of Anjou's household and his niece, Eleanor, daughter of Robert, married Richard Haute, who was a first cousin of Elizabeth and Anthony Woodville (Haute and Woodville were both executed by Richard, Duke of Gloucester in July 1483). The Haute family were themselves a literary family and later connected to the household of Thomas More. Sir Richard Roos was the translator of Alain Chartier's *La Belle Dame Sans Merci*,[43] a psychological study of love in which a lady refuses to accept the symbolic attributes of the Virgin Mary or to be the chivalric focus of men's projections of self-sacrifice and honour. In a coldly logical way she exposes the self-deceptions and self-absorption of the conventional courtly lover. She points out the folly of placing emotional store where there is no hope of it being requited, and that there is something self-absorbed and masochistic in conventional courtly love: 'To live in wo he hath gret fantasy'.[44] In the ensuing dialogue the lover admits he is restless in the prison of the self and that love is a way of escaping this prison by losing himself in another personality: 'It is greet duresse and discomfort/ To kepe a herte in so strayt a prisoun,/ That hath but oon body for his disport'.[45] She, in her complacent self-possession, sees such an interchange of personalities and the eventual return of the lovers to their separate selves as a perilous enterprise devoid of worship. She regards such a desire for self-transcendence as a mental aberration, suggesting the pain he is suffering has many origins, that love only aggravates it, and that he is attracted to her because she is not suffering but self-possessed: 'A sick body, his thought is al away/ From hem that fele no sorowe nor siknesse'.[46] In response to his request for pity she replies she can only love and respect he who is content with himself:

'Who loveth not himself, whatever he be/ In love, he stant forgete in every place;/ And of your wo if ye have no pite,/ others pite bileve not to purchace'.[47] Sir Richard Roos' translation of Chartier's *La Belle Dam Sans Merci* anatomizes another depressive delusion appropriate to the age, all-consuming courtly love. The lover, wearing black and adopting the pose of the melancholic, like Sydney's Astrophell, cannot accept that he cannot make a woman love him. He is forced, through the logic of his chosen woman, to come to terms with this folly of placing an emotional investment where there is no hope, the folly of projecting feelings and aspirations on to another person through his desire to escape from himself and his melancholy state of mind.

This new rationality and awareness of a sense that the self is a prison where there is no hope of any obvious chivalric or religious channel of transcendence is expressed in the poetry of another prisoner of war, Charles, Duke of Orleans, who had some connections with Roos and his circle. Robert Roos, possibly accompanied by his brother Richard, was in the escort that accompanied Charles of Orleans to Burgundy on his release in 1440.[48] From his earliest years Charles was exposed to the writings of antiquity. His grandfather was Charles V, the hero of Christine de Pisan, who built up the royal collection of Roman literature at the Louvre which was later pillaged by the Duke of Bedford and Fastolf; his father, Louis of Orleans, owned the works of Aristotle, Ovid, Horace, Lucan, Cicero and Virgil. In the court of Charles VI, where he grew up, he encountered humanist secretaries who studied the classics for their own sake. During his long imprisonment from 1415 to 1440 (much of it in solitary confinement in the White Tower in the Tower of London) Charles would come to rely on the stoic philosophy he imbued from these writers and from Chaucer's translation of Boethius (which he would have been introduced to by his friend and fellow poet, William de la Pole, the Duke of Suffolk and husband of Alice Chaucer, Geoffrey Chaucer's granddaughter).[49] In his poetry, which for him was a form of prayer, a way of presenting his mind and exploring his character, Charles indulged in a melancholy form of introspection that had nothing to do with traditional Christianity. Confronting the mysteries of personality, of the notion of the self and its feelings as a form of a prison, he developed the notion of the ego, the self, that was new in culture. In the fourteenth century and during the reign of Henry V clerical intellectuals in

England celebrated the solitary life, the detachment from human ties to a relationship with God; but Charles of Orleans depicted a solitary life in purely secular terms, describing his love of solitude, his constitutional melancholy and his retreat from his emotions. Such a retreat from social and emotional commitment was presented by Charles in secular and negative terms. Although he compared himself to a hermit alone in his cell, he described the self itself as a cell and himself as a prisoner within his personality, his feelings, memories and obsessions. This was far from the confident expectation of detachment from the emotions and worries of the self anticipated by the fourteenth-century mystics. During his long imprisonment Charles expressed, like Roos, his sense of being trapped within the prison of his melancholy feelings: 'Shall I ever see the end of your work, melancholy?'[50] This secular view of the self and its essential aloneness can account for the changing attitudes to death expressed in his writings. For Charles of Orleans, thought or consciousness often equalled pain, and he depicted life as a long wait for death. If the personality is perceived to be a prison and consciousness as pain, then death, if anticipated without a confident expectation of an existence in the hereafter, could be regarded as a release. The increasingly secular perspective encouraged by the popularity of pagan moral philosophers allowed Charles of Orleans, and many of his contemporaries, to express very different attitudes to death than those of clerical intellectuals of the previous generation. Showing little fear of an afterlife, they expressed a stoic view of life as something to be endured. Charles of Orleans frequently confessed his death wish in his poetry 'what is this liif or deth y lede/ Nay certes deth in liif is liklynes'. In 1458 in an oration in defence of his son-in-law, Alencon, who was threatened with capital punishment, he used Cicero as his model and argued that it was no punishment to execute an accused because in his own case death at Agincourt would have been easier for him to bear than his own life in prison, during which he had often desired death.[51] Charles of Orleans' strategy was to retreat from his emotions and relationships into the allegorical world, the landscape of the mind that he created within himself: 'All by myself, I shut myself up in my thoughts and build castles'.[52] Detached from himself and his pain he expressed his awareness that he was in danger of losing touch with reality. The way Charles chose to avoid his conviction that the self was a prison was to develop a multiplicity of selves, and he cultivated a variety of roles, of personae, such as the poet, lover, prince, soldier and prisoner, but above all the solitary melancholic. Anticipating such role players of the Renaissance as Sir Philip Sydney, he is a sign of the growing individuality of the fifteenth century and growing sense of the autonomy of the self.

In the surviving portraits of Richard III and in the poetry of these fifteenth-century prisoners and victims of fortune the image of melancholy dominates. The flexibility and theatricality that Roos and Orleans show towards the question of self-identity anticipates the posturing seen in Renaissance literature and in such roles as Hamlet. Such brooding, introspective types are obviously of interest to the literary scholar, but the individual of most interest to the historian is William Worcester (or Botoner). Worcester was also melancholic and moody. To a fellow sufferer, John Berney III, he complained in 1460 of his 'aduersyte, trouble yn my spryttes, thought and hevynesse' and to a servant of Waynflete (sole administrator of Fastolf's estate after 1472) he confessed that his poverty and the dead man's debtors and creditors 'make me noyed and werye'; and next to a saying in his translation of *The Dicts and Sayings of the Philosophers*, 'hevyness is a passion touching things passed and sorrow is a fear of things to come he added 'pro Botoner'.[53] Friar Brackley in a letter to John Paston I said of Worcester: 'do not confide in him he is a wretch full of spite and bad tempered'. He also observed Worcester's features as conforming to the classic, melancholy type, dark face with clear eyes[54] (like Durer's portrait of Melancholia); but for a man like Brackley the mercurial unpredictability he observed was a vice and in describing Worcester's dark swarthy complexion he was describing the classic features of the melancholic. Stephen Scrope in the *Epistle of Othea*, when discussing the influence of planets on behaviour advised the knight to model himself on the heavy considered wisdom of Saturn. Worcester would often sign himself with the sign of Saturn, identifying his antiquarian interests, his propensity to measure distances on the dimensions of buildings and his moodiness with the melancholic inspiration of this heavy planet that inspired scholars. Worcester kept despair at bay through thinking, cataloguing and intellectual exploration. An individualist who believed in private property and entrepreneurial activity,[55] he also saw that the despair that set in after his master Sir John Fastolf's death in 1460 could only be obviated by creating and maintaining friendships and links with the recent past, and studying history and the flora and fauna of his native land. He and those contemporaries who were holding these secular views on the nature of the self were all laymen. Any sense of intellectual detachment that they may have wrested from their private griefs had no reference to the ideal of negation espoused by the religious writers of the fourteenth century, their immediate intellectual predecessors. If Richard III's life demonstrates the destructiveness that can arise from delusions produced by excessive religious introspection, Worcester's life affirms the potential that can be realized if one can maintain a healthy balance of the active and contemplative lives and turn from the self to the outer world. His scientific spirit represented the most positive manifestation of the new secular outlook on which England's future developments would rest.

NOTES

CHAPTER 1

[1] Dominic Mancini, *The Usurpation of Richard III*, C.A.J. Armstrong (ed.), Gloucester, 1984, p. 61

[2] Ibid., pp. 91, 97

[3] *The Crowland Chronicle Continuations, 1459–1486*, N. Pronay and J. Cox (eds), London 1986, see intro, pp. 78–98

[4] Ibid., p. 129

[5] Ibid., p. 153

[6] Ibid., p. 175

[7] John Warkworth, *A Chronicle of the First Thirteen Years of the Reign of of Edward IV*, J.O. Halliwell (ed.), Camden Soc., 1839, p. 21; A.H. Thomas and I.D. Thornley (eds), *The Great Chronicle of London*, 1938, p. 220; R. Fabyan, *New Chronicles of England and of France*, H. Ellis (ed.), 1811, p. 662

[8] Philip de Commynes, *The Memoirs*, A.R. Scoble (ed.), London, 1911, vol. I, p. 394

[9] Ibid., pp. 358–9

[10] Ibid., p. 313

[11] 'John Rous' account of the reign of Richard III' in A. Hanham, *Richard III and His Early Historians*, Oxford, 1975, pp. 118–24

[12] Pamela Tudor-Craig, *Richard III (Catalogue of the 1973 Exhibition)*, 2nd edn, 1978, p. 53

[13] Sir Thomas More, *The History of Richard III*, R.S. Sylvester (ed.), Yale, 1976, p. 9

[14] Ibid., p. 42

[15] Ibid., pp. 86–9

[16] *Three Books of Polydore Vergil's English History Comprising the Reigns of King Henry VI, Edward IV, and Richard III*, H. Ellis (ed.), London, 1844, p. 156

[17] Ibid., p. 174

[18] Ibid., p. 187

[19] Ibid., p. 210

[20] Ibid., p. 227

[21] Lambeth Palace MS. 474, f. 182

[22] Mancini, p. 63

[23] More, *The History of Richard III*, p. 9

[24] Mancini, p. 63

[25] Ibid., p. 95

[26] Ibid., p. 97

[27] *Crowland Chronicle*, p. 190

[28] Tudor-Craig, *Richard III*, p. 95

[29] Hanham, *Richard III and His Early Historians*, p. 123

30   Vergil, *English History*, p. 167

31   Ibid., p. 174

32   Ibid., p. 178

33   Ibid., p. 191

34   Ibid., p. 200

35   Ibid., p. 205

36   Ibid., p. 205

37   More, *The History of Richard III*, p. 9

38   Ibid., p. 89

39   Hanham, *Richard III and His Early Historians*, p. 180; More, *English Works*, 1931, p. 83

40   More, *The History of Richard III*, p. 55

41   Ibid., pp. 55–6

42   Ibid., pp. 57–8

43   Ibid., pp. 55–6

44   Hanham, *Richard III and His Early Historians*, p. 180

45   More, *The History of Richard III*, p. 53

46   Sir George Buck, *The History of King Richard the Third*, A.N. Kincaid (ed.), Gloucester, 1979

47   Horace Walpole, *Historic Doubts on the Life and Reign of King Richard the Third*, London, 1768

48   William Hutton, *The Battle of Bosworth Field*, 1788

49   James Gairdner, *The Life and Reign of Richard III*, Cambridge, 1898, p. 247

50   Ibid., p. 249

51   C.R. Markham, *Richard III: His Life and Character*, 1906

52   P.M. Kendall, *Richard III*, London, 1955, pp. 16, 20, 314

53   Rosemary Hawley, *We Speak No Treason*, London, 1971, pp. 417–18

54   Tudor-Craig, *Richard III*, pp. 96–7

55   J.R. Lander, *Government and Community, England 1450–1509*, London, 1980, pp. 328–30

56   C. Ross, *Richard III*, London, 1980, p. 129

57   Ibid., pp. 141–4

58   Ibid., pp. 136–8

59   Ibid., p. 146

60   Ibid., p. 229

61   Rosemary Horrox, *Richard III, A Study in Service*, Cambridge, 1989, pp. 330–1

62   A.J. Pollard, *Richard III and the Princes in the Tower*, Stroud, 1991, p. 197

63   Ibid., p. 199

64   A.F. Sutton and L. Visser-Fuchs, *The Hours of Richard III*, Gloucester, 1991

65   Ibid., pp. 66–78

66   Virginia Renesburg, 'Prayer and the Book of Hours', in R.S. Wieck (ed.), *The Book of Hours in Medieval Art and Life*, London, 1988, pp. 39–44

67   Ibid., pp. 79–85

68   J. Bossy, 'Christian Life in the Middle Ages: Prayers', *TRHS*, 1991, p. 141

69   J. Bossy, 'Social History of Confession', *TRHS*, 1974

70   Bossy, 'Prayers', *TRHS*, pp. 140–8

71   E. Duffy, *The Stripping of the Altars*, Yale, 1992, p. 254

72   Ibid., 266 ff.

73   Ibid., p. 269

74   Duffy, *The Stripping of the Altars*, p. 223

75   J. Hughes, *Pastors and Visionaries: Religion and Secular Life in Late Medieval Yorkshire*, Woodbridge, 1988

76   YML 5 MS. Add. 2, fs 100v–101; the carvings of grateful mariners of ships delivered from storms can still be seen on a rood screen of the priory now in Flamborough parish church

77   Bodley MS. Lat Liturg. f2, fs 2, 12v, 19, 44

78   Hughes, *Pastors and Visonaries*, 331 ff.

79   Walter Hilton, *The Scale of Perfection*, E. Underhill (ed.), London, 1923, p. 214

80   Nicholas Love, *The Mirror of the Blessed Lyf of Jesu Crist*, L.F. Powell (ed.), Oxford, 1911, p. 213

81   Thomas à Kempis, *Earliest English Translations of the First Three Books of the De Imitatione Christi*, J.K. Ingram (ed.), EETS, London, 1893, p. 34

82   Ibid., p. 117

83   Ibid., p. 39

84   Ibid., pp. 12–13

85   J. Carey, *John Donne Life, Mind and Art*, London, 1981, pp. 13–14

86   A. Storr, *Feet of Clay: a Study of Gurus*, London, 1996, p. 18

87   M. Hicks, *Richard III, the Man Behind the Myth*, London, 1991, p. 163

CHAPTER 2

1   C. Weightman, *Margaret of York, Duchess of Burgundy 1446–1503*, Gloucester, 1989, pp. 94, 209–12; N.F. Blake, *William Caxton and English Culture*, London, 1991, pp. 89–98

2   Weightman, *Margaret of York*, pp. 37–9

3   Ibid., pp. 92–4; Livia Visser-Fuchs, 'Richard in Holland, 1470–1', *The Ricardian*, vi, no. 82, 1983, p. 221; C.L. Scofield, *The Life and Reign of Edward IV*, 2 vols, 1923, p. 562; M. Vale, 'England in the Low Countries' in C. Barron and N. Saul (eds), *England and the Low Countries in the Later Middle Ages*

4   Lambeth Palace MS. 265 f. 6

5   N.F. Blake, *William Caxton and English Literary Culture*, London, 1991, p. 75

6   W.J.B. Crotch (ed.), *The Prologues and Epilogues of William Caxton*, EETS, London, 1928, pp. 19–31

7   BL. MS. Harl. 4431

8   D. Bornstein, *The Middle English Translation of Christine de Pisan's Livre du Corps de Policie*, ed. from the MS. CUL k41.5, Heidelberg, 1977, p. 102

9   Ibid., p. 65

10   Ibid., p. 45

11   Ibid., pp. 107–8

12   Ibid., p. 104

13   William Worcester, *The Boke of Noblesse*, J.G. Nichols (ed.), London, 1860, p. 3

14   R. Deacon, *William Caxton*, London, 1976, p. 87

[15] J. Watts, '*De Consulatu Stilichonis*, Texts and Politics in the Reign of Henry VI', *Journal of Medieval History*, 16, 1990, pp. 251–66

[16] Watts, '*De Consulatu*' pp. 251–66. Watts maintains that the 1445 date is a scribal error and should read 1455, which fits the circumstances of York's assumption of the protectorate

[17] Palmer, 'Patrons and Letters in Norfolk and Suffolk in 1450', II, *PMLA*, (1913), 79 ff.

[18] *Parvus Cato Magnus Cato*, Benedict Burgh (transl. and ed.) from William Caxton's first edition, *c*. 1477, F. Kuriyawa (ed.), Tokyo, 1974, p. 77

[19] A. Sutton and L. Visser-Fuchs, 'Choosing a book in Late Fifteenth Century England and Burgundy', in C. Barron and N. Saul (eds), *England and the Low Countries in the Later Middle Ages*, pp. 61–98

[20] Crotch, *The Prologues and Epilogues of William Caxton*, pp. 10–16

[21] R.G. Davies, 'The Church and the Wars of the Roses' in A.J. Pollard (ed.), *The Wars of the Roses*, London, 1995, pp. 137; S.B. Crimes, *English Constitutional Ideas in the Fifteenth Century*, Cambridge, 1936, pp. 167–91

[22] Virgil, *Aeneid*, Bk VI ii, ll. 833–4. '*Oration Scotorum ad Regem Ricardum Tertium pro face firmanda inter Anglos et Scotos xii*', Sept. *MCCCL XXIV*, printed in D. Laing (ed.), *The Bannatyne Miscellany II*, Bannatyne Club, Edinburgh, 1886, pp. 41–8; A.J. Pollard (ed.), D. Shottle App. (tr.), *The North of England in the Age of Richard III*, Stroud, 1996, pp. 193–200

[23] A.F. Sutton and L. Visser Fuchs, 'Richard III's Books IV, Vegetius' *De re militari*', *The Ricardian*, 7, 1987, pp. 541–2

[24] T. Wright, *Political Poems and Songs Relating to English History from Edward III to Henry VIII*, 2 vols, RS, London, 1859–61, pp. 2, 71–82

[25] *The Governance of Princes*, James Yonge (transl.), 1422, EETS, Series 74, 1898

[26] A.J. Pollard, *North-Eastern England During the Wars of the Roses*, Oxford, 1990, pp. 232–44

[27] *Testamenta Eboracensia. III*, SS, 45, 1467–85, James Raine (ed.), 1864, p. 297

[28] Ibid., p. 279

[29] TE IV, p. 125

[30] TE III, p. 201

[31] TE IV, p. 116

[32] Pollard, *North-Eastern England*, 398 ff.

[33] C. Ross, *Edward IV*, London, 1974, p. 232; Commynes, II, pp. 54–9

[34] C. Richmond, '1485 and all that, or what was going on at the Battle of Bosworth', in P.W. Hammond (ed.), *Richard III, Loyalty, Lordship and Law*, London, 1984, pp. 172–206

[35] M.K. Jones, 'Richard III as a Soldier' in J. Gillingham (ed.), *Richard III A Medieval Kingship*, London, 1993, pp. 93–4

[36] Sir Thomas More, *The History of Richard III*, R.S. Slyvester (ed.), Yale, 1976, pp. 68–9

[37] Jones, 'Richard III as a Soldier', pp. 93–4

[38] Worcester, *The Boke of Noblesse*, pp. 22, 73

[39] A.F. Sutton and L. Visser-Fuchs, 'Richard III's Books IX, *The Grande Chroniques de France*', *The Ricardian*, VIII, Dec 1990, pp. 495–575

[40] A.F. Sutton and L. Visser-Fuchs, 'Richard III's Books V, Aegidius Romanus *De regimine principum*', *The Ricardian* Vol. 7, 1985–7, pp. 541–52

[41] M. Thiebaux, 'The Mouth of the Boar', *Romance Philology*, 22 (1969), pp. 281–9; Geoffrey of Monmouth, History of the Kings of Britain, C. Thorpe (transl.), 1966, p. 176; 'Richard III's Books VIII, 'Historia Regum Britanniae with the Prophecy of the Eagle and Commentary', *The Ricardian*, VIII, pp. 108, 351–62; 'Richard III's Books VII, Guido delle Colonne's *Historia Destructionis Troiae*', *The Ricardian*, vol. 7, 1985–7

[42] A.F. Sutton and L. Visser-Fuchs, 'Richard III's Books XI, Ramon Lull's *Order of Chivalry* translated by William Caxton', *The Ricardian*, ix, 114, Sep. 1991, pp. 110–30; A.T.P. Byles, (ed.), '*The Book of the Ordre of Chyvalry* translated by William Caxton', EETS, OS, 168, 1926

[43] A.F. Sutton and L Visser-Fuchs, 'Richard III's Books: Chivalric Ideals and Reality', *The Ricardian* ix, 116, March 1922, 190–206; and 'Richard III's Books IV, Vegetius' *De re militari*', *The Ricardian* vol. 7, 1987, 541–52; G. Lester (ed.), *The Earliest English Translation of Vegetius' De re militari*, Middle English Texts, 21, Heidelberg, 1988, pp. 103–4

[44] 'British Library Harleian Manuscript 433', R. Horrox and P.W. Hammond (eds), 3 vols, *Richard III Society*, 1979, vol. III, pp. 124–51

[45] J.L. Watts, 'Ideas, Principles and Politics' in A.J. Pollard (ed.), *The Wars of the Roses*, London, 1995, pp. 110–33

[46] *Grants etc from the Crown during the reign of Edward the Fifth . . .*, J.G. Nichols (ed.), Camden Soc., 1854, 1– lxvii; BL. MS. Cotton Vitellius E.x Art 23, ff. 170–6

[47] A.F. Sutton and L.Visser-Fuchs, 'A Curious Searcher of Our Common Weal Public: Richard III, Piety, Chivalry and the Concept of the Good Prince', in Hammond (ed.), *Richard III Loyalty, Lordship and Law*

[48] BL. Harl. MS. 433, ii, pp. 48–9

[49] Harl. 433, p. 124

[50] A.J. Pollard, *Richard III and the Princes in the Tower*, Stroud, 1991, p. 154; Harleian 433, iii, p. 107

[51] *Statutes of the Realm 1107–1703, Record Commission 1810–28*, Rich. III, ch 2; P.W. Hammond and A. Sutton, *Richard III, The Road to Bosworth Field*, London, 1985, p. 160

[52] Rosemary Horrox, *Richard III, A Study in Service*, Cambridge, 1989, p. 330

[53] Idley, Peter, *Instructions to his Son*, C. D'Evelyn (ed.), London, 1935

[54] Ibid., ll. 885

[55] Ibid., ll. 739

[56] *The Curiale made by Mayster Alain Chartier, tranls William Caxton 1484*, EETS, ES, 54

[57] *Le Quadrilogue Invectif*, p. 246

[58] P.W. Fleming, 'The Hautes and their Circle', in *Culture and the English Gentry in England in the Fifteenth Century*

[59] Bornstein, *Christine de Pisan's Livre Du Corps De Policie*, ed. from MS. CU.L K.K. 1.5, Heidelberg, 1977

[60] *Exerpta Historica*, London, 1831

[61] *Book of Policy*, p. 116

[62] R.J. Mitchell, *John Tiptoft, 1427–1470*, London, 1938, pp. 176–8

[63] For the text see Mitchell, *John Tiptoft*, Appendix, pp. 215–41

[64] *The Declamacion of Noblesse*, pp. 236–7

[65]   Ibid., p. 240

[66]   *The Paston Letters and Papers of the Fifteenth Century*, N. Davis (ed.), 2 vols, Oxford, 1971–6, pp. 574–5, 577

[67]   A. Sutton and L. Visser-Fuchs, 'Choosing a book in late fifteenth century England and Burgundy' in C. Barron and N. Saul (eds) *England and the Low Countries*, pp. 61–98

[68]   Crotch, *Prologues*, pp. 41–4

[69]   Ibid., pp. 89–90

[70]   Ibid., pp. 76–80

[71]   Idley, *Instructions to his Son*, ll. 1427

[72]   Vespasiano de Bistici, *Vite di uomini illustri del secolo XV*, L. Frati (ed.), I (1892), p. 322

[73]   Mitchell, *John Tiptoft*, pp. 64–79

[74]   PL ii (Davis), 494; *Exerpta Historica* 245

[75]   A. Sutton and L. Visser Fuchs, 'Choosing a Book in Late Fifteenth Century England and Burgundy' in C. Barron and N. Saul (eds), *England in the Low Countries in the Late Middle Ages*, pp. 61–98

[76]   Anne Payne, 'The Salisbury Roll of Arms *c.* 1463 in the fifteenth century', in D. Williams (ed.), *England in the Fifteenth Century*, Woodbridge, 1987, pp. 187–96; A.F. Sutton and L. Visser-Fuchs, 'Richard III's Books, Ancestry and True Nobility', *The Ricardian*, IX, Dec. 1992, pp. 343–51

[77]   BL. MS. Cotton Julius EIV; see f. 28r for drawing of Richard III and Anne Neville; William, Earl of Carysfort (ed.), *The Pageants of Richard Beauchamp, Earl of Warwick*, Oxford, 1908

[78]   C. Ross, 'Some "Servants and Lovers" of Richard in his youth', *The Ricardian*, 55, pp. 2–5

[79]   A. Sutton and L. Visser-Fuchs, 'Richard III's Books VI, The Anonymous FitzHugh Chronicle', *The Ricardian*, vol. 8, 1988–90, pp. 104–19

[80]   Thomas Hobbes, *Leviathan*, C.B. Macpherson (ed.), London, 1968, ch xiii

[81]   J. Watts, 'Ideas, Principles and Politics', in Pollard (ed.), *The Wars of the Roses*, pp. 110–33

CHAPTER 3

[1]   *Dicts and Sayings*, pp. 24, 174

[2]   Benedict Burgh, *Magnus Cato*, p. 12

[3]   Ibid., p. 43

[4]   *Dicts and Sayings*, p. 12

[5]   Ibid., p. 175

[6]   *Christine de Pisan's Moral Proverbs, trans. by Earl Rivers and repr. from orig. edit. by Caxton A.D. 1478*, W. Blades (ed.), London, 1859

[7]   *Dicts and Sayings*, p. 146

[8]   Ibid., pp. 172, 106

[9]   H.G. Wright, *Boccacio in England from Chaucer to Tennyson*, London, 1957

[10]   Magdalen College, Oxford, MS. 198

[11]   BL. MS. Harl. 103

[12]   W.J.B. Crotch, *Prologues and Epilogues of William Caxton*, EETS, 176, 1929, pp. 36–8

[13]   R. Deacon, *William Caxton*; *The Curiale made by Mayster Alain Chartier, transl. William Caxton 1484*, EETS, ES

[14] Caxton, *The Curiale*, p. 3

[15] Ibid., p. 7

[16] Ibid., p. 10

[17] Ibid., p. 11

[18] Ibid., p. 12

[19] Caxton, *Prologues and Epilogues*, pp. 38–40

[20] Ibid., pp. 111–12

[21] John Rous, *Historia Regum Angliae*, T. Hearne (ed.), Oxford, 1975, Chronicle, p. 214

[22] William Worcester, *The Boke of Noblesse*, J.G. Nichols (ed.), London, 1860, pp. 50–3

[23] *English translation of Le Quadrilogue Invectif*, Prologue, p. 151

[24] *Le Quadrilogue Invectif*, p. 150

[25] Christine de Pisan, *Livre du Corps de Policie*, pp. 63–4

[26] R. Weis, *Humanism in England During the Fifteen Century*, Oxford, 1967, pp. 120–1; Mitchell, *John Tiptoft*, pp. 26–35

[27] Vespasiano de Bisticci, *Vite uonimi illlustri del secolo XV*, p. 322; *Warkworth Chronicle*, pp. 38–9

[28] Kenneth Dover, *Marginal Comments*, London, 1994

[29] *Le Quadrilogue Invectif*, p. 20

[30] R.B. Emden, *A Biographical Register of the University of Cambridge to 1500*, Cambridge, 1963, p. 6

[31] *CPR*, 1467–77, p. 450; *BRUC*, p. 489

[32] *BRUC*, pp. 229–30

[33] *BRUC*, pp. 229–30

[34] *VCH*, 1449–50

[35] *TE, III*, pp. 140–1; A.F. Leach, *The Schools of Medieval England*, London, 1915, pp. 275–6

[36] R. Willis and J.W. Clark, *Architectural History of the University of Cambridge*, 4 vols, Cambridge, 1886, iii, pp. 14–15

[37] M. Underwood, 'John Fisher and the Promotion of Learning', in *Humanism, Reform and the Reformation: and the Career of Bishop John Fisher*, Cambridge, 1989, p. 128

[38] *VCH*, iii, p. 419; D. Leader, *A History of the University of Cambridge, vol. i, The University to 1546*, Cambridge, 1988, pp. 270–5

[39] Ibid., pp. 275–85

[40] *Mons perfeccionis, the hyll of perfeccion; In die innocencium sermo pro episcopo puerorum*; an English sermon on Luke viii *Qui habet aures audiendi: audiat; Desponsacio virginis Christo, Sponsage of a virgin to cryste*

[41] *Gallicantus ad confratres suos curatos in sinodo apud Barnwell*, Pynson, 1498, RSTC, 277, 74

[42] C.I. Scofield, *The Life and Reign of Edward IV*, 2 vols, London, vol. ii, p. 168

[43] *BRUC*, pp. 490–1

[44] Ibid., p. 401; *Historians of the Church of York (RS)* ii, xxv

[45] *BRUC*, p. 6; CUL MS. Add. 3468, f. 9

[46] D. Leader, *A History of the University of Cambridge, Vol. 1, The University to 1546*, Cambridge, 1988, pp. 275–81

[47] A.G. Dickens, *The English Reformation*, 2nd edn, London, 1989, p. 73

[48] *EDR*, 1908, p. 88

[49] John Alcock, *Gallicantus Johannis alcok (RSTC 277)*, Pynson, 1498

[50] Bradshaw and Duffy (eds), *Humanism, Reform and the Reformation: the Career of Bishop John Fisher*, Cambridge, 1989, p. 60

[51] Leader, *Medieval Cambridge*, p. 272

[52] John Alcock, *An Exhortacyon made to Religyous Systers (Sponsage of a Virgin to Christ)*, Westminster, Wynken de Worde (STC 287) in *The English Experience*, No 638, its record in early printed books published in facsimile, Amsterdam, 1974

[53] Tait, 'The Letters of John Tiptoft, Earl of Worcester and Archbishop Neville to the University of Oxford, *EHR*, xxv (1920), pp. 573–4; Weis, *Humanism in England During the Fifteenth Century*, pp. 148–52

[54] Bradshaw and Duffy, p. 90

[55] *The Crowland Chronicle Continuations*, pp. 81–94

[56] Ibid., p. 75

[57] Commynes, *Memoirs*, p. 313

[58] *Crowland Chronicle*, p. 75

[59] Smith, 'A Preaching Bishop', p. 513

[60] John Alcock, *Sermon on Luke VIII, Sermo – Qui habet aures audiendi*, Westminster, Wynkyn de Worde, STC 284 (microfilm). Alcock addressed parishioners on obeying their priests and conforming to the sacraments and addresses his closing remarks to 'my frends' to the 'spirytualtye who are to be holy in conversation' and to 'syres' and the 'masters of the temporalities who are to remember the bill of justice'

[61] Walter Hilton, *The Scale of Perfection*, 245–9; J. Hughes, 'The Administration of Confession in the diocese of York in the Fourteenth Century', in D. Smith (ed.), *Studies in Clergy and Ministry in Medieval England*, Borthwick Studies in History, York, 1991, p. 153

[62] Alcock, *Qui habet aures audiendi*

[63] Ibid.

[64] Julia Smith, 'An image of a Preaching Bishop in Late Medieval England: the 1498 Portrait of Bishop John Alcock', *Viator*, 1990; John Alcock, *Gallicantus*, title page, Bodley MS Auct. Q1 5.33, 513 ff.

[65] J. Hughes, *Pastors and Visionaries: Religion and Secular Life in Late Medieval Yorkshire*, Woodbridge, 1988, 269 ff.

[66] E. Duffy, 'The Career of Bishop Fisher, in Bradshaw and Duffy (eds), *Humanism, Reform and the Reformation: The Career of Bishop Fisher*, Cambridge, 1989, pp. 219–22

[67] Hughes, 'The Administration of Confession', 158 ff.

[68] C. Ross, *Richard III*, 12, London, 1980, pp. 28–9

[69] A.J. Pollard, *North-Eastern England During the Wars of the Roses*, Oxford, 1990, p. 343

[70] Ibid., p. 329; L.C. Atreed, 'An Indenture between Richard Duke of Gloucester and the Scrope family of Masham and Upsall', *Speculum*, 58, 1983, pp. 1018–25

[71] Mancini, *The Usurpation of Richard III*, pp. 62–5

[72] A.J. Pollard, *Richard III and The Princes in the Tower*, Stroud, 1991, p. 78

[73] *YCR* I, p. 73

[74] Ibid., pp. 342–6

[75] York Civic Records, A. Raine (ed.), vol 1, 1939; *Yorkshire Archaeological Society Record Series*, vol 98, p. 18

[76] York House Books 2/4 f. 169b

77 Ross, 'Some "Servants and Lovers" of Richard in his Youth', *The Ricardian*, 55, pp. 2–5

78 Hughes, *Pastors and Visionaries*, p. 264

79 Ibid., p. 100

80 C.A.J. Armstrong, 'The Piety of Cicely, Duchess of York' in D. Woodruff (ed.), *For Hilaire Belloc*, 1942

81 Stonor, *Letters*, 3rd ser., xxx, p. 14

82 Armstrong, 'The Piety of Cicely, Duchess of York', p. 82

83 *Wills from Doctor's Commons*, p. 3

84 For christening ceremony see Herald's Aut in BL. Add. MS. 6113; *Gentleman's Magazine*, 1831, p. 25

85 Armstrong, 'The Piety of Cicely, Duchess of York', pp. 190–6

86 W. Prevenier and W. Blackmans, *The Burgundian Netherlands, 1330–1530*, 1986, p. 249

87 M.J. Hughes, 'Margaret of York', *The Private Library*, 3rd ser., vols 7 and 2, Spring and Summer 1984

88 Bodley MS. Douce 365

89 K.B. McFarlane, *Hans Memling*, Oxford, 1971

90 Vickers, *Humphrey duke of Gloucester*, 1967, pp. 234, 445–6

91 C. Weightman, *Margaret of York, Duchess of Burgundy, 1446–1503*, Gloucester, 1989, p. 48

92 Ibid., pp. 91–2; L. Visser-Fuchs, 'Richard in Holland 1470–1', *The Ricardian*, p. 221

93 Weightman, *Margaret of York*, pp. 98–9; J. Molinet, *Chroniques*, G. Doutrepont and O. Jodogne (eds), 3 vols, Brussels, 1935–7, pp. 106–8; Commynes, *Memoires*, pp. 1, 292–5, ii, 34–6; J. Varsen and E. Charavay, *Lettres de Louis XI*, 12 vols, Paris, 1883–1909, v, p. 366

94 N.H. Nicolas, *Wardrobe Accounts of Edward IV*, 1830, pp. 126, 141–2, 144–5, 153, 166; C. Scofield, *The Life and Reign of Edward IV*, pp. 284, 295

95 John Rous, *The Rous Roll*, W. Couthorpe (ed.), new edn, Gloucester, 1980, item 56

96 *TE*, IV, p. 149

97 L.C. Atreed, 'An Indenture between Richard Duke of Gloucester and the Scrope family of Masham and Upsall', *Speculum* 58, 1983 , p. 1018

98 Leland, *Collectanea* vi, Thomas Hearne (ed.), 1774, pp. 2–14

99 A.F. Sutton and L. Visser-Fuchs, 'Richard III's Books Observed', *The Ricardian*, ix, no. 120, March 1993, p. 385

100 *Crowland Chronicle*, p. 133

101 Vergil, pp. 200, 227

102 *Oratio Scotorum*, pp. 41–8

103 *Foedera*, T. Rymer (ed.), London, 1707, pp. 12, 265

104 Lambeth Palace MS. 474, fs. 124–6

105 BL. Harl. 433 f. 121

106 Mancini, p. 97

107 *Christ Church Letters*, J.B. Shephard (ed.), Camden New Ser. 19, 1877, p. 46

108 *BRUO*, i, p. 358

109 Bodley MS. Laud Misc. 501; Tudor-Craig, *Richard III*, p. 41; Henry Ansgar-Kelly, *Divine Providence in the England of Shakespeare's Histories*, Harvard, 1970, pp. 73–4

110 Anatonia Gransden, *Historical Writing in England c. 550–c. 1307*, London, 1974, ii, p. 315;

BL. MS. Add. 48976, no. 64

111 *Annals of Cambridge*, i, pp. 228–9

112 *BRUC*, pp. 352–3

113 Ibid., pp. 524–5

114 Harl. iii, 58

115 Borthwick Institute Reg. Neville, xxii, f. 316, CCR, 1476–85, Emden, *BRUO*

116 *BRUC*, p. 60

117 Ibid., pp. 275–6

118 Ibid., pp. 40–1

119 Ibid., pp. 190–1

120 *CPR*, 1467–77, p. 401

121 *BRUO*, iii, 1609–10; *Historians of Richard III*, J.R. Lumby (ed.), p. 23

122 *BRUO*, iii, 1776–9

123 *Crowland Chronicle*, p. 133

124 Mancini, p. 93

125 J.Raine, 'The Statutes ordained by Richard duke of Gloucester, for the college of Middleham', *The Archeological Journal*, vol. 14, 1857, pp. 160–70

126 Ross, *Richard III*, p. 135; *CPR*, p. 477

127 Ibid., pp. 135–6

128 *Annals Cambridge*, 1, pp. 228–9

129 Lambeth Palace MS. 474, ff. 139v–140v; *Horae Ebor*, 125; Bennet, p. 247

130 *The Coronation of Richard III*, A.F. Sutton and P.W. Hammond (eds), Gloucester, 1983, p. 340

131 Harl. iii, p. 123

132 *Hours of Richard III*, p. 112

133 Ross, *Richard III*, p. 142

134 Lambeth Palace MS. 474, ff. 184–184v

135 *A Middle English Paraphrase of the Old Testament III*, U. Ohlander (ed.), Goteburg, 1966, ll. 13, 100

136 *CPR*, p. 67; Ross, *Richard III*, p. 130

137 'Statutes of Middleham', pp. 160–70

138 R.B. Dobson, 'Richard III and the Church of York', in R.A. Griffiths and J. Sherbourne (eds), *Kings and Nobles in the Late Middle Ages*

139 Pollard, *Richard III and the Princes*, p. 193

140 Watts, *De Consulatu*, p. 258

141 Sir Thomas More, *The History of King Richard III*, R.S. Slyvester (ed.), Yale, 1976, p. 63

142 F. Sandford, *Genealogical History of the Kings and Queens of England*, London, 1707, pp. 391–2

143 *The Coronation of Richard III*, Sutton and Hammond, 6; Marc Bloch, *The Royal Touch, Sacred Monarchy and Scrofula in England and France*, English translation, London, 1973, pp. 128–30; B. Spencer, 'Henry of Windsor and the London Pilgrim', in *Collectanea Londinensia* presented to R. Merrifield, *London and Middlesex Aracheological Society*, Special Paper 2, 1978, p. 241; P. Grosjean (ed.), *Henrici VI Angliae Miracula Postuma ex Codice Musei Britannici Regio 143 C.VIII*, Brussels, 1935, note 18 no. 40

144 *The Coronation of Richard III*, Sutton and Hammond, pp. 4–11; Bloch, *The Royal Touch, Sacred Monarchy and Scrofula in England and France*, pp. 18–19

[145] Ibid.

[146] Harl. iii, 83; *Richard III the Road to Bosworth Field*, Hammond and Sutton, p. 137

[147] 'Ballad of Bosworth Field', *Bishop Percy's Folio Manuscript*, III (1868), J.W. Hales and F.J. Furnivall (eds), 233–59

[148] *Guild of Corpus Christi*, Skaife (ed.), xii

[149] A.F. Johnston, 'The Religious Plays of the Religious Guilds of York: The Creed Play and the Pater Noster Play', *Speculum*, 1975

[150] Pamela Tudor-Craig, 'Richard III's Triumphant Entry into York, August 29 1483', in R. Horrox (ed.), *Richard III and the North*, Hull, 1986, 110 ff.

[151] Mancini, *The Usurpation of Richard III*, p. 26

[152] Ibid., p. 66

[153] Commynes, *Memoirs*, p. 374

[154] Harl. 433, iii, p. 108

[155] For such a view see Ross, *Richard III*, 136 ff. and 'Rumour, Propoganda and Popular Opinion during the Wars of the Roses', in R.A. Griffiths (ed.), *Patronage, the Crown and the Provinces*, Gloucester, 1981, pp. 22–8

[156] *Calendar of Letter Books of the City of London*, R.R. Sharpe (ed.), 1912, p. 206

[157] *TE*, III, p. 350; J.H. Tillotson, *Marrick Priory, a Nunnery in Late Medieval Yorkshire*, p. 43

[158] Harl. iii, p. 35

[159] Idley, *Instructions to His Son*, ll. 1695 ff.

[160] Mancini, p. 94–7

[161] Mancini, p. 61

[162] *The Itinerary of King Richard III, 1483–1485*, Rhoda Edwards, Richard III Society, 1983, xi

[163] Weightman, 'Margaret of York', p. 186

[164] Harl. 433, iii, p. 29

[165] Ibid.

[166] Harl. iii, p. 124

[167] *Foedera*, vol. 12, p. 204

[168] Ibid.

[169] Harl. ii, pp. 228–30

[170] Mancini, p. 69; More, *The History of King Richard III*, pp. 10–11

[171] P.M. Kendall, *Richard III*, London, 1955 pp. 322–3

[172] Mancini, p. 94

[173] S.B. Crimes, *English Constitutional Ideas in the Fifteenth Century*, Cambridge, 1936, p. 173

[174] Harl. iii, p. 54

[175] Ibid., p. 12

[176] *Crowland Chronicle*, p. 151

[177] John Alcock, *Qui habet aures audiendi audiat*

[178] Harl. 4333 iii, p. 139

[179] Ibid., p. 139

[180] Tudor-Craig, *Richard III*, p. 11

[181] R. Lovatt, 'A Collection of Apocryphal Anecdotes: John Blacman Revisited', in A.J. Pollard

(ed.), *Property and Politics, Essays in Late Medieval English History*, Gloucester, 1984, pp. 172–97

    [182] John Blacman, *Henry the Sixth. A Reprint of John Blacman's Memoir*, M.R. James (ed. and transl.), Cambridge, 1919

    [183] *Itinerary of Richard III*, xiv; Kendall, *Richard III*, pp. 343, 346

CHAPTER 4

    [1] Lambeth MS. 474, f. 7v

    [2] Ibid., f. 25

    [3] Ibid., fs 129v; 179–79v; A. Sutton and L. Visser-Fuchs, *The Hours of Richard III*, Gloucester, 1991, 50 ff.

    [4] Harl. iii, p. 112

    [5] Harl. 11, p. 163

    [6] Mancini, *The Usurpation of Richard III*, pp. 97, 137

    [7] 'The Statutes ordained by Richard Duke of Gloucester for the College of Middleham', J. Raine (ed.), *The Archaeological Journal*, 14, 1857, p. 169

    [8] Longleat MS. 257; 'A ME Metrical Paraphrase of the Old Testament' I, H. Kalen (ed.), Goteborgs Hogskolas Arsskrift, 28, 1922, clvii; 'A Metrical Paraphrase of the Old Testament' II, U. Ohlander (ed.), Goteborgs Universitets Arsskritt LXI, Stockholm, 1955; 'A ME Metrical Paraphrase of the Old Testament' III, U. Ohlander (ed.), Gothenburg, 1960; 'A ME Metrical Paraphrase of the Old Testament' IV, U. Ohlander (ed.), Gothenburg Studies in English, 16, 1963. A.F. Sutton and L. Visser-Fuchs, 'Richard III's Books II, A Collection of Romances and Old Testament Stories'

    [9] *The Itinerary of King Richard III 1483–1485*, Rhoda Edwards, Richard III Society, 1983, pp. 7, 20

    [10] Ibid., p. 37; F.B. Burbidge, *Old Coventry and Lady Godiva*, 1952, p. 222

    [11] P.W. Hammond, 'Richard III's Books III. Vegetius De Re Militari, The Siege of Thebes and the New English Bible', *The Ricardian*, vol. 7, 1987, pp. 479–85

    [12] The text owned by Anne Neville and Richard of Gloucester is BL. Egerton MS. 2006 and their names occur on the fly leaf. This copy of the English translation of Mechtild's revelations has been edited by Theresa A. Halligan, *The Booke of Gostlye Grace of Mechtild of Hackeborn*, Pontifical Institute of Medieval Studies, Toronto, 1979. The other surviving copy of the English translation is Bodley MS. 220. See also A. Sutton and L. Visser-Fuchs, 'Richard III's Books: I. *The Book of Gostlye Grace of Mechtild of Hackeborn*', *The Ricardian*, vol. 7, 1985–7, pp. 278–92

    [13] *The Pageants of Richard Beauchamp, Earl of Warwick*, William, Earl of Carysfort (ed.), Oxford, 1908

    [14] BL. Egerton MS. 2006, ff. 185b–186b

    [15] BL. MS. Lambeth 474; Sutton and Visser-Fuchs *The Hours of Richard III*, p. 39

    [16] W.M. Ormrod, 'The Personal Religion of Edward III', *Speculum*, 64, 1989, 848–877

    [17] E.F. Rickert, 'King Richard II's Books', *The Library* xiii, pp. 144–7

    [18] J. Payne Collier (ed.), *Household Books of John, duke of Norfolk*, Roxburghe Club, 1844, p. 277

    [19] Sutton and Visser-Fuchs, *The Hours of Richard III*, p. 38; M.R. James, *A Descriptive Catalogue of the Manuscripts in the Library of Lambeth Palace: the Medieval Manuscripts*, Cambridge, 1932; BL. MS. Add. 42131; Bodley Rawl. Liturg. d.1

20 Ross Fuller, *The Brotherhood of the Common Life and its Influence*, Albany, 1995, p. 26

21 Ibid., Fuller, *The Brotherhood of the Common Life*

22 Bodley MS. 365

23 Thompson, 'Registers of Archdeacons of Richmond', *YAS*, 30, pp. 116–18, 131, Pt 2, *YAS*, 32, 1936, p. 119; *TE*, III, pp. 345, 348–9

24 For English text of the book of hours see H. Littlehales, *The Prymer or Lay folk's Prayer Book*, EETS, OS, vols 105, 109

25 Bodley MS. Lat. Liturg. f2; N.J. Rogers 'Books of Hours Produced in the Low countries for the English Market in the fifteenth Century', 2 vols, Camb. M.Litt. thesis, 1982, pp. 136–42

26 *The Academy*, 16, 1876, pp. 230–2

27 *TE*, II, pp. 59–61

28 Daniel Williams, 'The Hastily Drawn will of William Catesby', *Leicester Archeological and Historical Soc. Trans.*, 51, 1975–6, pp. 45–51

29 *TE*, IV, p. 106

30 *TE*, IV, p. 210

31 *TE*, II, p. 175; *CPR*, 1461–7, p. 447

32 E.F. Bosanquet, 'The Personal Prayer Book of John of Lancaster, duke of Bedford K.G.', *The Library*, 4th ser. xiii, pp. 148–54

33 W. Couthorpe (ed.), *The Rous Roll*, Gloucester, 1980, item 54

34 eg. Lambeth Palace MS. 474, ff. 112–122v; Sutton and Visser-Fuchs, *The Hours of Richard III*, p. 97, n. 135

35 T. Stapleton (ed.), *The Plumpton Correspondence*, Camden Soc., 1839, p. 8

36 R.S. Wieck (ed.), *The Book of Hours in Medieval Art and Life*, London, 1988

37 S.B Meech and H.E. Allen (eds), *The Book of Margery Kempe*, London, EETS, 1940, pp. 164, 202

38 *TE*, IV, pp. 164–7

39 Ibid., p. 139

40 Lambeth Palace MS. 474, fs 72–90

41 *TE*, III, p. 212

42 J.W. Hales and F.J. Furnivall (eds), *Bishop Parry's Folio Manuscript*, vol. 3, 1868, p. 246

43 *TE*, V, pp. 88–91

44 N. Pevsner (ed.), *The Buildings of England Yorkshire: York and the East Riding*, Harmondsworth, 1972, p. 230

45 *TE*, V, pp. 88–91

46 *TE*, III, p. 212

47 Ibid., pp. 264–8

48 Ibid., p. 265

49 William Christian, *Reason and God in a Spanish Valley*, New York, 1972, p. 132

50 Lambeth Palace MS. 474, f. 169

51 Ibid., fs 182–183

52 Ushaw 10, f. 25; Bodley MS. Laud Lat. 15, f. 30v

53 Wieck, *Book of Hours*, pp. 163–4; *Horae Ebor*, pp. 66–7; Lambeth Palace, MS. 474, ff. 158–60

54 *TE*, IV, p. 15

55   Lambert Palace MS. 474, fs 167–8; J.A.W. Bennet, *Devotional Pieces in Verse and Prose from MS Arundel and MS Harleian 6919*, Scottish Text Soc. 3rd ser., vol. 23, Edinburgh, 1955, p. 287

56   Lambeth Palace MS. 474, pp. 168–9

57   Ibid., fs 156v–8; Wieck, *Book of Hours*, p. 164; *Horae Ebor*, pp. 67–8

58   Hughes, 'The Administration of Confession in the Diocese of York in the Fourteenth Century' in *Studies in Clergy and Ministry in Medieval England*, D. Smith (ed.), Borthwick Studies in History, York, 1991, 117; *The Prick of Conscience*, R. Morris (ed.), Berlin, 1863, ll. 3, 380–83

59   Ibid., fs 173–4; YML Add. MS. 2, fs 171v–2; Wieck, *Book of Hours*, pp. 104–5; *Horae Ebor*, pp. 134–5

60   Ibid., fs 145v–151v; Bennet, 'Devotional Pieces', pp. 170–80; *Horae Ebor*, pp. 76–80

61   Bodley MS. Lat. Liturg. f. 2, ff. 10v, 124–140, 147v, 171v

62   Rogers, 'Books of Hours'

63   *TE*, III, p. 256

64   Waller Hilton, *The Scale of Perfection*, E. Underhill (ed.), London, 1923, Bk II, ch. 22

65   V. Reinburg, 'Prayer and the Book of Hours' in Wieck, *The Book of Hours in Medieval Art and Life*, pp. 39–44

66   J. Hughes, *Pastors and Visionaries: Religion and Secular Life in Late Medieval Yorkshire*, Woodbridge, 1988, 208 ff.

67   YML Add MS., 2m fs 166v–7

68   Bodley MS. Laud Lat. 15, f. 114v

69   Ibid., fs 113v–14

70   YML MS. XVI. K.6 fs 83–4

71   Ushaw 10, ff. 12v–13; Rogers, p. 168

72   *EDR*, 1909, 11 ff.

73   John Alcock, *Mons Perfectionis*, Wynkyn de Worde, Wesminster, 1497, in *The English Experience*, no. 706

74   Richard Rolle, M. Deanesly (ed.), *Incendium Amoris*, Manchester 1915, ch. 15

75   *TE*, IV, p. 138

76   *TE*, IV, pp. 251–63

77   E. Duffy, 'The Spirituality of John Fisher', in *Humanism, Reform and the Reformation*, pp. 218, 223

78   *The Coronation of Richard III*, A. Sutton and P.W. Hammond (eds), Gloucester, 1983, pp. 28–9

79   Hilton, *Scale of Perfection*, Bk ii, ch 22

80   *King Richard III*, Act III, Sc. vii, ll. 97–8, The Arden Shakespeare

81   Sutton and Visser-Fuchs, *The Hours of Richard III*, p. 39; M.K. Jones, 'Sir William Stanley of Holt: Politics and Family in the Late Fifteenth Century', *Welsh History Review*, vol. 14, 1988

82   Bosanquet, 'The Personal Prayer-book of John of Lancaster', pp. 148–55

83   BL. MS. Add. 38603, ff. 57v–58; Sutton and Visser-Fuchs, *The Hours of Richard III*, p. 105

84   See William Christian, *Reason and God in a Spanish Valley*, New York, 1972, p. 131 for comparative observations among twentieth-century Catholics in rural Spain

85   Lambeth MS. 474 f. 183v

86   'Statutes of Middleham', pp. 160–70

87   Lambeth Palace MS. 474, fs 180v–181

88 *Secreta Secretorum*, p. 203

89 Ibid., p. 211

90 John Alcock, *Mons Perfectionis*, 1498

91 C. Horstmann (ed.), *Yorkshire Writers*, London, 1895, pp. 376–7

92 E. Duffy, *The Stripping of the Altars*, Yale, 1992, p. 267; Balliol Coll. MS., p. 354

93 Sutton and Visser-Fuchs, *The Hours of Richard III*, pp. 83–5

94 Duffy, *Stripping of the Altars*, p. 268

95 *The Paston Letters and Papers of the Fifteenth Century*, N. Davis (ed.), Oxford, 1971–6, vol. i, 7; C. Richmond, *The Paston Family in the Fifteenth Century*, Cambridge, 1990, pp. 36, 169

96 Ibid.

97 *The Romance of Sir Degrevant*, C.F. Casson (ed.), EETS, OS, 221, 1949, repr. London, 1970, lxvii

98 Horstman, *Yorkshire Writers*, i, p. 376

99 *The Thornton Manuscript, Lincoln Cath, MS. 91, A Facsimile*, London, 1977, f. 265; *Yorkshire Writers*, i, p. 400; *Liber de Diversis Medicines*, M.S. Ogden (ed.), EETS, OS, 207, London, xii–xiii

100 *A Metrical Old Testament*, ll. 770–96

101 Ibid., ll. 885–9

102 Lambeth MS. 474, f. 179v

103 Ps 77.9.10

104 Lambeth MS. 474, fs 131–2

105 Ibid., fs 139v–140v; Bennet, p. 247

106 Metrical Old Testament, ll. 7325–46

107 Psalm 121 (Terce)

108 MS. Harl. 787, f. 2; *op. cit.* J. Gairdner, *The Life and Reign of Richard III*, Cambridge, 1989, p. 244

109 Harl. III, p. 58

110 *The Road to Bosworth Field*, 145, PRO C81/1392/6; *Crowland Chronicle*, p. 568; Ellis, *Original Letters*, 2nd series, pp. 159–60

111 M. Hicks, 'Richard III as Duke of Gloucester: A Study in Character', *Borthwick Paper*, 1986, pp. 32–4

112 *J.E.B. Major (ed.), The English Works of John Fisher*, Part I, EETS, Ext Ser 27, London, p. 88

113 Ibid., p. 74

114 S. Greenblatt, *Renaissance Self Fashioning, from More to Shakespeare*, Chicago, 1986

115 Psalm 54 (Prime)

116 Psalm 118

117 Psalm 37 (penitential psalms)

118 Psalm 22

119 Psalm 63 (Lauds)

120 Psalm 129 (penitential psalms)

121 Psalm 138 (Office of the Dead); Kelly, *Divine Providence in Shakespeare's Histories*, p. 38; *Town Chronicles of England*, R. Fleney (ed.), Oxford, 1911, p. 118; Jean de Waurin, *Anchiennes Chroniques d'Engleterre*, E. Dupont (ed.), 3 vols, Paris, 1853–63, pp. 1, 4–5, 111, 342, 350

122 Lambeth MS. 474 fs 179–179v

123 Ibid., f. 98v

[124] B. Wolffe, *Henry VI*, London, 1981, p. 17; K.A. Kelly, *Divine Providence in the England of Shakespeare's Histories*, 1970, p. 63

[125] *Crowland Chronicle*, p. 181

[126] F.P. Titchwell, 40

[127] *PL* iii (Gairdner), pp. 209, 256

[128] W. Blackmans, 'The Devotion of a Lonely Duchess', in T. Kren (ed.), *Margaret of York and the Visions of Tondal*, Malibu, 1992, pp. 29–44

[129] N. Morgan, 'Some Remarks on the Character and Content of the Library of Margaret of York', in *Margaret of York and the Visions of Tondal*, p. 63; BL. MS. Add., 7970

[130] BL. MS. Add. 7970; S. Lewes, 'The Apocalypse of Margaret of York', in *Margaret of York and the Visons of Tondal*, p. 84

[131] Vergil, p. 222. Pamela Tudor-Craig, 'The Hours of Edward IV and William Lord Hastings: British Library Manuscript Aditional 54782' in D. Williams (ed.), *England in the Fifteenth Century, Proceedings of the 1986 Harlaxton Symposium*, Woodbridge, 1987, 343 ff.

[132] H. Ellis (ed.), *The New Chronicles of England and France*, London, 1911, pp. 671–2; Mancini p. 92

[133] Tudor-Craig, 'The Hours of Edward IV', p. 346; BL. MS. Add. 54782, fs 42b–43

[134] Shakespeare's *King Richard III*, The Arden Shakespeare, Act IV Sc. III ll. 12–16

[135] J. Hughes, 'Stephen Scrope and the Intellectual of Sir John Fastolf: Moral and Intellectual Outlooks', in *Medieval Knighthood IV*, Papers form the fifth Strawberry Hill Conference, 1990, C. Harper-Bill and Ruth Harvey (eds), Woodbridge, 1993, pp. 103–47

[136] J. Chipps-Smith, 'Margaret of York and the Burgundian Portrait Tradition', in *Margaret of York and the Visions of Tondal*, pp. 47–57

[137] Bodley MS. Douce 365, f. 115

[138] Chipps-Smith, 'Margaret of York and the Burgundian Portrait Tradition', p. 52

[139] C. Weightman, *Margaret of York, Duchess of Burgundy 1446–1503*, Gloucester, 1989, pp. 91–2; J. Molinet, *Chroniques*, pp. 106–8, P. Commynes, *Memoires*, i, pp. 292–5, ii, pp. 34–6; Vaarsen and Charavay, *Lettres de Louis XI*, v, p. 366

[140] F. Hepburn, *Portraits of the Later Plantagenets*, 1986, p. 32, 71 ff.

[141] P. Tudor-Craig, *Richard III*, 1978, pp. 92–3

[142] The manuscript owned by Richard III and Anne Neville, which will be cited, is BL. Egerton MS. 2006, edited by T.A. Halligan as *The Book of Gostlye Grace of Mechtild of Hakeborn*, Pontifical Institute of Medieval Studies, Toronto, 1979. The Latin original, *Liber Specialis Gratie*, is printed in *Revelationes Gertrudianae as Mechtildianae, cura Solesmensium*, ii vols, Paris, 1877

[143] Eithne Wilkins, *The Rose Garden Game*, London, 1969, pp. 106–10, 165–6, 173

[144] *Plumpton Correspondence*, p. 50

[145] E. Maclagan and C.C. Oman, 'An English gold rosary of about 1500', Archeologia, 1935, lxxxv, pp. 1–22

[146] BL. Egerton MS. 2006, f. 107r; *The Booke of Gostlye Grace*, pp. 326–7

[147] BL. Add. MS. 7970, f. 1v; see also the borders of Bodley MS. Douce 365

[148] BL. Egerton, MS. 2006, f. 35r; *The Book of Gostlye Grace*, p. 112

[149] BL. Egerton, MS. 2006, f. 55r; *The Booke of Gostlye Grace*, p. 173

[150] Hepburn, *Portraits of Later Plantagenets*, p. 73

151 BL. Egerton, MS. 2006, f. 94r; *The Book of Gostlye Grace*, p. 288

152 BL. Egerton, MS. 2006, f. 33v; *The Book of Gostlye Grace*, p. 123

153 Bodley MS. Douce 219, f. 40; Otto Pacht, *The Master of Mary of Burgundy*, London, 1948, p. 38

154 BL. Egerton MS. 2006, f. 118r; *The Booke of Gostlye Grace*, p. 358

155 BL. Egerton MS. 2006, f. 40

156 Fuller, *The Brotherhood of the Common Life*, p. 98

157 BL. Egerton MS. 2006, f. 137r–137v; *The Booke of Gostlye Grace*, p. 408

158 BL. Egerton MS. 2006, f. 186–186v; *The Booke of Gostlye Grace*, pp. 542–5

CHAPTER 5

1   From *The Office of the Dead*, iii, iii Job, 8–12

2   M. Hicks, 'Richard III as Duke of Gloucester: a Study in Character', *Borwick Paper*, 1986, pp. 32–4

3   Psalm 119, l. 98

4   Psalm 119, l. 121

5   Harl. MS. *433*, vol. 2, p. 42

6   *The Book of the Order of Chivalry printed by William Caxton*, A.T.B. Byles (ed.), EETS, OS, 168, 1926, pp. 121–5

7   Fisher, *English Works*, p. 3

8   Metrical Old Testament, ll. 8223–32

9   Lambeth MS. 474, fs 184–84v; Sutton and Visser-Fuchs, *The Hours of Richard III*, pp. 62–4

10 J. Fisher, *The English Works*, J.E.B. Major (ed.), EETS, Ex. Ser. 27, p. 3

11 Ibid., p. 71

12 Lambeth MS. 474, fs 214–6

13 Ibid., f. 180v; for an alternative view see A.F. Sutton and L. Visser-Fuchs, in 'Richard III and St Julian, a new Myth', *Ricardian*. They do not see any link between the two prayers. For St Julian's legend see *Analecta Bollandiana* 63, 1945, pp. 145–219

14 Lambeth MS. 474, f. 181

15 Ibid., fs 184–184v

16 *The Revelations of St Birgitta*, W.P. Cumming (ed.), EETS, London, 1929, pp. 75–83

17 Lambeth MS. 474 fs 179–179v

18 Ibid., f. 179v

19 Ibid., fs 169–76

20 Ibid., fs 174–6v; see also J. Barre, *Prieres Anciennes de L'Occident A La Mere Du Sauveur*, Paris, 1963

21 *Vergil's English History*, p. 227

22 Marjorie Weeks, 'The Personality of Richard III: Some Opinions of a Psychiatrist based on his Portraits', *The Ricardian*, IV, no. 56, 1977

23 *Crowland Chronicle*, p. 181

24 Vergil, p. 222

25 *The New Chronicles of England and France*, H. Ellis (ed.), London, 1911, pp. 671–2

26 Rosemary Horrox, *Richard III, A Study in Service*, Cambridge, 1989, p. 289

27   M. Jones and M.G. Underwood, *The King's Mother*, Cambridge, 1922, p. 257; 'Remembraunce had at the moneth mynde of the Noble Prynces Margarete Countesse of Rychemonde and Darbye, emprynted by Wynkyn de Worde', in *The English Works of John Fisher*, part I, 289–310

28   BL. Egerton MS. 2341; Reg. Guild of Holy Trinity of Luton, H. Clough (ed.), London, 1906, pp. 16–17

29   *The King's Mother*, pp. 256–8

30   Ibid., p. 71

31   Lambeth Palace MS. 474, fs 138v–9

32   *A Middle English Old Testament* III, ll. 13100 ff.

33   Ibid., ll. 13, 1100 ff.

34   *TE*, IV, p. 21

35   P. Lewis, *Later Medieval France: The Polity*, 1968, pp. 17–18; L. Richmond, 'The Visual Culture of Fifteenth Century England' in A.J. Pollard (ed.), *The Wars of the Roses*, London, 1995, pp. 207–8. Richmond sees in these extremes of Richard III a complexity that contrasted with the provincial complacency of his countrymen.

36   *Crowland Chronicle*, p. 133

37   *Chronicles of England and France*, p. 238

38   Vergil, p. 192

39   J. Hughes, 'Stephen Scrope and the Circle of Sir John Fastolf: Intellectual and Moral Outlooks', in *Medieval Knighthood IV Papers from the 5th Strawberry Hill Conference*, 1991, C. Harper-Bill and R. Harrey (eds), Woodbridge, 1993, pp. 103–7

40   *Dicts and Sayings*, p. 12

41   I am preparing a book on this subject.

42   Ethel Seaton, *Sir Richard Roos Lancastrian Poet*, London, 1961; CUL. MS. Ee z 17

43   Ibid., p. 99. There are six surviving manuscripts. The one bearing Roos' ascription is BL. MS. Harl. 372. For text of *La Belle Dame Sans Merci* see edition in *The Complete Works of Geoffrey Chaucer vii Chaucerian and other Pieces*, W.W. Skeat (ed.), Oxford, 1897

44   *La Belle Dame Sans Merci*, ll. 261

45   Ibid., ll. 561–4

46   Ibid., ll. 599–600

47   Ibid., ll. 661

48   N.C. Goodrich, *Charles of Orleans A Study of Themes in his French and in his English Poetry*, Geneva, 1967, p. 55

49   MacCracken, 'An English Friend of Charles of Orleans', *PMLA*, xxvi, 1910, pp. 55, 142

50   John Fox, *The Lyric Poetry of Charles of Orleans*, Oxford, 1969, p. 50

51   Goodrich, *Charles of Orleans*

52   Fox, *The Lyric Poetry of Charles of Orleans*, p. 60

53   Emmanuel College, Cambridge, MS. 1210, f. 11b

54   *PL* iii (Gairdner), p. 229

55   E.M. Carus-Wilson, 'Evidences of Industrial Growth on some Fifteenth Century Manors', *Economic History Review*, 2nd ser. xii, (1959–60), pp. 190–205

BIBLIOGRAPHY

PRIMARY SOURCES

Manuscripts

British Library

BL. MS. Harl. 787
BL. MS. Add. 38603
BL. MS. Add. 42131
BL. MS. Add. 48967 no. 64
BL. MS. Add. 6113
BL. MS. Cotton Julius EIV
BL. MS. Cotton Vitellius Ex Art 23 (Sermon of Bishop Russel)
BL. Egerton MS. 2006 (Richard III and Anne Neville's copy of *The Revelations of St Mechtild*)
BL. Egerton 2341
BL. MS. Harl. 103. (Tiptoft's copy of Lydgate's *Fall of Princes*)
BL. MS. Harl. 4431
BL. MS. Harl. 433
BL. MS. Harl. 787

Cambridge University

CUL. MS. Add. 3468
Emmanuel Coll., Cambridge MS. 1210 (Worcester's annotated copy of *The Dicts and Sayings of the Philosophers*)

Oxford University

Bodley MS. 220 (*The Revelations of St Mechtild*)
Bodley MS. 365 (Book of Hours)
Bodley MS. Douce 219 (Book of Hours)
Bodley MS. Douce 365 (Book of Hours)
Bodley MS. Lat. Liturg. f 2 (Book of Hours)

Bodley MS. Laud Misc 501 (Carmeliano's *Life of St Catherine*)
Bodley MS. Laud Lat. 15 (Book of Hours)
Bodley MS. Auct. Q1 533 (John Alcock, *Gallicantus* title page)
Magdalen College, Oxford, MS. 198. (Worcester's notebook)
Magdalen College, Oxford, Fatolf Paper Titchwell 40

Lambeth Palace

Lambeth MS. 265 (Wydeville's *The Dicts and Sayings of the Philosophers*)
Lambeth MS. 474 (Richard III's Book of Hours)

York

York Minster Library MS. Add. 2 (Book of Hours)
YML MS. XVI K.6. (Book of Hours)
Borthwick Institute of Historical Research Register Probate Register, George Neville

Others

Longleat MS. 257 (Richard III's Old Testament)
Ushaw, St Cuthbert's College MS. 10 (Book of Hours)

Printed Sources

The Academy 16, 1876
Alcock, John, *An English Sermon on Luke Viii*, Westminster, Wynkyn de Worde, STC 284 (microfilm)
—— *Desponsacio virginis Christo; Gallicantus ad Confratres*, Pynson, 1498, RSTC 277, 74
—— *An Exhortation made to Religious Sisters*, Westminster, Wynkyn de Worde, STC 287, in *The English Experience*, no. 630
—— *Mons Perfectiones*, Wynkyn de Worde, Westminster, 1497, in *The English Experience*, no. 706
Analecta Bollandiana 63, 1945 (Legend of St Julian)
Annals of Cambridge
'Ballad of Bosworth Field', *Bishop Percy's Folio Manuscript*, III (1868), J.W. Hales and F.J. Furnivall (eds), 233–59
Bannatyne Miscellany II, D. Laing (ed.), Bannatyne Club, Edinburgh, 1886
'BL. Harl. MS 433', R. Horrox and P.W. Hammond (eds), 3 vols, Richard III Soc., 1979
The Booke of Gostlye Grace of Mechtild of Hackeborn, Theresa A. Halligan (ed.), Pontifical

Institute of Medieval Studies, Toronto, 1979

The Book of Margery Kempe, J.B. Meech and H.E. Allen (eds), London, EETS, 1940

The Book of the Order of Chivalry, printed by Caxton, A.T.B. Byles (ed.), Os, 168, 1926

Calendar of Letter Books of the City of London, R.R. Sharpe (ed.), 1912

Calendar of Patent Rolls

Caxton, William, *Prologues and Epilogues*, W.J.B. Crotch (ed.), EETS, 176, 1929

Christ Church Letters, J.B. Shepherd (ed.), Camden New Ser. 19, 1877

Christine de Pisan's Moral Proverbs, transl by the Earl of Rivers and repr. from orig. ed. by Caxton AD 1478, W. Blades (ed.), London, 1859

Commynes, Philip de, *The Memoirs*, A.R. Scoble (ed.), London, 1911

The Complete Works of Geoffrey Chaucer, vii, Chaucerian and other Pieces, W.W. Skeat (ed.), Oxford, 1897

The Coronation of Richard III, A. Sutton and P.W. Hammond (eds), Gloucester, 1983

The Crowland Chronicle 1459–1486, N. Pronay and J. Cox (eds), London, 1986

The Curiale made by Mayster Alain Chartier translated by William Caxton, 1484, EETS, Es. 54

The Earliest English translation of Vegetius De re militari, G. Lester (ed.), Middle English Texts, 21, Heidelberg, 1988

Ely Diocesan Register, Cambridge, 1893–6

Excerpta Historica, London, 1831

Fabyan, R., *New Chronicles of England and France*, H. Ellis (ed.), 1811

A Fifteenth Century Translation of Alain of Chartier's le Traite de L'Esperaunce and le Quadrilogue Invectif, M.S. Blayney (ed.), EETS, 1974

Fisher, J., *The English Works Part 1*, J.E.B. Major (ed.), EETS, Ext. Ser. 27

Foedera, T. Rymer (ed.), London, 1707, vol. 4

The Governance of Princes, James Yonge (transl.) 1422, EETS, Ex. Ser. 74, 1898

Grants etc from the Crown during the Reign of Edward the Fifth, J.G. Nichols (ed.), Camden Soc., 1854

The Great Chronicle of London, A.H. Thomas and I.D. Thornley (eds), 1938

Henrici VI Angiae Miracula Postuma ex Codice e Musei Britannici Regio 143 C VIII, Brussels, 1935

Hilton, Walter, *The Scale of Perfection*, E. Underhill (ed.), London, 1923

Historians of Richard III, J.R. Lumley (ed.)

Horstmann, C., *Yorkshire Writers*, London, 1895

Idley, Peter, *Instructions to his Son*, C. D'Evelyn (ed.), London, 1935

The Itinerary of King Richard III, 1483–1485, Rhoda Edwards, Richard III Society, 1983

John Blacman, Henry the Sixth. A Reprint of John Blacman's Memoir, M.R. James (ed. and transl.), Cambridge, 1919

'John Rous' "Account of the Reign of Richard III"', in A. Hanham, *Richard III and his Early Historian*, Oxford, 1975

Kempis, Thomas à, *Earliest English Translations of the First Three Books of the De Imitatione Christi*, J.K. Ingram (ed.), EETS, London, 1893

Love, Nicholas, *The Mirror of the Blessed Lyf of Jesu Crist*, L.F. Powell (ed.), Oxford, 1911

Leland, *Collectanea*, vi, T. Hearne (ed.), 1774

Lettres des Louis XI, 12 vols, J. Varsen and E. Charavay (eds), Paris, 1883–1909

Liber de Diversis Medicines, M.S. Ogden (ed.), EETS, Os. 207, London

Mancini, Dominic, *The Usurpation of Richard III*, C.A.J. Armstrong (ed.), Gloucester, 1984

A Middle English Paraphrase of the Old Testament, I, H. Kalen (ed.), Goteborgs Hogskolas, Arssknift, 28, 1922

A Middle English Paraphrase of the Old Testament, II, U. Ohlander (ed.), Goteburgs Universitets Arsskrift LXI, Stockholm, 1955

A Middle English Paraphrase of the Old Testament, III, U. Ohlander (ed.), Gothenburg, 1966

A Middle English Paraphrase of the Old Testament, IV, U. Ohlander (ed.), Gothenburg Studies in English, 16, 1963

Molinet, J. *Chronique*, G. Doutrepont and O. Jodogne (eds), 3 vols, Brussels, 1935–7

Monmouth, Geoffrey of, *History of the Kings of Britain*, C. Thorpe (tr.), 1966

More, Sir Thomas, *The History of Richard III*, R.S. Sylvester (ed.), Yale, 1976

The New Chronicles of England and France, H. Ellis (ed.), London, 1911

The Pageants of Richard Beauchamp, Earl of Warwick, William, Earl of Carysfort (ed.), Oxford, 1908

Parvus Cato, transl. Benedict Burgh, from William Caxton's first edn, *c.* 1477, F. Kuriyama (ed.), Tokyo, 1974

The Paston Letters and Papers of the Fifteenth Century, N. Davis (ed.), 3 vols, Oxford, 1971–6

Pisan, Christine de, *Livre Du Corps De Policie*, from MS. CUL KK 1.5, Diane Bornstein (ed.), Heidelberg, 1977

The Plumpton Correspondence, T. Stapleton (ed.), Camden Soc., 1839

Political Poems and Songs Relating to English History from Edward III to Henry VIII, 2 vols, Rolls Ser., London, 1859–61

The Prick of Conscience, R. Morris (ed.), Berlin, 1863

The Primer of Layfolk's Prayer Book, H. Littlehales (ed.), EETS, Os. vols 105, 109

Register of the Guild of Corpus Christi, R.H. Skaife (ed.), Surtees Society, 57, 1871

Revelationes Gertrudianae Mechtildianae cura Solesmensium 2 vols, Paris, 1877

The Revelations of St Birgitta, W.P. Cumming (ed.), EETS, London, 1929

Richard III, The Road to Bosworth Field, P.W. Hammond, and A. Sutton (eds), London, 1985

Rolle, Richard, *Incendium Amoris*, M. Deanesly (ed.), Manchester, 1915

The Romance of Sir Degrevant, C.F. Casson (ed.), EETS, Os, 221, 1949, repr. London, 1970

Rous, John, *Historia Regum Angliae*, T. Hearne (ed.), Oxford, 1975

—— *The Rous Roll*, W. Couthorpe (ed.), new edn, Gloucester, 1980

King Richard III, The Arden Shakespeare

'The Statutes ordained by Richard Duke of Gloucester for the College of Middleham', J. Raine (ed.), *The Archaeological Journal*, 14, 1857

Statutes of the Realm, 1107–1703, Record Commission, 1810–23

Testamenta Eboracensia II, 1429–67; Testamenta Eboracensia III, 1467–85, J. Raine (ed.), SS, 45, 1864

Three Books of Polydore Vergil's English History comprising the Reigns of King Henry VI, Edward IV, and Richard III, H. Ellis (ed.), London, 1844

The Thornton Manuscript, Lincoln Cath. Ms. 91, a Facsimile, London, 1977

Town Chronicles of England, R. Flency (ed.), Oxford, 1911

Vespasiano de Bistici, Vite di uomini illustri del Seculo xv, L. Frati (ed.), i, 1892

Wardrobe Accounts of Edward IV, N.H. Nicolas (ed.), 1830

Warkworth, John, *A Chronicle of the first thirteen years of the Reign of Edward IV*, J.B. Halliwell (ed.), Camden Soc., 1839

Waurin, Jean de, *Anchiennes Chroniques d'Engleterre*, E. Dupont (ed.), 3 vols, Paris, 1853–63

Wills from Doctors Commons

Worcester, William, *The Boke of Noblesse*, J.G. Nichols (ed.), London, 1868

York Civic Records, A. Raine (ed.), vol. I, 1939, *Yorkshire Archaeological Society Record Series*, vol. 98, p. 78

SECONDARY SOURCES

Ansgar-Kelly, H., *Divine Providence in the England of Shakespeare's Histories*, Harvard, 1970

Armstrong, C.A.J., 'The Piety of Cicely Duchess of York, a Study in late Medieval Culture', in D. Woodruff (ed.), *For Hilaire Belloc, Essays in honour of 72nd birthday*, 1942

Atreed, L.C., 'An indenture between Richard Duke of Gloucester and the Scrope family of Masham and Upsall', *Speculum*, 58, 1983

Barre, J., *Prieres Anciennes de L'Occident à la mere Du Sauveur*, Paris, 1963

Bennet, J.A.W., 'Devotional Pieces in Verse and Prose from MS. Arundel and MS. Harleian 6919', *Scottish Text Soc.*, 3rd ser. vol. 23, Edinburgh, 1955

Blackmans, W., 'The Devotion of a Lonely Duchess', in T. Kren (ed.), *Margaret of York and the Visions of Tondal*, Malibu, 1992

Blake, N.F., *William Caxton and English Literary Culture*, London, 1991

Bloch, Marc, *The Royal Touch, Sacred Monarchy and Scrofula in England and France*, English translation, London, 1973

Bosanquet, E.F., 'The Personal Prayer Book of John of Lancaster, duke of Bedford K.G., *The Library*, 4th ser. xii

Bossy, J., 'Social History of Confession', *TRHS*, 1974

—— 'Christian Life in the Middle Ages: Prayers', *TRHS*, 1991

Buck, Sir George, *The History of King Richard the third*, A.N. Kincaid (ed.), Gloucester, 1979

Burbidge, F.B., *Old Coventry and Lady Godiva*, 1952

Carey, J., *John Donne, Life, Mind and Art*, London, 1981

Carus-Wilson, E.M., 'Evidences of Industrial Growth on some Fifteenth Century Manors', *Economic History Review*, 2nd ser. xii, 1959–60

Chipps-Smith, J., 'Margaret of York and the Burgundian Portrait Tradition', in T. Kren (ed.), *Margaret of York and the Visions of Tondal*, Malibu, 1992

Christian, William, *Reason and God in a Spanish Valley*, New York, 1972

Collier, J.P., (ed.), *Household Books of John Duke of Norfolk and Thomas, Earl of Surrey, 1481–1490*, Roxburghe Club, 1848

Crimes, S.B., *English Constitutional Ideas in the Fifteenth Century*, Cambridge, 1936

Davies, R.G., 'The Church and the Wars of the Roses' in A.J. Pollard (ed.), *The Wars of the Roses*, London, 1995

Deacon, R., *William Caxton*, London, 1976

Dickens, A.G., *The English Reformation*, 2nd edn, London, 1987

Dobson, R.B., 'Richard III and the Church of York', in *Kings and Nobles in the Late Middle Ages: a Tribute to Charles Ross*, R.A. Griffiths and J. Sherbourne (eds), Gloucester, 1986

Dover, Kenneth, *Marginal Comments*, London, 1994

Duffy, E., *The Stripping of the Altars*, Yale, 1992

Emden, R.B., *A Biographical Register of the University of Cambridge*, Cambridge, 1963

—— *A Biographical Register of the University of Oxford*, 3 vols, Oxford, 1957–9

Fleming, P.W., 'The Hautes and their Circle', in *Culture and the English Gentry in England in the Fifteenth Century*

Fox, J., *The Lyric Poetry of Charles of Orleans*, Oxford, 1969

Fuller, Ross, *The Brotherhood of the Common Life and its Influence*, Albany, 1995

Gairdner, James, *The Life and Reign of Richard III*, Cambridge, 1989

Gentleman's Magazine, 1831

Gransden, Anatonia, *Historical Writing in England c. 550–c. 1307*, London, 1974

Greenblat, S., *Renaissance Self Fashioning from More to Shakespeare*, Chicago, 1981

Hammond, P.W., 'Richard III's Books III Vegetius' *De Re Militari, The Siege of Thebes* and the *New English Bible*', *The Ricardian*, 7, 1987

—— (ed.), *Richard III, Loyalty, Lordship and Law*, London, 1984

Hanham, A., *Richard III and his Early Historians*, Oxford, 1975

Hawley, Rosemary, *We Speak no Treason*, London, 1971

Hepburn, F., *Portraits of the Later Plantagenets*, 1986

Hicks, M., 'Richard III as Duke of Gloucester: a Study in Character', *Borthwick Paper*, 1986

—— *Richard III, the Man Behind the Myth*, London, 1991

Hobbes, Thomas, *Leviathan*, C.P. Macpherson (ed.), London, 1968

Horrox, Rosemary, *Richard III, A Study in Service*, Cambridge, 1989

Hughes, J., *Pastors and Visionaries: Religion and Secular Life in Late Medieval Yorkshire*, Woodbridge, 1988

—— 'The Administration of Confession in the Diocese of York in the Fourteenth Century', in *Studies in Clergy and Ministry in Medieval England*, D. Smith (ed.), Borthwick Studies in History, York, 1991

—— 'Stephen Scrope and the Circle of Sir John Fastolf: Intellectual and Moral Outlooks', in *Medieval Knighthood IV Papers from the 5th Strawberry Hill Conference*, 1991, C. Harper-Bill and R. Harvey (eds), Woodbridge, 1993

Hughes, M.J., 'Margaret of York', *The Private Library*, 3rd ser. vols 2 and 7, 1984

Hutton, William, *The Battle of Bosworth Field*, 1788

James, M.R., *A Descriptive Catalogue of the Manuscripts in the Library of Lambeth Palace in the Medieval Manuscripts*, Cambridge, 1932

Johnston, 'The Religious Plays of the Guilds of York. The Creed Play and the Pater Noster Play', *Speculum*, 1975

Jones, M.K., and Underwood, M.G., *The King's Mother*, Cambridge, 1922

—— 'Richard III as a Soldier', in *Richard III a Medieval Kingship*, J. Gillingham (ed.), History Today, 1993

—— 'Sir William Stanley of Holt: Politics and family in the Late Fifteenth Century', *Welsh History Review*, vol. 14

Kelly, H.A., *Divine Providence in the England of Shakespeare's Histories*, 1970

Kendall, P.M., *Richard III*, London, 1955

Kren, T. (ed.), *Margaret of York, Simon Marmion and the Visions of Tondal*, Malibu, 1992

Lander, J.R., *Government and Community, England 1450–1509*, London, 1980

Leader, D., *A History of the University of Cambridge, vol. I, The University to 1546*, Cambridge, 1988

Leech, A.F., *The Schools of Medieval England*, London, 1915, repr. 1969

Lewes, S., 'The Apocalypse of Margaret of York', in *Margaret of York and the Visions of Tondal*, Malibu, 1992

Lewis, P., *Later Medieval France: The Polity*, 1968

Lovatt, R., 'A Collection of Apocryphal Anecdotes: John Blacman Revisited', in A.J. Pollard (ed.), *Property and Politics, Essays in Late Medieval English History*, Gloucester, 1984

Maclagan, E. and Oman, C.C., 'An English Gold Rosary of about 1500', *Archeologia*, 1935

MacCracken, 'An English Friend of Charles of Orleans', *PMLA*, xxvi, 1910

McFarlane, K.B., *Hans Memling*, Oxford, 1971

Markham, C.R., *Richard III: His Life and Character*, 1906

Mitchell, R.J., *John Tiptoft, 1427–1470*, London, 1938

Morgan, N., 'Some Remarks on the Character and Content of the Library of Margaret of York', in T. Kren (ed.), *Margaret of York and the Visions of Tondal*, Malibu, 1992

Ormrod, W.M., 'The Personal Religion of Edward III', *Speculum*, 64, 1989

Pacht, Otto, *The Master of Mary of Burgundy*, London, 1948

Palmer, 'Patrons and Letters in Norfolk and Suffolk in 1450 II', *PMLA*, 1913

Payne, Anne, 'The Salisbury Roll of Arms *c.* 1463 in the Fifteenth Century' in D. Williams (ed.), *England in the Fifteenth Century*, Woodbridge, 1987

Pevsner, N., *The Buildings of England Yorkshire: York and the East Riding*, Harmondsworth, 1972

Pollard, A.J., *North-Eastern England During the Wars of the Roses*, Oxford, 1990

—— (ed.), *The North of England in the Age of Richard III*, Stroud, 1996

—— *Richard III and the Princes in the Tower*, Stroud, 1991

—— *The Wars of the Roses*, London, 1995

Prevenier, W. and Blackmans W., *The Burgundian Netherlands 1330–1530*, 1986

Richmond, C., *The Paston Family in the Fifteenth Century*, Cambridge, 1990

—— 'The Visual Culture of Fifteenth Century England' in A.J. Pollard (ed.), *The Wars of the Roses*, London, 1995

—— '1485 and all that, or what was going on at the Battle of Bosworth', in P.W. Hammond (ed.), *Richard III, Loyalty, Lordship and Law*, London, 1984

Rickert, E.F., King Richard II's Books, *The Library*, xiii

Rogers, N.J., 'The Books of Hours Produced in the Low Countries for the English Market in the Fifteenth Century', 2 vols, Cambridge M. Litt. thesis, 1982

Ross, C., *Edward IV*, London, 1974

—— *Richard III*, London, 1980

—— 'Rumour, Propoganda and Popular Opinion during the Wars of the Roses', in R.A. Griffiths (ed.), *Patronage, the Crown and the Provinces*, Gloucester, 1981

—— 'Some "Servants and Lovers" of Richard in his youth', *The Ricardian*, 55

Routh, P., and Knowles, R., *The Medieval Monuments of Harewood*, Wakefield, 1993

Sandford, F., *Genealogical History of the Kings and Queens of England*, London, 1707

Scofield, C., *The Life and Reign of Edward IV*, 2 vols, 1923

Seaton, Ethel, *Sir Richard Roos Lancastrian Poet*, London, 1961

Smith, Julia, 'An image of a Preaching Bishop in Late Medieval England: the 1498 portrait of Bishop John Alcock', *Viator*, 1990

Spencer, B., 'Henry of Windsor and the London Pilgrim', in *Collectanea Londinensia presented to R Merringfield*, London and Middlesex Archeological Soc. Special Paper 2, 1978

Storr, A., *Feet of Clay: a Study of Gurus*, London, 1996

Sutton A., and Visser-Fuchs L., *The Hours of Richard III*, Gloucester, 1991

—— 'A Curious Searcher of Our Common Weal Public: Richard III Piety, Chivalry and the Concept of a good prince', in P.W. Hammond (ed.), *Richard III Loyalty and Law*, London, 1986

—— 'Choosing a Book in Late Fifteenth Century England and Burgundy', in C. Barron and N. Saul (eds), *England and the Low Countries in the Late Middle Ages*

—— 'Richard III's Books II, A Collection of Romances and Old Testament Stories,' *The Ricardian*, 1985

—— '*The Booke of Gostelye Grace* of Mechtild of Hackeborn', *The Ricardian*, 7, 1985–7

—— 'Richard III's Books V, Aegidius Romanus *De Regimine Principum*', *The Ricardian*, 7, 1985–7

—— 'Richard III's Books IV, Vegetius' *De Re Militari*', *The Ricardian*, 7, 1987

—— 'Richard III's Books VII, *Guido delle Colonne's Historia Destructionis Troiae*', *The Ricardian* 7, 1985–7

—— 'Richard III's Books VI, the Anonymous FitzHugh Chronicle', *The Ricardian* 8, 1988–90

—— 'Richard III's Books VIII, *Historia Regum Britanniae* with the prophecy of the Eagle and Commentary', *The Ricardian* 8

—— 'Richard III's Books IX, The Grande Chroniques de France', *The Ricardian*, VIII, 1990

—— 'Richard III's Books X, Raymond Lull's *Order of Chivaly* translated by William Caxton', *The Ricardian* 9, 1991

—— 'Richard III's Books, Chivalric Ideals and Reality', *The Ricardian*, 1992

—— 'Richard III's Books, Ancestry and True Nobility', *The Ricardian*, 1992

—— 'Richard III's Books, Books Observed', *The Ricardian* 9, 1993

Tait, 'The Letters of John Tiptoft, Earl of Worcester and Archbishop Neville to the University of Oxford, *EHR*, xxv, 1920

Thieboux, 'The Mouth of the Boar', *Romance Philology*, 22, 1969

Tillotson, J.H., *Marrick Priory a Nunnery in Late Medieval Yorkshire*

Tudor-Craig, P., 'Richard III's Triumphant Entry into York, Aug 29 1483', in R. Horrox (ed.), *Richard III and the North*, Hull, 1986

—— 'The Hours of Edward IV and William Lord Hastings: British Library MS. Add. 54782' in D. Wilkins (ed.), *England in the Fifteenth Century, Proceedings of the 1986 Harlaxton Symposium*, Woodbridge, 1987

—— *Richard III, Catalogue of the 1973 Richard III Exhibition*, 2nd edn, 1978

Underwood, M., 'John Fisher and the Promotion of Learning' in B. Bradshaw and E. Duffy (eds) *Humanism, Reform and the Reformation: the Career of Bishop John Fisher*, Cambridge, 1989

Vale, M. 'England and the Low Countries', Barron and Saul (eds), *England and the Low Countries in the Late Middle Ages*

Vickers, K.H., *Humphrey Duke of Goucester*, London, 1967

Victoria County History, Yorkshire, East Riding, W. Page (ed.), 1907

Visser-Fuchs, L., 'Richard III in Holland 1470–1', *The Ricardian*, VI, no. 82, 1983

Walpole, Sir Horace, *Historic Doubts on the Life and Reign of King Richard the Third*, London, 1768

Watts, J., '*De Consalatu Stilichonis*, texts and politics in the Reign of Henry VI', *Journal of Medieval Studies*, 16, 1990

Watts, J.L., 'Ideas, Principles and Politics' in A.J. Pollard (ed.), *The Wars of the Roses*, London, 1995

Weeks, M., 'The Personality of Richard III: Some Opinions of a Psychiatrist based on his Portraits', *The Ricardian*, IV, No. 56, 1977

Weightman, C., *Margaret of York, Duchess of Burgundy 1446–1503*, Gloucester, 1989

Weis, R., *Humanism in England During the Fifteenth Century*, Oxford, 1967

Wieck, R.S. (ed.), *The Book of Hours in Medieval Art and Life*, London, 1988

Wilkins, Eithne, *The Rose Garden Game*, London, 1969

Willis R. and Clark J.W., *Architectural History of the University of Cambridge, 4 vols*, Cambridge, 1986

Wolffe, B., *Henry VI*, London, 1981

Wright, H.G., *Boccacio in England from Chaucer to Tennyson*, London, 1957

INDEX